# Mastering
Practical Criticism

# Palgrave Master Series

Accounting
Accounting Skills
Advanced English Language
Advanced Pure Mathematics
Arabic
Basic Management
Biology
British Politics
Business Communication
Business Environment
C Programming
C++ Programming
Chemistry
COBOL Programming
Communication
Computing
Counselling Skills
Counselling Theory
Customer Relations
Database Design
Delphi Programming
Desktop Publishing
e-Business
Economic and Social History
Economics
Electrical Engineering
Electronics
Employee Development
English Grammar
English Language
English Literature
Fashion Buying and Merchandising
  Management
Fashion Marketing
Fashion Styling
Financial Management
Geography
Global Information Systems

Globalization of Business
Human Resource Management
International Trade
Internet
Java
Language of Literature
Management Skills
Marketing Management
Mathematics
Microsoft Office
Microsoft Windows, Novell
  NetWare and UNIX
Modern British History
Modern German History
Modern European History
Modern United States History
Modern World History
Novels of Jane Austen
Organisational Behaviour
Pascal and Delphi Programming
Philosophy
Physics
Poetry
Practical Criticism
Psychology
Public Relations
Shakespeare
Social Welfare
Sociology
Spanish
Statistics
Strategic Management
Systems Analysis and Design
Team Leadership
Theology
Twentieth-Century Russian History
Visual Basic
World Religions

www.palgravemasterseries.com

## Palgrave Master Series
### Series Standing Order ISBN 0–333–69343–4
*(outside North America only)*

You can receive future titles in this series as they are published by placing a standing order. Please contact your bookseller or, in case of difficulty, write to us at the address below with your name and address, the title of the series and the ISBN quoted above.

Customer Services Department, Macmillan Distribution Ltd
Houndmills, Basingstoke, Hampshire RG21 6XS, England

# Mastering
## Practical Criticism

Lindy Miller

palgrave

© Lindy Miller 2001

All rights reserved. No reproduction, copy or transmission of
this publication may be made without written permission.

No paragraph of this publication may be reproduced, copied or
transmitted save with written permission or in accordance with
the provisions of the Copyright, Designs and Patents Act 1988,
or under the terms of any licence permitting limited copying
issued by the Copyright Licensing Agency, 90 Tottenham Court
Road, London W1T 4LP.

Any person who does any unauthorised act in relation to this
publication may be liable to criminal prosecution and civil
claims for damages.

The author has asserted her right to be identified as the author
of this work in accordance with the Copyright, Designs and
Patents Act 1988.

First published 2001 by
PALGRAVE
Houndmills, Basingstoke, Hampshire RG21 6XS and
175 Fifth Avenue, New York, N. Y. 10010
Companies and representatives throughout the world

PALGRAVE is the new global academic imprint of
St. Martin's Press LLC Scholarly and Reference Division and
Palgrave Publishers Ltd (formerly Macmillan Press Ltd).

ISBN 978-0-333-80270-0
ISBN 0-333-80270-5

This book is printed on paper suitable for recycling and
made from fully managed and sustained forest sources.
Logging, pulping and manufacturing processes are
expected to conform to the environmental regulations
of the country of origin.

A catalogue record for this book is available
from the British Library.

10  9  8  7  6  5  4
10  09  08  07

Printed and bound in China

I dedicate this book to the memory of my Father

I dedicate this book to the memory of my father

# Contents

# ◼ ⌄ Acknowledgements

My thanks go to Emma Miller (BA Hons, MA) for the sample essays and for her academic support throughout. The following colleagues and students have helped me through discussion and debate: Richard Swan, Pat Argar and Julian Hill. I am grateful to my daughter, Jess, for her encouragement, to Dario, for help with indexing, and to my mother, Beatrice, for her support and endless cups of tea. My thanks go also to colleagues and sixth-form pupils of the Harvey Grammar School from whom I have learnt so much.

The author and publishers would like to thank the following for permission to reproduce copyright material: AQA (AEB) examination questions are reproduced by permission of the Assessment of Qualifications Alliance; Gillon Aitken Associates Ltd on behalf of the estate of the author for material from Bruce Chatwin, *On the Black Hill* (1982) pp. 38–41, Copyright © 1982 Bruce Chatwin; Margo Ewart for Gavin Ewart, 'They Flee From Me That Sometimes Did Me Seek' from *Selected Poems* by Gavin Ewart, Hutchinson; Faber & Faber Ltd for an extract from Samuel Beckett, *Waiting for Godot* (1955) pp. 13–15, and with Farrar, Straus & Giroux, LLC for Seamus Heaney, 'The Wife's Tale' from *Door into the Dark/Selected Poems 1966–1987* by Seamus Heaney, Copyright © 1990 by Seamus Heaney, and with Random House, Inc. for W. H. Auden, 'Funeral Blues' from *Collected Poems* by W. H. Auden, Copyright © 1940 and renewed 1968 by W. H. Auden; Peters, Fraser & Dunlop Ltd on behalf of the author for Roger McGough, '40 Love' from *After the Mersey Sound* by Roger McGough, Penguin (1983); Rosemary A. Thurber and the Barbara Hogenson Agency for James Thurber, 'The Little Girl and the Wolf' from *Fables for Our Time* by James Thurber, Copyright © 1940 by James Thurber, Copyright © renewed 1968 by Helen Thurber and Rosemary A. Thurber; Vernon Scannell for 'A Case of Murder' from *Collected Poems 1950–1993* by Vernon Scannell. Every effort has been made to trace all the copyright-holders, but if any have been inadvertently overlooked the publishers will be pleased to make the necessary arrangement at the first opportunity.

# ▮ ✓ ❙ Introduction

## How to use the book

This book has been written specifically for Advanced level and undergraduate students, to help them to learn the skills of practical criticism. Without these skills it is impossible to achieve a real understanding or appreciation of literature, as *these skills underpin all literary study*. It is therefore *essential* that you:

- *Read the whole book; and*
- *Read it chronologically.*

Only by doing this will you really understand the process and see how it leads you to a detailed analysis of texts. This will take time if you read it carefully and follow the examples closely, but practical criticism is an essential skill for all scholars of literature, both in coursework and examinations, and therefore it will be an investment for your future, whatever the level of study you pursue.

## What to expect from the book

By the time you have finished reading this book you should be able to:

- Analyse an unseen text from any genre.
- Read closely and understand issues beneath the surface.
- Understand and be able to use all the relevant elements of analysis to form a response that reflects understanding and appreciation.
- Organise and plan before writing your essay.
- Express yourself appropriately.
- See the pitfalls but approach the process with confidence.

## Who should read the book

- All Advanced level English Literature and English Literature/Language students.
- All English Literature undergraduates.
- All Advanced level Modern Foreign Language students (all modern foreign language courses contain a literature element).
- All Modern Foreign Language undergraduates (for the same reason).
- PGCE students on English courses.

- Teachers of English.
- Lecturers in English.
- Teachers of Modern Foreign Languages.

## The design of the book

First there will be a general discussion of practical criticism and all that is entailed in the acquisition of this skill. Then there will be advice on essay writing, with detailed examples of practical criticism in action for each of the three genres. Sample essays are provided with every exercise. These essays are *possible* responses to the questions set and they do not constitute the *only* acceptable answers. They are *not* realistic examples of a typical A-level, or even undergraduate, response to the question *in one hour under examination conditions*. However, they *are* detailed and well expressed and they illuminate the texts; as such, they are examples of the standard of response to which you should aspire – always aim high to allow for gravity. The essays should be read with this in mind.

Later, the focus will be on the student's questions and problems, followed by a reference section which can be used to help you when you are actually undertaking practical criticism for your coursework or examination preparation. There is a glossary of terms towards the end of the book.

# ◼ ☑ 2 Practical criticism

## Advanced level (A-level)

Advanced level English Literature syllabuses stress that students should be able to show a personal response, critical sense and independent judgement, and examiners want to see evidence of your careful reading and thorough understanding of a text as well as *your own* ideas about it. It is for this reason that practical criticism is unseen, and is also why it is thought to be such an important aspect of the study of English Literature at *all* levels. It is your opportunity to respond in *your own* way to texts without feeling some underlying need or pressure to replicate the 'received wisdom' of your teachers or lecturers.

Practical criticism (also referred to as 'critical appreciation' or 'critical analysis') is a *compulsory element* of *all* English A-level courses and it is the essence of a deep understanding and appreciation of **all** literature at Advanced level.

## Degree level

Practical criticism underpins *everything* you do in terms of literary study, and it is essential that you acquire the necessary skills if you are to produce a sensitive, informed and critical response to texts. It is an entirely text-centred approach and *nothing* can replace critical appreciation as an essential tool for literary study; it must become a natural part of the way you learn to look at literature if you are to succeed in this field.

## What is practical criticism?

Practical criticism is an exercise in which you analyse closely a previously unseen piece of writing without any additional information about the material or the writer; in other words you read closely, looking at 'the words on the page' (Richards, 1929) in front of you and *nothing else*. You will be given a question that you must answer in essay form.

It relies entirely upon your willingness and ability to read *closely*, focusing on every word and exploring its *effect* on the piece and its contribution to the building of the larger issues at work within it. The other half of the process involves your ability to write a clear and well-organised essay.

*All* General Certificate of Secondary Education (GCSE) and A-level students have used these skills to some degree and if you are studying either for A-levels or for a degree, you will have already acquired at least some of the skills necessary to succeed in this. You now just need to develop and refine them, and that is what this book is intended to help you to do.

## Technical aspects

As practical criticism involves far more than just comprehension, candidates need to look as much at the '**how**' as at the '**what**'. Perhaps it would be helpful to think of the '**what**' in terms of the *content* of a poem or passage; what it is *about*, whereas the '**how**' is more to do with the *style* of a piece, the *way* in which a writer writes.

Both of these aspects are made accessible to us by an understanding of critical terms, not because the vocabulary has any intrinsic value in itself, but because, like all language, it gives a name to an idea. These terms give us a common language with which to discuss the ideas; that is, after all, how all language works. It matters little whether we call a chair a 'chair' or a 'flurb'; what matters is that we all *agree* upon what to call it. 'Chair' has become the accepted name for the article that usually has four legs and a seat upon which to sit. It is simply easier to give this item a commonly agreed name; it is a form of shorthand for the *concept* of a chair.

In discussion of '**how**' a writer communicates his or her ideas, you will need to be able to handle a range of critical terms, but you should look at these merely as a set of tools to help you, *not* as an end in themselves or as a means to sounding learned! It is of little use to embark upon an exercise of mere 'technique spotting'; the only value in discussing critical terms at all is in your discussion of the *effect* they have on the text. Always ask yourself, '**How** do they *contribute to meaning*? **Why** has the writer used them here?' These are the key questions for analysis, and we shall be asking these and seeking to answer them in some detail.

Do not be tempted to have by you a list of critical terms and use these as a form of checklist against which you tick off which features are, or are not, present in the piece set for analysis. If you do this, your reading will be a sterile and impersonal affair that lacks the *personal engagement* that is so central to the skill of practical criticism. You are aiming to communicate to the examiners your *personal experience* of the effects of the text on *you* as a reader; a mere check list of critical terms will in no way help you to achieve this.

## Informed personal response

Examiners are looking for evidence of an *informed, personal response* from the candidate, and this invites you to *engage with* the text and to *explore layers of meanings*. What does an '**informed**' response mean? An 'informed' opinion is one that is formed from *more* than just one's own personal reaction to something. If an opinion is informed, it has been created from a blend of knowledge, understanding and experience; it is *your* response but one that operates within a context of objective information, gained from outside yourself.

Where does this 'information' come from?

- From teachers/lecturers in school/college/university.
  Teachers and lecturers have valuable stores of information at their fingertips and students should use this expertise constructively to build up their own hoard of knowledge about literature and how it works.
- From reading a variety of criticism on literary works.
  Read the work of numerous critics and consider the ways in which they look at literature.
- From studying books such as this.
  This book will teach you not only the skills of practical criticism but also a great deal about *how literature works*. You can then apply this to your own experience of reading prose, poetry and drama.

What does '**personal**' mean? This aspect is probably far easier to understand; it is *yours*. It is the part of the response that is likely to differ from that of the candidate sitting next to you in the examination. It relates to the effect that the text has on *you*.

To every act of communication we bring a multitude of assumptions, experiences, prejudices and, perhaps, even 'hang-ups'. In short, we carry a life history with us that inevitably comes into play whenever we interact with texts, be they literature, film, art or music. It is important to remember that we respond *as people* to literature, *not only as students* of it. Students are, first and foremost *people* (as indeed are examiners, although there are times when that fact seems harder to accept!). Our responses to literature can sometimes tell us a great deal about ourselves as human beings. This is where the '**personal**' response comes in, but it is essential to remember also the discussion about the '**informed**' element so that there is a balance of the two. It is, then, in some senses, a mixture of the *objective* (outside knowledge and information) and the *subjective* (inner thoughts and feelings). If we can achieve this mixture, we shall have created a response that is knowledgeable about literature and how it works because it is 'informed', as well as being alive and individual because it is 'personal'.

There is a fuller discussion about our personal responses to literature in Chapter 5.

## Helping to make meaning

When a text and a reader meet it is an *active* process in which the reader *works together with* the writer and helps to construct readings that may differ in emphasis and ideas from reader to reader. The reader does not just passively receive a sealed package of meaning and blindly accept this as the truth, the whole truth and nothing but the truth. Texts, it could be argued, come to life when they are *read*. Meaning is *re*created when reader interacts with text, and *both* reader and text contribute to this process of making meaning. Naturally, meaning is created when a writer writes a text, but the process of making meaning is repeated when the reader reads it. The process of communication consists of transmitting *and* receiving, and some will argue that the process is incomplete until the message has been received.

Receiving is not always a straightforward matter, however, and meaning is *not* always immediately accessible. 'Good' literature invariably presents us with challenges and it is rarely completely understood straight away. It requires us to *work at* discovering its meanings, but it is in these murky areas of ambiguity that the process offers us the most excitement and reward.

Meaning can also differ on different occasions. This statement might be hard to accept on first reading. 'Why should literature mean one thing on Monday and another on Tuesday?' you ask. Try to think of a film that you have seen more than once. While there are obvious constant, invariable elements in each viewing, many things will change each time you watch it:

- **Familiarity** is a key issue. Knowing the film well changes your responses to it.
- Your **mood** at the time is relevant. Watching a black comedy in a rather gloomy and miserable mood, you might see more of the black and less of the comedy.
- Recent **experiences** will change your responses to the film (as they will to much of your life); seeing a film containing death after you have gone through the experience of losing someone will cause a reaction that is inevitably very different in nature from that which you would have had *before* the loss. You will understand and empathise in a different way, and you will notice things that you did not see before.
- **Time** between viewings spent thinking about the ideas in the film will alter how you see it at a later date. Experiences and reflections will perhaps change our responses.
- **Information** gathered about the film since the last viewing will affect your response. Perhaps you discover something about the director's or scriptwriter's intentions which changes the way you respond to the text.
- **Discussion with others and personal reflection** are also likely to affect your response. We are often able to see our own ideas more objectively, and even critically, when we discuss them with someone else, and the opinions of others sometimes cause us to reconsider our standpoint.

What is important to understand at this stage is that meaning is *not* a case of there being only *one* 'correct' reading of a text; intelligent, creative reading can produce multiple meanings that can all coexist quite satisfactorily within an area of acceptable interpretation. Reading closely is a *personal, creative* and *dynamic* process; it is *not* a finite product set in stone.

# A 'DO' list for reading and analysis

## Read the question *carefully*

This might seem like an obvious thing to say, but it is surprising just how many students rush into a practical criticism exercise without following this advice. An acute sense of panic is often behind their somewhat frantic dash, but it is vital to remain in control and approach the question *calmly*. Panic invariably clouds our thinking and has a proven detrimental effect on our powers of creativity.

Read *every word* of the question *at least twice* and do a focusing exercise on it *before* you begin to read the text set for analysis. You may well be familiar already with this process, but if you are not it is really very simple and extremely effective. Let us look at a typical example question:

> *Read the poem carefully several times until you have the feel of it. What do you find interesting about the way in which the poet has chosen to describe the relationship of this couple?*

**Focusing** involves reading the question closely and then homing in on *key* words, which serves to focus your mind on the demands of the task. We have in the first sentence of the example essentially two sentences: (i) 'Read the poem carefully several times until you have the feel of it' is merely an instruction, but one that you should follow closely. (Note that you are asked to read the poem 'several times'; this is dealt with later in detail.)

'Until you have the feel of it' is a telling clause. You can accept as standard that 'until you have the feel' of a poem you cannot hope to even make a start on an analysis of it. Getting the feel of a text is to do with *engaging with the feelings in it*. Poetry is essentially about *emotion*, and if you are unable to get the feel of it you can safely assume that you have *not understood it*. If this is the case, you must *keep reading* until you do understand it.

The next sentence, (ii) 'What do you find interesting about the way in which the poet has chosen to describe the relationship of this couple?' is the actual question to be answered, and you should focus closely on the most important words: 'What do **you find interesting** about **the way** in which the poet has chosen to **describe** the **relationship** between this couple?' The words in bold are those that would be highlighted in a focusing exercise. Let us consider them one by one.

▶ *you* We focus on this because it reminds the candidate that a **personal response** is called for. The examiner wants to know how *you* respond to the text; and what effect it has on *you*? Remember the discussion above on **personal response**?

▶ *find interesting* These words can be interpreted widely and offer you the chance to take any aspect of the text upon which you feel able to comment in an interesting way and discuss the effect it has on *you*.

- It could be that the *imagery* is rather unusual and reveals the narrator's attitude to a character or situation. How does this affect your reading of the text?
- You might be able to comment on an interesting *structure* or *form* that helps the writer to develop a line of argument.
- Perhaps the *sound* of the language is telling. Are there 's' sounds that suggest something threatening or unpleasant because they seem to hiss? Or are the 's'

sounds soothing and sweet? Do long vowel sounds and soft consonants create a sense of calm and peace?

These are just three brief suggestions. **How** to look at literature will be dealt with in detail in Chapter 4; see 'Tools of analysis – features of text'.

▶ **the way**   This quite clearly deals with the '**how**' of the text. Focus here needs to be firmly on style and how this relates to the content. As all elements of analysis tend to blend together in a text, you will find that this aspect can be closely linked to '*interesting*', dealt with above. Again, this will be discussed in detail in Chapter 4 in 'Tools of analysis – features of text'.

▶ **describe**   This word is important because it asks you to focus on a particular aspect of the text: the *description*. Again, this draws attention to the '**how**' of the piece. The way in which a writer describes a character or situation tells us a great deal about how he or she feels about it; in other words his/her attitude, and this is central to a full understanding of any piece of literature. It is not enough to say that a poet is dealing with a marriage in a poem; you must be able to comment on his/her *attitude* to it or feelings about it and this is revealed through the way in which he/she *describes* it.

▶ **relationship**   This is primarily a reminder of what you should be focusing on in all of the above. In the case of a marriage, it would be reasonable to suppose that a poet would describe both the husband and the wife, possibly separately, but focusing on *relationship* will serve as a reminder that it is the interaction between the two parties that is to be discussed. How does the marriage work? How do they respond to each other? What are the dynamics of the partnership?

**This focusing exercise should be carried out carefully EACH TIME you approach a question on a text set for practical criticism**. Only after doing this can you be sure that your answer will be focused. If you fail to complete this exercise thoroughly, you run the risk of merely 'writing about' the poem in some vague way; unless you define the question precisely and then answer it closely, you cannot expect to gain good marks. Ultimately, your task in an examination is to *answer the question*, and you cannot do this if you have not clearly defined what it is.

## Read the text *carefully*

This may seem like another rather obvious thing to say, but this piece of advice cannot be stressed too heavily. You must read the piece *several times*. The first time you read it, you will probably have no more than a rough idea of what the piece or poem is 'about', but each time you read it a fuller sense of the meaning will become apparent, as will the wider issues at work in the passage.

Remember that the quality of your writing depends largely on the quality of your *reading*. However well you write, you can only discuss the meaning that you have discovered in the text, and it is in *reading closely* and *thinking* that this meaning is found.

# How and why we read

Our lives are full of examples of reading and we use this skill for a wide range and variety of purposes. It might be enlightening to make a mental or actual note of examples of 'texts' that we read in an average day, and the purposes for which we read them:

- An alarm clock, to check our progress on getting up;
- The labels on cosmetics, to help us to wash or apply make-up;
- The labels on medicines, to ensure that we take the right drug in the correct dosage;
- The cereal packet, perhaps to take advantage of special offers or to check contents;
- The newspaper, to be informed;
- The back of a lorry in a traffic jam, to read about available products or services;
- The shopping list which we wrote, to remind us what to buy; and so on.

We could go on but I shall stop there; the point is clear enough.

Let us consider for a moment the example of a shopping list. 'Close reading' of the sort needed for practical criticism is simply not required in this case. If we write 'eggs' on our list there is little more to do than simply connect the words 'eggs' with the food that we boil or fry or scramble, or eat with bacon. We do not need to do anything else. There is little ambiguity *in the context of a shopping list*. 'Eggs' means simply that – eggs, although we could argue that still leaves us with the choice of hens' eggs, fish eggs or Easter eggs! The purpose of reading in this example is straightforward, as indeed is the language.

Change *the context*, however, and you have a different story. 'Eggs' in a literary text opens up all sorts of possibilities. It brings to mind ideas about new life, the cyclical nature of existence, religious and pagan symbolism and perhaps much more. Its meaning may be *ambiguous* in a text such as a poem, calling for us as readers to interpret and help to *make* meaning that is relevant *within the context of the text as a whole*. So, the *purpose* for which we read determines the *way* in which we read.

Much of the shopping-list type of reading involves skimming, scanning or 'checking' and has little to do with the entirely different but similarly named 'close reading' you will be asked to do for practical criticism. It is therefore important, at this stage, to try, to some extent, to **forget** the process of '**ordinary**' reading and focus instead upon this very *different* variety.

Reading for the purposes of practical criticism has to be *very close*. Whilst being realistic about the inevitable restraints of time imposed by all examinations, ideally you should aim to *read closely every word in the text*. However, you cannot be expected to comment on every word in such detail under examination conditions. This does not mean, however, that you should not *try* to consider the *significance* of every word to the text as a whole.

For example, when a writer uses 'he' and 'I' and not 'we', this could be important and worthy of note (and probably comment), depending on the context of the whole poem or text. If the writer sometimes uses 'we' and sometimes 'he and

I' there is undoubtedly a reason for this which needs to be *explored*. Ask yourself, 'Why does he/she use 'we' here and 'he' and 'I' somewhere else?'

## Make connections and organise relevant material around key words

It is essential to remember that **nothing in good literature is ever random**. It is not a slip of the pen or a lapse in concentration that makes the writer suddenly change from 'we' to 'he' and 'I'. Depending on the context of the whole piece, close reading here *could* tell us that at times the narrator sees a unity between the two characters (when he uses 'we') and at others he or she senses separation (as when 'he' and 'I' appears).

This could well be a train of thought that is worth following. Once you have spotted this idea, you can start to track it elsewhere in the text. Are there other clues that suggest a similar theme?

- Is the **language** used *by* the characters different?
- Is the **language** used to *describe* these characters different?
- Is the **imagery** used to describe these characters different?
- Is the **tone** employed when talking about them different?
- Are the characters presented in different **settings**?
- Do they have different **roles**?
- Are the **feelings** experienced by the characters different?

This could result in an extremely fruitful discussion around some of the key words we highlighted in the focusing exercise. Remember that those words are our guides as to what exactly should be the focus of our discussion. We picked out the '*way*' the poet chooses to '*describe*' the '*relationship*' between the couple and this point about the use of 'I' or 'we' relates to *all* these elements of the question. Let us return to our focusing exercise begun on page 7.

> ▶ **the way** – *how* does he/she talk about the relationship? He/she does it by sometimes using 'I' and sometimes 'we', suggesting that on occasions there is a unity between them, but at other times they are separate from one another.
> ▶ **describe** – what language does the author use to describe them? He/she uses 'I' to show a distinction between the two, and 'we' to denote togetherness.
> ▶ **relationship** – how does this appear to us? Sometimes they are united, sometimes separate, suggesting that there is a unity between them, but that this can alter and they can become defined more separately as individuals.

I am not suggesting that you spend great lengths of time discussing the 'I'/'we' point so thoroughly, but it is important that you see how *central* this issue is to so many vital elements of the question we identified when we did the focusing exercise. It could be discussed in some detail, once only, in relation to one of these elements, and perhaps touched on when you are focusing on the other two aspects.

A consideration of the use of 'I' and 'we' would therefore be *central* to these elements of the question. How did we come upon this crucial concept? We analysed the *language*.

It should be clear by now that focusing closely on the language is the *first and most important step* in this skill of practical criticism. Analysing language can show us 'signposts' in the text, which can lead us towards a deeper understanding of the text as a whole. The language is perhaps the single most important indicator of the existence of the larger issues at work in a piece.

If you think about it, what else is there? Surely all literature is 'merely' *words on a page*, and unless these words are read *carefully*, then *real, complete* meaning is lost to us.

# A 'DO' list for writing

## Be clear

For communication to be effective it *has* to be clear. Perhaps the most important and seemingly simple rule to follow at all times when you are writing is to *be clear*. This sounds straightforward enough, but many candidates fail to achieve this essential clarity when they write. Why is this? There are several possible reasons.

### The candidate's thinking is not clear

What you write down on paper is a result of what is going on in your head. If your thinking is muddled it is inevitable that your writing will be also.

- Why might your thinking be confused? Perhaps you have not read the passage/poem carefully enough. If there appear to be contrasts or differences, have you reconciled these; found explanations for them? Let us go back to our 'I'/'we' example. If you have not seen this distinction through close reading, your grasp of the relationship will be shallow and when other issues to do with separation or unity occur in the piece, this lack of understanding may well lead to confusion in your thinking or an inability to make connections and develop themes.

### The candidate's expression is not clear

Whatever level of clarity you may have achieved in terms of your *thinking*, if your *expression* is cloudy, then the message will also be unclear. Expression is simply the way in which you express your thoughts, feelings and ideas. Writing at A-level or undergraduate level implies that candidates are dealing with rather complex issues. Therefore it is even more important that the way in which you express these ideas is straightforward and clear. Do not be tempted to assume (as do some of the weaker candidates) that if a long word is used where a short one will do, you will impress the examiner with your sophisticated vocabulary. The secret is to use the most *appropriate* and *accurate* word; this may be short or long. Examiners are not fooled by 'mock learning'. They see through all sorts of tricks that desperate candidates try to bluff their way to a good grade.

## The candidate's organisation is poor

You may have some perceptive and insightful things to say about a text but if your essay is a haphazard affair with little sense of direction, development or order, the examiner is going to find it difficult to follow your argument. Organisation depends on two essential elements: *structure* and *direction*.

- *Structure*   This relates to how you *construct* your argument. Let us think of a building. Before a builder positions windows, doors and roof, a firm layer of 'foundation' is laid down at the *start* of the process, below the ground floor. After this, each layer of construction is laid carefully close to the last. The whole process is monitored closely and organised thoughtfully, and it is essential that, if the building is to stay upright and look good, it must be *structured* properly. The *order* is of primary importance. Imagine a house with the foundations half way up the walls, the roof where the foundations should be, and the doors where the roof should go. Yet this analogy serves well in a comparison with many an essay of which examiners are supposed to make sense. Build your argument carefully and logically.
- *Direction*   This relates to *where your argument is going*. Where are you aiming to get to by the end of your essay? Does your essay lead the examiner along a path that he or she can follow, to a definite destination? Perhaps putting it more simply, *what are you trying to say?* It is important to achieve a sense of *movement* in your writing. The examiner needs to feel that he or she has *gone somewhere* with you. In essence, what you are doing when you write an essay is metaphorically taking the examiner by the hand and saying, 'Come with me. I'm going to show you what I think and feel about this.' Be sure that you lead the reader somewhere *clearly*, however, and not just take him/her into a cul-de-sac, or round in circles.

## Be formal

Written expression is rarely more formal than when required of a candidate in A-level or degree examinations. This means that colloquialisms and slang are *not* acceptable.

Every year A-level examiners comment upon the work of candidates who use expressions such as 'laid back' or 'no hassle' to describe the tone of a text, and it is important to realise at the outset of your study that this is simply *inappropriate* language for the task that you have been set.

Formality in language is increasingly rare as we enter the twenty-first century, and informality has become fashionable and desirable in many areas of behaviour. However, it is *essential* to put that informality to one side and ensure that a suitably formal, and therefore precise, style of language is adopted in your practical criticism paper.

What alternatives could our less formal candidates have offered instead of 'laid back' or 'no hassle'? 'Calm', 'serene' and 'tranquil' would all have been appropriate options. A wide descriptive vocabulary is an *essential* element of good essay-writing and if yours is poor I suggest that you apply yourself to improving it *early* in your course. Do *not* leave this until the last minute; it takes time and effort to acquire a wide vocabulary and this cannot be achieved in the two weeks before your final examination. Reading good-quality literature with a dictionary and thesaurus by your side is a useful method. Write down any new words that you do not understand, look them up in a dictionary and thesaurus and make a note of them. Then try to *use* in conversation the new words that you've learnt. 'If you don't use it you lose it'; it is the same with any skill.

The requirement to use good English is not unreasonable. Students of English at Advanced and degree levels *should* be able to use their language proficiently, and such a skill is *key* in differentiating the higher grades from the lower. I have been to numerous conferences where teachers and lecturers read and assess students' written material, and the most commonly recurring feature of these events is assessors establishing content in common with many essays, but agreeing that what distinguishes those that deserve the higher grades is the *quality of the expression*.

An essay that bears evidence of a wide and formal vocabulary does a great deal to convince an examiner that he or she should be considering the higher grades, and it does this because it is more precise and analytical as well as more elegant and convincing. Anyone can use language such as 'laid back'.

## Provide evidence

Remember that *every* point that you make about a text needs to be *supported with evidence from it*. It is very easy with a subject like English Literature to be carried away on a cloud of personal response and engagement and to forget that practical criticism is an academic exercise. It is, in fact, a pleasing combination of the personal and the objective, as was discussed earlier. For every response you have to the text you *must* explain the reasons for it and to do this you should provide *close textual reference*. This means quite simply that you refer closely to the text *each time you make a claim*.

You would not dream of going into a court of law and making comments (either complimentary or defamatory) about a person's character without expecting to have to substantiate them. It is the same for practical criticism. In effect, you are making claims about a text and about the effect it has on you. Expect to have to *provide evidence* for *each one* of those claims.

### Types of evidence

- This evidence can be in the form of **close reference**, which is what we do when we (rather obviously) refer closely to the text. Discussing Seamus Heaney's 'A Wife's Tale', an example of this could be a candidate saying, 'The poet suggests that the man and wife sometimes feel divided in their relationship because he portrays them as having different roles; he is a farmer and she operates in a domestic area. They are then seen as being more together when she brings lunch to him in the field.' Here the candidate has *referred closely* to the text to support his/her argument *without using any of the actual words used by the poet*.

- The other type of evidence available is, of course, **quotation**. An example of this is the same candidate saying, 'The poet suggests that the man and wife sometimes feel divided in their relationship because he distinguishes them as individuals by using "I" but then portrays them as a couple when the man calls them "we".' Here the candidate has *quoted exactly the actual words used by the poet* to support his/her argument.

Both methods are acceptable, but it is wise to aim for a generous sprinkling of *embedded quotation* throughout your essay. Detailed advice on using quotation effectively is given later (see pages 242–3).

## Think about an order

If we return briefly to our discussion about structure, you will remember that order is an essential element. Remember the foundations, walls, doors, windows and roof? Everything has to be laid down in the *correct order* to enable the building to stay upright and look good. It is the same with your essay.

Allow yourself time to consider the significance of the material that you have collected. Think about ways in which you could *combine* and *order* your observations *in relation to the question*. This is where your focusing exercise can be very helpful. Could two similar points be dealt with in one paragraph perhaps, or in two adjoining sections? This will add smoothness to your work and show the examiner that you have taken the time and trouble to make his/her journey through your responses easier.

You will see that your material tends to fall into 'natural patterns'. Think carefully about the *direction* of your argument and consider the ways in which your responses can be used to *support and develop it*.

## Draw up a provisional plan

For your essay to be well structured and have a sense of direction it is important to have a provisional plan with which to work as you progress. This need not be written in stone and it can be modified at any time and in any way.
The plan should contain:

- The *main stages* of your essay and a conditional, 'working' *conclusion*;
- *Key points related to the question* (go back and look at what you did in the focusing exercise) in each main stage; and
- Highlighted *relevant quotations*.

There will be detailed guidance on how to annotate texts and prepare answers later (see pages 83–4, 205–8).

Remember that the plan is *provisional* and that it can be altered in any way at any stage of the process. It is often necessary to reshape material in the light of emerging thoughts and ideas. What a provisional plan does is to provide your essay with a sense of direction from the start. It is similar to the motorist finding a road sign as soon as he or she leaves his/her house, and not waiting until he/she gets lost before looking for one.

# ◼ ☑ 3 Ambiguity and meaning

## Ambiguity

We know, from our use of everyday language, that words do not always have a single constant meaning. If this were the case, why would solicitors need to be so careful to avoid ambiguity in legal documents?

*The Concise Oxford Dictionary* offers '*a double meaning which is either deliberate or caused by inexactness of expression*' and '*an expression able to be interpreted in more than one way*' as definitions of the word 'ambiguity'. Both have something valuable to offer the student of practical criticism.

We shall focus on the following:

- Inexactness of expression; and
- Ability to be interpreted in more than one way.

As any student of poetry will know, one of the key characteristics of the genre is ambiguity. People do not write poetry because they wish to express themselves *precisely*, but because it is the most effective vehicle for communicating *power-fully*. Therefore 'inexactness of expression' is likely to be everywhere and it is something that any student of literature will have to take in his/her stride.

## Multiple meanings

It is precisely *because* the expression is inexact that we can interpret it in more than one way, and this is one of the reasons why the study of poetry is so interesting and challenging. You have only to question a group of literature students as they strive to analyse a complex piece of poetry to see that individuals can derive *different* meanings from the same text, while still operating in a mutually agreed area of overall meaning.

You may be wondering how the student is supposed to establish meaning if he/she is always surrounded by such vagueness. What can he/she be sure of, if anything? The answer is to *look at the context*.

# Context

Perhaps one of the most obvious examples of language changing its meaning according to its context is the word 'gay'. Not that long ago the word suggested a feeling of happiness and light-heartedness; however, in its twenty-first century context it carries not only different connotations but also very different denotative meanings.

Let us consider a simple example from literature – Vernon Scannell's 'A Case of Murder', which tells of a young boy who is left alone in a flat with the family cat and, terrified of the creature, kills it:

> They should not have left him alone,
> Alone that is except for the cat.
> He was only nine, not old enough
> To be left alone in a basement flat,
> Alone, that is, except for the cat.
> A dog would have been a different thing,
> A big gruff dog with slashing jaws,
> But a cat with round eyes mad as gold,
> Plump as a cushion with tucked-in paws –
> Better have left him with a fair-sized rat!
> But what they did was leave him with a cat.
> He hated that cat; he watched it sit,
> A buzzing machine of soft black stuff,
> He sat and watched and he hated it,
> Snug in its fur, hot blood in a muff,
> And its mad gold stare and the way it sat
> Crooning dark warmth: he loathed all that.
> So he took Daddy's stick and he hit the cat.
> Then quick as a sudden crack in glass
> It hissed, black flash, to a hiding place
> In the dust and dark beneath the couch,
> And he followed the grin on his new-made face,
> A wide-eyed, frightened snarl of a grin,
> And he took the stick and he thrust it in,
> Hard and quick in the furry dark,
> The black fur squealed and he felt his skin
> Prickle with sparks of dry delight.
> Then the cat again came into sight,
> Shot for the door that wasn't quite shut,
> But the boy, quick too, slammed fast the door:
> The cat, half-through, was cracked like a nut
> And the soft black thud was dumped on the floor.
> Then the boy was suddenly terrified
> And he bit his knuckles and cried and cried;
> But he had to do something with the dead thing there.
> His eyes squeezed beads of salty prayer

But the wound of fear gaped wide and raw;
He dared not touch the thing with his hands
So he fetched a spade and shovelled it
And dumped the load of heavy fur
In the spidery cupboard under the stair
Where it's been for years, and though it died
It's grown in that cupboard and its hot low purr
Grows slowly louder year by year:
There'll not be a corner for the boy to hide
When the cupboard swells and all sides split
And the huge black cat pads out of it.

In the second line of the poem, the reader is told clearly about 'the cat'. There is little ambiguity in this and the word holds no unusual connotations (associations) at this point, although there is a suggestion of something rather threatening in, 'Alone that is except for the cat', especially when those words are repeated verbatim two lines later. However, in terms of ambiguity, there is little; 'cat' quite simply refers to a cat.

Later on this creature is described variously:

- 'Plump as a cushion with tucked-in paws';
- 'A buzzing machine of soft black stuff';
- 'hot blood in a muff';
- 'Crooning dark warmth';
- 'black flash';
- 'the furry dark';
- 'The black fur';
- 'the soft black thud';
- 'the dead thing';
- 'the thing'; and
- 'the load of heavy fur'.

Notice that *these descriptions are ambiguous* in that they *could* refer to things other than a cat. However, we can be reasonably sure that they *do* refer to the cat in the flat with the boy, *because we have a context into which to place these ambiguous descriptions*; we have already been told quite clearly in line 2 that he is alone in a flat with 'the cat'.

Our interpretation of these ambiguous descriptions takes place against a backdrop of information – a context. Once we are safe in the knowledge that Scannell is representing a cat in the descriptions above, we are then free to consider which specific *characteristic* he is focusing upon in each of those representations.

- 'Plump as a cushion with tucked-in paws' suggests a certain smugness and complacency in the cat. He sits there fat and happy.
- 'A buzzing machine of soft black stuff' creates a harsher feeling; 'buzzing machine' is unpleasant and sounds cold and feelingless.

Notice the way in which the descriptions change after the cat's death. The animal becomes:

- a 'soft black thud', which sounds heavy and lifeless; and
- 'the load of heavy fur', which again lacks vitality.

## Mind the gap (semiotics)

Ambiguity provides a *gap between the description of something and the thing itself* and it is in this gap that the reader/audience gets to work to help to make meaning. If you are familiar with semiotics (the science of signs) you will recognise 'the signifier' in 'the description of something' and 'the signified' in 'the thing itself'. (There is a brief discussion of semiotics at the end of Chapter 4 – in Tools of analysis – features of text.) Ambiguity often calls for hard work from the reader/audience but it is in doing this that the reader/audience becomes *involved* in the text and it is *here* that many of literature's greatest challenges lie.

The key is always to *look at the context*; once you are secure in that, you can safely explore the muddy waters of ambiguity knowing that you have a solid foundation upon which to build your interpretations.

# ■ ⋎ 4 Tools of analysis – features of text

## How *not* to use this chapter – beware!

This chapter should be read *thoroughly* and preferably chronologically, but obviously not all at one sitting. It is *not* to be thought of as representing a definitive and comprehensive body of knowledge and 'facts' about literary devices, all of which you *must* know, remember and use at *all* times if you are ever to understand and appreciate literature completely.

## How to use this chapter

The purpose of this chapter is to introduce you to, or to help you to consolidate your understanding of the various tools of critical analysis – the features of text – and of the ways in which they work in literature. While many of these tools of analysis are to be found in poetry, they also frequently characterise much prose and drama. I have often not distinguished between the three genres in terms of *where* these features tend to occur because, as you will discover, the boundaries between the genres are less rigid than is often thought.

For these reasons I have selected examples from all genres. Once you have understood the features of a text and how they affect it, you will be able to recognise them in *any* genre and appreciate their function in a specific text.

## A-level

If you are an A-level student, you may be encountering some of the concepts for the first time, although you should be familiar with others from your GCSE English and English Literature courses. The ideas contained in this chapter are central to the practice of practical criticism and, while they do not constitute a definitive or exhaustive list of tools of analysis, they *will* help you to acquire a good understanding of many of the techniques that writers use and the *effect* that these have upon a text.

This understanding is *essential*, not only for the practical criticism component of your A-level paper but also for your study of *all literature, at all levels*. You cannot ever hope truly to understand and appreciate literature without having first acquired the skills of practical criticism. This chapter resembles a tool-kit that will help you to unlock the text.

## Undergraduate

If you are an undergraduate, you should be familiar with many of these ideas already from your A-level English course, and because of this you may be tempted to ignore this chapter. I earnestly recommend that you read it carefully because you will find that the method of learning in a university is quite different from what you will have been used to in either school or college.

The focus in university is more on knowledge and exploration than it is on learning (as it was at school). Your lecturers and tutors will not consider it their responsibility to 'teach' you anything as fundamental to the study of literature as the skills of practical criticism. You will be expected to have mastered these skills already to a high level of competence, and the work you do at university will *start* from that point of proficiency; it will be *assumed* that you are skilled in the art of critical analysis. Unless you feel that you have absolutely nothing to revise or learn about the tools of analysis, I suggest you read this chapter thoroughly. If you find that you are familiar with all the techniques *and* with the effects that they have upon a text, then it should only serve to add to your confidence and consolidate what you already know, which can only be a good thing.

You will notice a considerable difference between university and school or college in terms of your own learning; feeling confident about ground already covered should help you to bridge this gap more smoothly.

## A piece of woven fabric

If we look at literature in terms of a piece of woven material, it could be said that it consists of various *elements* or threads that contribute to its overall colour, texture and design. Our job, in practical criticism, is to analyse these elements and see **how** they *are woven together* to create and support the *whole fabric.*

Some would criticise this dissectional view of a text, and maintain that in carrying out this analysis we destroy the whole and kill the life of the piece. However, it is only in this close consideration of the text's various elements and of the ways in which they *all work together* that we can gain any sense of the process of *crafting* the text has undergone at the hands of its creator. An appreciation of this process and an understanding of the way in which it works is something that can give us a great deal of pleasure.

## Intention

Students have often expressed surprise at the fact that study of a text discloses similar messages in tone, imagery, language, and indeed in *all* its various elements. 'Are you sure that that's what the writer meant, or are you just seeing those things because you want to?' is a question I am asked frequently. How do I answer it? It is quite straightforward. 'Can you find evidence in the text for your claim?' If you can then it is, quite simply, there. *Evidence is what turns your assertions into 'facts'.*

**Nothing in good literature is ever random**. It is *not* accidental that the tone, the imagery, the language, or indeed any of the elements, reflect one another *and* the overall meaning. It is *not* a happy coincidence that you could trace the theme or central idea throughout many elements of the text. It simply does not happen by chance. Part of the skill of a good writer is the ability to *craft* a text so that it reflects the key ideas in many if not all of its major elements.

A safe theory to work on is, 'If it's there, it's there for a purpose'. And if it is there for a purpose, your job of practical criticism is to try to establish exactly *what* that purpose is.

It is never enough merely to 'technique spot', however. You are given little credit for simply acknowledging that the writer has used a certain type of imagery. What is required is that you then *discuss the reason* for this use of imagery and the *effect* it has on the text.

Let us look, for example, at Shakespeare's character, Macbeth, who receives prophecies from three witches about his future rise to power. He takes these predictions seriously and, spurred on by a manipulative and forceful wife, murders his way to the throne. Not at ease with himself, he continues to destroy all those whom he feels pose a threat to his security, and is himself finally destroyed by Macduff, whose wife, children and servants he had put to death.

Malcolm, son of the murdered king, refers to Macbeth as a 'hell-kite'. To note that Malcolm has used the imagery of a 'kite' or bird of prey is a *start*, but we need to go further than that. *Why* does he refer to Macbeth in those terms? What is the *significance* of the metaphor?

Malcolm calls him a 'kite' because 'kite' is another word for a bird of prey. What is the significance of a bird of prey in this context? A bird of prey feeds on other animals. Those who fall prey to it are its victims. Macbeth preys on numerous innocent victims in the play and this makes him an animalistic hunter and destroyer of other people.

Shakespeare adds 'hell' to 'kite', thus *doubling* the effect of the metaphor and giving the title an evil edge. Should the audience be in any doubt as to Macbeth's intentions, 'hell' reminds us that he is devilish. Consider the two words together and you have an evil animal that preys on other creatures. The image is unpleasant, and because of the associations we have with the words 'hell' and 'prey', the extent of Macbeth's evil is increased.

Only in *moving on* from the initial stage of spotting the imagery do we gain an insight into the writer's intentions. By asking ourselves, '*Why* did he use that word?' and, 'What *effect* does it have on the text?' we understand the *reasoning behind* his use of language and therefore his *intention*. In this example, his intention is to portray Macbeth as evil and animalistic at this point in the play.

It is important to remember that our main focus must remain the *whole* text, the writer's intention and what he or she is trying to communicate. Our analysis of different threads of the fabric is only valuable in that it helps us to understand the grand design, the larger pattern; *it is not an end in itself.*

# Technique spotting

It is futile to have a checklist of textual features through which to work, ticking off what is present and (even worse) commenting on what is *not*. Candidates must approach each text by focusing on the elements that *are there* and commenting on the *effect* that they have on it, highlighting the features *which contribute most to its meaning*. It is pointless to work your way down a long catalogue of techniques if you fail to connect these to the *meaning of the text as a whole*. This is why it is useful to have a good knowledge and understanding of *all* the tools of analysis so that you can focus on those that are most influential in the text you are studying.

In order to help you to do this it is necessary to approach this section in a slightly arbitrary way, considering each element separately and, to some extent, in isolation. It is important to remember though, that while this might be a practical way of undertaking the study of these elements, *they do not work in isolation in literature*; the threads are woven closely together, with each thread crossing over and supporting the others, and you must make these connections clear.

# Remember the 4 Cs when dealing with a new analysis

The 4 Cs are:

- calm
- confidence
- close reading
- concentration

It is important to bear in mind that your success at practical criticism in examinations demands a certain approach. Facing a previously *unseen* text under exam conditions against the clock requires a level of cool-headedness greater than that needed in tests of knowledge and understanding of *set* texts.

# Don't panic

Our analytical and creative thinking is seriously impaired when we panic; we tend to 'freeze' and to do so will do you no good in the examination. Remember that the ideas with which the writer is dealing are unlikely to be beyond your grasp; examiners set questions with which they think candidates will be able to *engage*, because without this engagement the whole process is unviable. Markers want to see evidence that you have responded personally to the challenge. In purely practical terms, remember that examining boards at all levels want their candidates to succeed; they are unlikely to set you texts for analysis that are utterly beyond your ability to analyse.

# Tools of analysis – features of text

Every text is like a piece of woven fabric and *all* its threads, or features are connected. Although these tools of analysis are, inevitably, dealt with separately here, it should be remembered that they reflect, enhance and interact with one another in intricate and sometimes inextricable ways in literature.

## Meaning

### Subject

I shall deal with this element first, as it is perhaps the most important hurdle to overcome in our journey towards an understanding of a text. We need to establish, in broad terms only at this stage, the subject matter or **theme**. Ask yourself the simple question, 'What is it *about*?'

After one or two readings you should be able to come up with a reasonably accurate, if not detailed, response. If you find this difficult, try to summarise the text, focusing solely for now on *the content*. Comprehension is absolutely essential to the process of practical criticism. It is your starting point, part of your foundations (remember the discussion earlier about a house and its structure?) and if these foundations are shaky, so too will be the whole building.

*Do not underestimate this element of analysis.* Before rushing in to deal with perhaps more interesting aspects of criticism, a solid 'layer' of basic comprehension *must* be established. Everything else is built upon this. Students will concede that this stage of making sense of a piece is vitally important to the whole process, yet I regularly see them skimp on this and dash headlong into a discussion of deeper issues long before they have safely fixed a *meaning* in their minds.

Concentrate on what the writer is saying. This stage of the process will inevitably entail a close study of the way in which the poem, prose or drama is structured. What are the connections between the stanzas, paragraphs or speeches? Is there an argument, exposition or emotion developing?

Your initial observations cannot hope to explain the writer's intentions or the wider issues at work in the piece and they will inevitably be somewhat superficial. This does not matter at this stage. They simply constitute an essential *framework*, which will guide and direct your analysis of the other elements.

## Sentence structure analysis

Valuable insights into meaning can be gained from a careful analysis of the way in which texts are structured. Consider this aspect of 'To His Coy Mistress' by Andrew Marvell. (See later, pp. 116–17.) The poem's narrator exhorts the object of his desire to agree to his wish for sexual intercourse; he urges her to 'seize the day' and procrastinate no more. His address to her is divided into three sections, the first beginning with 'Had we . . .', the second with 'But . . .' and the last with 'Now therefore. . .'.

- *Section 1*

> **Had we** but world enough, and time,
> This coyness, Lady, were no crime.

- *Section 2*

> **But** at my back I always hear
> Time's wingèd chariot hurrying near;

- *Section 3*

> **Now therefore**, while the youthful hue
> Sits on thy skin like morning dew,
> And while thy willing soul transpires
> At every pore with instant fires,
> Now let us sport us while we may;

'Had we' is merely another form of '*if* we had'. What is emerging now is a clear *shape* to the verse, based on a traditionally structured argument – that of '**if . . . but . . . therefore**'. Here we can see three distinct *stages* to the text. This is the way in which Marvell has chosen to *build* his verse. It has a direction, and a purpose. He argues '*if*' we had all the time in the world I *would* spend ages wooing you, '*but*' we don't, so '*therefore*' let's do it now.

It is important to notice also the way in which verb forms complement this structure. The 'if' section takes the *conditional* form of the verb 'to have' – 'had we'; the 'but' section uses the *present* tense of the verb 'to hear' – 'I always hear'; and the 'therefore' part at the end employs the *imperative* form of the verb 'to sport' – 'Now let us sport us while we may'. Notice the way in which the force of the argument increases; the conditional is just that – uncertain; the present is the actual state of things – the truth (as the narrator sees it); and the imperative issues a command. So the '**if . . . but . . . therefore**' structure of the argument is reinforced by the **conditional . . . present . . . imperative** use of verbs.

Look at this example of the way in which Virginia Woolf manipulates her sentence structure in *Mrs Dalloway*.

> A sound interrupted him; a frail quivering sound, a voice bubbling up without direction, vigour, beginning or end, running weakly and shrilly and with an absence of all human meaning into
>
> > ee um fah um so
> > foo swee too eem oo –
>
> the voice of no age or sex, the voice of an ancient spring spouting from the earth; which issued, just opposite Regent's Park Tube Station, from a tall quivering shape, like a funnel, like a rusty pump, like a wind-beaten tree for ever barren of leaves which lets the wind run up and down its branches singing
>
> > ee um fah um so
> > foo swee too eem oo
>
> and rocks and creaks and moans in the eternal breeze.

A far cry from the ordered use of verb forms and carefully staged arguments in verse with which Marvell presents us, this extract offers us prose that streams poetically in a sentence of 118 words. However, this is not to say that it has no structure. This prose is shaped and built by its repetition, rhythm, punctuation, rhyme and diction.

The repetition of 'a' at the start of the extract, of the vowel sounds in the 'chorus', of 'like' and of 'and' in the last sentence, all invest the text with a dreamy wistfulness and a sense that the sound is endless.

The rhythm is achieved by the grouping of certain words using commas and semi-colons. This gives the piece a lilting effect – a gentle movement – but also a feeling of continuity and smoothness, because the abrupt and absolute interruptions of full stops are absent: 'like a funnel, like a rusty pump, like a wind-beaten tree'. The five monosyllabic sounds in each line of the chorus create the sense of a constant, haunting pulse.

The rhyme that threads its way through the two-line chorus gives it unity and smoothness together with a feeling of perpetuity; this voice is timeless – the repetition suggests this also.

The diction also gives it shape. The use of 'a' numerous times maintains a feeling of vagueness throughout the extract, which is reinforced by the repetition of 'like'. The narrator seems to be searching for a way to define the sound; using 'like' three times suggests that she cannot. It is unique, yet indistinct and imprecise.

The 118-word sentence creates a sense of continuity and the ethereal, which runs alongside the gentle, lilting movement achieved by grouping words inside commas and semi-colons. This stream suggests a sense of timelessness, which is reinforced by words such as 'ancient' and 'eternal'.

Looking at sentence structure is an important tool for analysis and yet is one that students frequently overlook. The sentence is where the words 'live' and it tells us a great deal about the text's meanings. Like all other features or 'how's, it reflects the 'what' and can provide us with valuable insights into the writer's intention.

# Problems and solutions

You may well encounter difficulties at this stage, but none of them is insurmountable. It is as well to be prepared from the outset for some of the problems you might face in the examination.

## Problem: difficult vocabulary or diction

It is possible that the text will contain unfamiliar words that you find hard to understand.

*Action*

• Look at the *context*. It is often possible to make an intelligent guess at a word by considering the words around it. How does it 'fit in'?

- If it is a long word, break it down into smaller parts. Does it have a prefix or a suffix that can guide you towards its meaning?
- Be prepared for this by reading widely from the start of your course and ensure that you build a reasonable vocabulary, appropriate for the study of Advanced- and degree-level English Literature, which will also help you to express yourself fluently and concisely when you write.
- If the vocabulary is at all specialised or technical, *you must not panic*. Technical terms or specific jargon will be explained or, if it is not explained, you will not be expected to understand it, and this will have been taken into account when the paper was set.

## Problem: complex syntax

It is possible that the syntax (which is simply the grammatical arrangement of words) is not entirely straightforward. This may be because the subject matter of the piece is complex and the writer's syntax simply reflects that complexity. There may be complicated sentence structures, which are hard to follow.

*Action*

- Close reading and careful analysis is *essential*. Follow the 'path' that each sentence takes and try hard to 'hang on' to meaning as you discover it. Sloppy reading and lack of concentration are your greatest enemies in this situation. There is little that close focus and meticulous reading will not solve.
- The other cause of difficulties with syntax is likely to be related to the period during which the text was written. It is surprising how quickly writing styles change, and pre-twentieth-century texts can present some candidates with problems.
- Be prepared for this from the outset of the course and *read widely* across the eras. If you confine your reading to twentieth-century texts your reading experience will be impoverished and you will feel uncomfortable with a text from any other period.
- *Do not panic in the examination*. If you allow this to happen you will give your mind permission to seize up in the very areas in which it needs to function both analytically and creatively. The difficulties are likely to be *superficial*, centring on spelling, punctuation and organisation of words, but these are *not* insurmountable and calm thinking will soon 'straighten out' complex constructions.

## Problem: strange or alien settings, events or characters

One of the many benefits that wide reading can provide is the opportunity to experience vicariously a variety of settings, events and characters that are foreign to us. Is that not why many people read, in fact – to taste something that is *outside* their own experience? Literature can transport us to different countries and times; it can introduce us to strange people and unusual events. It is, in a sense, a form of travel, and we must not be afraid to leave temporarily what is familiar and routine to us in order to enrich our experience of life, albeit through somebody else. We cannot hope to have experienced personally all that we encounter in literature. Indeed, literature would seem dull if that were the case!

*Action*

- Go with the flow. *Imagination and a willingness to follow the writer into unknown territory are essential.* If you resist what is new and different you will not get anywhere, either in life or in your study of literature.
- *Be sensitive and empathise.* Try to feel what the writer is feeling. Look at life through his/her eyes.
- Taste the foreign flavours of this new land and *enter into the experience* wholeheartedly. It is the only way to benefit from your travels, from your experience of literature. If you don't, there is little point in studying literature at all.

## Problem: complex ideas

Good literature often deals with ideas or concepts that can be difficult to grasp, and many texts offer A-level and degree-level students intellectual challenges.

*Action*

- Don't shy away from the challenge. One of the most exciting aspects of practical criticism is grappling with complex ideas. Instead of retreating in the face of such demands, try to ask yourself, 'What is the thrust of the writer's argument here?'

## Motif

A motif is much smaller than a theme. It is an image or event that occurs frequently in a text, just as a motif on a piece of fabric appears at regular intervals in its design. An example is the 'nothing' motif in *King Lear*. It should not be confused with the *theme* of a text but it does still add to its meaning.

## Form and structure

Form is to do with *the way in which something is written*. To establish this element of analysis, ask yourself, 'What *form* does it take?' Quite simply, '*How* is this written?'

Why do we bother to discuss form? Some students assume that this is a random decision made by a writer on a whim, and that it matters little what form a text takes; but they could not be more wrong. *Writers choose the form to suit the content.* Form is an aspect of the '**how**' of a text and as such it *must* be appropriate to the '**what**', the content.

Once you have established the subject of the piece, as discussed above, you can then go on to think about the form, because the form will be appropriate to the content or subject.

Poetry is comparatively straightforward in this respect, as there are distinct forms, which are easy to recognise. We shall deal with this genre first.

- Is the poem written in the form of an **ode** or a **sonnet** and so on?

There are a number of other questions, which you will also need to ask yourself:

- Does the structure **emphasise significant features**?
  - (a) Perhaps a particular line is isolated for emphasis?
  - (b) Does repetition enforce an idea or emotion?
  - (c) Can you see an emerging argument, which relies on the structure for its effect?
- Do you notice anything interesting in the **layout** on the page?

In the following poem, '40 Love' by Roger McGough, the layout (or form) visually reinforces the content.

### 40 Love

| | |
|---|---|
| middle | aged |
| couple | playing |
| ten | nis |
| when | the |
| game | ends |
| and | they |
| go | home |
| the | net |
| will | still |
| be | be |
| tween | them |

Here we see the text *mirroring* a tennis court, with an imaginary net down the middle of the page. Notice what happens to your eyes as you read this; they bounce back and forth across the page as a ball would across a court, reflecting the way in which the couple are on opposite sides, separated by a net, hurling words, perhaps even insults at each other across the gap that exists between them.

This is a simple, perhaps somewhat extreme, but effective example of form suiting content, or the '**how**' mirroring the '**what**'.

- Is there a noticeable **rhythm** which falls into a pattern?

Rhythm helps to provide a sense of *movement* in a text. Think about *how* the rhythm in this poem is created. What effect does it have on the text? Does it emphasise a particular idea or emotion?

- Look for **pauses**.

Much is to be gained from an examination of these, and this is an aspect of practical criticism that is frequently overlooked. Pauses, like everything else in good literature, are there for a reason. They often create drama and their location is vital. The usual position for a pause in poetry is at the *end* of a line and this is sometimes reinforced by punctuation such as a comma, full stop or semi-colon.

The very fact that the line of verse ends and another begins is sufficient to cause a slight pause as we read.

Where there are breaks *within* a line, we should always ask, '*Why?*'

- Look at the *intensity* of the pause; a full stop is more intense than a comma, for example. Is it a mild pause or a strong one? How much drama is created by this pause?
- Examine what is *before* and *after* the pause. Why is there a pause at that particular point in the poem?
- What *effect* does the pause create? It halts the flow of the verse, so what does this do to the verse?
- *What idea is isolated* by the pause? How important is it? How relevant is it to the central meaning of the poem?

Remember that:

- Each device that is used by a writer will have an *effect* on the whole piece.
- Each device is in someway *linked to the meaning* of the whole piece.

*Always* ask yourself, '*Why* is that pause there?'

- **End stop** and **enjambment** greatly affect the movement of a poem.

*Where* are they? *Why* are they *there*? Enjambment, or 'run-on' lines, creates a sense of continuity, whereas end stop (simply stopping at the end of a line, denoted by punctuation such as commas, full stops, question marks or exclamation marks, semi-colons or colons) causes a pause and can be used to emphasise what is on either side of that punctuation.

- **Length of stanza** should be considered.

What is the effect of a short or long stanza? What happens in the poem when there is a mixture of short and long stanzas? Are there any patterns emerging in the stanzas that can be connected to length?

- **Metre** should be looked at.

This relates to the combination of stressed and unstressed syllables. Metre was thought to keep a text tightly held together, and evidence of this can still be seen in limericks and nursery rhymes. Look at where the stresses fall. Are these places significant? If you are unsure about metre and its function in literature, do not worry about this aspect now; it is dealt with in detail later.

- Is the poem written in **blank verse**?

This is unrhymed iambic pentameters. It is a form that is commonly used for narratives and for communicating thoughts and feelings. Its rhythms are consistent and help to give the writing a sense of purpose and direction.

- Is it written in **free verse**?

This is poetry that seldom rhymes and does not have lines of regular length. The feeling is one of freedom; poetic conventions have been done away with. It is a popular mode for twentieth-century poets. Again, a fuller discussion of free verse occurs under 'Rhythm' (see pages 54–7).

- Are there any **rhyming couplets**?

This is rhymed iambic pentameter in which the lines rhyme in twos, so that line one rhymes with line two, line three with line four and so on. Fuller discussion of rhyming couplets appears under 'Rhyme' on pages 42–5.

## Tone

Tone is an element of analysis with which students often struggle. They know it is a key ingredient of all literature, but frequently find it difficult to define. It is, like all these aspects of a text, entwined in the fabric of the writing; just another thread in the material, but one that is key to discovering the writer's *intention*. It is the tone that creates the feel of the text and it is essential to establish this if you are to discuss meaning successfully.

So how is the tone of a text determined? A rule that generations of students have found helpful is to read the poem or passage through several times and then decide which *tone of voice* you would use to read it *aloud*. Anyone who has had experience of drama or theatre will be aware of the importance that is placed upon the tone of voice in which a line is delivered. **Changing the tone can entirely change the meaning**. You may well have heard the expression, 'The medium *is* the message'. If we think of 'medium' as meaning 'how', then we see that 'how' something is said really establishes 'what' is being said.

Take a few moments to try a simple exercise to see if this idea works.

- Think of as many *different* ways as you can to say aloud, 'Where are you going?'
- Say them *all aloud*.
- Now think of the adjectives that you would use to describe your different tones of voice for example, 'angry', 'curious', 'pleading', 'challenging' and so on.

Perhaps you have heard the expression, 'It's not what you say, it's the way that you say it'. It is as true in literature as it is in life. Your angry 'Where are you going?' does not mean the same as the identical question put in a pleading tone. *It is not the same question put another way; it is a **different** question*. Why? Because your *tone of voice reveals your attitude* and attitude is an important part of the meaning.

Your angry 'Where are you going?' means that you are communicating your anger by demanding to know where another person is going. You are challenging that person, showing your displeasure. Your angry tone *means* that you are angry.

A pleading 'Where are you going?' suggests that you are begging that person not to go. You are imploring him/her, showing your weakness and need. Your beseeching tone *means* that you are desperate.

So, you see that **tone establishes meaning**. It is not an add-on element, which we might or might not choose to discuss; it is *essential* to any consideration of meaning or content.

Imagine an extract from an early-twentieth-century piece of writing about the emancipation of women. You have to discuss the content or subject. To do this you *must* consider the tone. Picture the different outcomes if the piece were:

- an angry outcry against women's continuing equality and freedom in which the writer expresses his (or her, but this is unlikely) indignation and displeasure at changing social trends

or

- a triumphant celebration of the positive and long overdue changes in the position of women in which the writer shares with us his (or her) pleasure and excitement at changing social trends.

The two extracts **mean** different things. They are *not* the same thing said in two different ways. Tone informs us about attitude, and *attitude is part of meaning*.

## Figurative language

### Allegory

Allegory is a narrative in which the surface events represent abstract ideas. Sometimes writers find they can comment upon and satirise characters more effectively by presenting them as someone or something else. John Bunyan's *The Pilgrim's Progress* is a famous example which personifies abstract concepts and vices in characters such as Lechery, Pride, Mr Worldly-Wise and Christian, the pilgrim. Another well-known example is *Animal Farm*, in which George Orwell illustrates the correspondence between certain animals and key characters in the Russian Revolution; for example, Napoleon the pig, and Stalin.

Allegory and satire sometimes work together; it is a convenient way of thinly disguising identity so as to ridicule individuals or systems.

### Conceit

This is an elaborate, improbable and extended metaphor that compares two very different things. It is common in metaphysical poetry; for example, in John Donne's 'The Flea', in which he compares himself and his lover to a flea which, having sucked the blood of both, acts as a unifying force in their relationship.

Another example is in 'A Valediction: Forbidding Mourning', Donne's comparison of lovers' spirits with the two feet of a pair of compasses in that the movements of one are influenced by those of the other.

Although our initial response to some conceits is to think of them as unlikely and strange, the intention is that they be seen as imaginative and proof of astute observation on the part of the writer. Metaphysical poets were trying hard to come to terms with a changing world and much of their work reflects what might seem to be rather odd ways of understanding and relating human experience. Conceits can present the reader with a challenge, but as with any metaphor, we approach them by establishing what features both elements have in common. This exercise can be a refreshing one; in seeking to understand the mind of the writer, we are presented with new ways of looking at the world and at our experiences of it.

## Diction

This refers to the selection and organisation of words in a text. In everyday language, the word is similar to 'vocabulary'. A writer's choice of words provides us with important clues to the meaning of a text and it gives us a great deal of information about his/her attitude to the subject. Just as we learn about people in real life from the language they use, a writer's diction contains much that is potentially useful in our discussion of any text and its author's intentions.

Notice the difference between the diction in Oliver Goldsmith's *The Deserted Village* and Brian Patten's 'Dead Thick', respectively:

> While words of learned length and thundering sound
> Amaz'd the gazing rustics rang'd around,

and

> It's exhausting. The kids are thick.
> They've nothing between their ears.

Diction can help us to establish such things as attitude, temperament, social class and context. This will be evident in Chapter 12, in the discussion of the original and adapted versions of 'They Flee From Me That Sometime Did Me Seek', where the issue is discussed in detail.

## Imagery

In simple terms, imagery refers to the 'pictures' or 'images' that a writer helps to create in the reader's mind through the language that he or she uses. However, these 'pictures' are not always concerned with what we *see*. They can be:

- **visual** – to do with what we *see*;
- **aural** – relating to what we *hear*;
- **tactile** – concerned with what we can *feel* or *touch*;
- **olfactory** – about what we *smell*; or
- **gustorial** – to do with the sensations of *flavour* and *texture* in the mouth.

It is important to remember that different types of imagery can overlap. What seems perhaps to be only visual can cross the boundaries between sight and tangibility, and offer us also some sense of what is felt.

### Visual imagery

> I see the dawn creep round the world
> Here damm'd a moment backward by great hills
> Robert Louis Stevenson, 'Song at Dawn'

The visual imagery in these lines is straightforward. Stevenson's use of 'see' immediately signposts the visual aspect for us. A visual picture of a sunrise comes to mind and the second line further embellishes the image because we are told that the dawn is 'damn'd a moment backward by great hills', suggesting that the hills are somehow holding it back so that the light seems to be amassing behind the mountains. We can then expect an enormous outflow of light when the dawn bursts the banks of the dam.

The word 'creep' personifies the dawn as moving forward surreptitiously, while 'damm'd' suggests a halting of that movement. Both references to movement add to the visual impact of the lines.

The long, open vowels of 'see', 'dawn', 'creep', 'round' and 'world' all slow down this movement and reinforce the meaning of 'creep'. The *sound* of individual words must also be considered in a discussion of imagery.

## Aural imagery

> And thud! flump! thud! down the steep steps came thumping
> And splashing in the flood, deluging muck –
> The sentry's body.
>
> Wilfred Owen, 'The Sentry'

Here Owen's impact lies in the aural imagery in the lines. The arrival of the sentry's body is heralded by numerous references to the sounds it makes as it falls into the dug-out. These sounds – 'thud', 'flump', 'thump' and 'splash' – are all onomatopoeic and suggest heaviness.

The dead German's body thunders down the opening to the dug-out and lands unceremoniously in the midst of its enemy. By using this type of aural imagery Owen creates a 'sound picture' of the scene which serves to enhance his message about the gruesome inhumanity of war.

## Tactile imagery

> And he took the stick and he thrust it in
> Hard and quick in the furry dark,
> The black fur squealed and he felt his skin
> Prickle with sparks of dry delight.
>
> Vernon Scannell, 'A Case of Murder'

The aspect of touch is very evident in this extract. The word 'stick' suggests a harshness, something hard, as does 'thrust'. The 'hard' of line 2 reinforces this, and this impenetrability is contrasted with 'furry dark', which has a yielding, resilient feel to it. Once again, softness is suggested with the word 'fur' and then 'felt' is a clear indicator of the tactile element in the verse. Further references to 'skin', 'prickle' and 'dry delight' all clearly develop this idea of touch.

Notice the 'texture' of the language. The 'stick', 'hard' and 'quick' of the first two lines 'feel' harsh. The consonants are hard, the vowels short. The hard 'k' in 'quick', 'dark', 'prickle' and 'sparks' emphasises the viciousness of the attack on the cat. The contrast between the hard stick and the soft cat highlights the brutal nature of the injury.

## Olfactory imagery

> Season of mists and mellow fruitfulness,
> Close bosom friend of the maturing sun,

> Conspiring with him how to load and bless
> With fruit the vines that round the thatch-eaves run:
>
> John Keats, 'To Autumn'

Notice how words such as 'mists', 'mellow fruitfulness', 'maturing sun', 'fruit', 'vines' and even 'thatch-eaves' evoke a typical autumn smell. Keats is appealing heavily to our experience of smell as he works to create a sense of place and time in the first stanza of the poem. The result is a heady mixture of fruit and late summer sun, so evocative of autumn days. It is as if we breathe our way into the verse.

## Gustorial imagery

The imagery of taste is exemplified in Keats's 'The Eve of St Agnes':

> With jellies soother than the creamy curd,
> And lucent syrops, tinct with cinnamon;

The sweetness of jelly is combined with its smoothness and this texture is emphasised by 'creamy'. The word 'syrops' also suggests a smooth sweetness, and there is the other flavour of 'cinnamon'. Two lines to make your mouth water.

The imagery of taste, smell and touch can add a certain sensuousness to a text. This means simply that there is an appeal to one or more of the five senses: sight, sound, touch, taste and smell. This should not be confused with another useful term in practical criticism – '*sensual*'. This differs from '*sensuous*' in that 'sensual' is to do with the more fleshly or erotic side of feeling; it is pleasing in a more sexual way.

That is not to suggest that the two are always entirely separate. Writers make much of the link between food and sex, and this association is often exploited in our media today. Nor is this concept new; D. H. Lawrence makes some vivid connections in this respect in his 'Sea and Sardinia'.

## Mixed imagery

Imagery frequently falls into more than one category; the boundaries between categories are often blurred. Take, for example, Andrew Marvell's 'To His Coy Mistress':

> Now therefore, while the youthful hue
> Sits on thy skin like morning dew,

Notice that 'youthful' is perhaps at first associated with the visual aspects of a description, but it is also to do with the tactile. Skin that is young *looks* youthful, but it also *feels* young; it is tighter, smoother and softer than older skin.

The same applies to 'morning dew'. Although dew is visually discernible we are also aware of its tactile properties; it is damp and fresh, and perhaps cool. There is a beauty and a purity about it which we perceive both through its visual *and* its tactile qualities.

Another way of looking at imagery is to think of it as a writer describing something *in terms of something else*.

Imagery is an area that students sometimes find difficult to discuss, but it is essential to establish in your mind exactly what it means and to be able to spot it in a text and talk about it meaningfully in an essay. It is about *the emotional response that the writer evokes in you, the reader, and about the feelings or the atmosphere that he or she creates in the text.*

Perhaps the most important aspect of all is that imagery tells us about *how the writer feels towards the subject about which he or she is writing.* In *Macbeth*, when Malcolm refers to Macbeth as a 'hell-kite', this imagery of both a bird of prey and a creature from hell tells us what Malcolm is feeling about Macbeth, therefore it informs us about Shakespeare's *attitude* as the writer, in this case to a character.

By using imagery, a writer has a way of communicating *a feeling about his/her subject*. Perhaps without realising it, we use imagery in everyday language; what are we doing, for example, when we describe someone as 'sweet' or 'bitter'? We are using the imagery of taste to communicate *the way that we feel about that person*. Imagery is not a *literal* use of language; when we employ it we are using language *figuratively*. That person would not *literally* be sweet if you taste him or her, nor is he or she *literally* bitter.

Another everyday is example is the term 'laid-back'. When we describe someone in this way we are not suggesting that he/she is literally lying down; we merely mean that he/she is calm or easy-going. We are given an *image* of someone in a physically relaxed position to suggest a person who has a placid disposition.

What imagery does is make the writer's language more

- intense;
- precise; and
- direct.

In short, it adds a great deal of **power** to a text.

Still under the heading of 'imagery' we should now consider some different examples of figurative or non-literal language use.

## Simile

When a writer chooses to compare one thing with another by using words such as 'like' or 'as' it is called a simile. Again, it is an example of a writer describing one thing in terms of another. However, when using a simile he or she is not saying that one thing *is* another, but only that it is *like* another. See, for example, William Wordsworth's untitled poem, 'I wandered lonely as a cloud', commonly known as 'Daffodils':

> I wandered lonely **as** a cloud
> That floats on high o'er vales and hills

He is not suggesting that he *is* a cloud, only that he felt like one in his loneliness.

An important question to ask yourself is '*Why* is he like a cloud? *In what ways* does he resemble a cloud?' We could think of a few explanations:

- Clouds are *lonely* in a sense.
- They are somewhat *inconstant*, ever-changing.

- They *merge* at times with other clouds then *break away* into solitude again.
- They are *removed from the rest of us in a world of their own*, looking down on humanity from an elevated position.
- They are *natural*, and not only are they products of nature but they are also subject to its laws and influences. Mankind has no control over them.

By establishing the qualities of clouds we have come a long way towards an understanding of Wordsworth's narrator's view of himself (he likens himself to a cloud, after all) as well as his *intentions and attitudes*, and it is *only* by *analysing the nature of imagery* that we can hope to gain any understanding of *how* the writer *sees* the object of it.

In short, the best way to appreciate the attitude of the writer is to analyse his/her imagery. We shall best understand *what* he/she has written and *how* he/she has written it if we try to establish *why* it was written. The *why* question can be answered by gaining an understanding of the imagery.

## Metaphor

When a writer chooses to compare one thing with another so strongly that he/she says that one thing *is* another we call it metaphor. A *figurative* word or group of words actually replaces the *literal* meaning. See the examples in D. H. Lawrence's 'Last Lesson of the Afternoon':

> How long have they **tugged the leash**, and **strained apart**
> My **pack of unruly hounds**! I cannot start
> Them again on a **quarry** of knowledge they hate to **hunt**,
> I can **haul** them and **urge** them no more.

Here Lawrence uses the metaphor of a pack of hounds to describe the actions of the narrator's pupils. Words and phrases such as 'tugged the leash', 'strained apart', 'pack of unruly hounds', 'quarry', 'hunt', 'haul' and 'urge' all relate to hounds. The narrator does not say that his pupils are *like* hounds; he says that *they are one and the same*.

Metaphor helps a writer to make concrete what are often rather abstract ideas, thereby enabling the reader to understand these concepts more clearly.

It is always necessary to ask, '*Why* has the writer chosen this type of metaphor? What are the *connections* between hounds and schoolboys?' These questions are the key to understanding the nature of the metaphor used and therefore the attitude of the writer. Lawrence quite clearly sees the boys *in terms of a pack of hounds*. The boys are eager to be free of his control and they are undisciplined. The narrator concedes that he cannot direct them towards a search for learning in which they are reluctant to engage; he seems weary with the effort. It does not take a great deal of imagination to connect this description with a class of reluctant pupils.

Metaphors often have the effect of making us look at the world in a different way – the way the writer sees it. They link the familiar with the unfamiliar at times – what is known with what is often at first sight *very* different. This is why it is essential to ask that question, '*Why* has the writer used this imagery? What is it about school boys that makes him connect them with hounds?' Once you have answered that question you are well on the way to a real understanding of the text.

Metaphors tend to be concentrated, somewhat condensed and compact, and for this reason they can sometimes be difficult to 'unpack'. There is an intensity in metaphor that is lacking in simile; it is remarkable what a difference the addition of 'as' or 'like' can make.

## Personification

This is when characteristics that are normally associated with human beings are attributed to abstract ideas or inanimate objects. *Why* should a writer choose to do this? *The effect* is that the idea or the object seems more tangible to us, easier to 'get hold of', and turning it into something human helps us to relate to it as we would to another person.

Personification also gives the writer greater scope; there is more you can *do* with a person than an idea or an object. People can act out types of behaviour, which exemplify their characters.

In 'To Autumn' Keats personifies autumn:

> . . . sitting careless on a granary floor,
> Thy hair soft-lifted by the winnowing wind;

'Sitting careless' gives 'her' a sense of abandon, a certain mellowness and ease. She is on the granary floor because it is her efforts that are responsible for the harvest and the wind gently lifts her hair as it winnows. She is affected by the forces of nature; the same wind that winnows the crop stirs her hair.

We hear that she is 'drowsed with the fume of poppies', which again creates a softness mixed with a heavy fullness that Keats sees as characterising autumn. Turning the season into a woman has given the poet seemingly endless opportunities to help the reader to relate to the idea of autumn.

When we read in this example from a pupil's work, 'fear gripped my throat and stomach with its iron grasp', it is easier for us to imagine fear as this writer has done; someone who has his (or her) hands around the narrator's throat and stomach. The fact that it is 'iron' suggests hardness and coldness. The intensity of the fear is greatly enhanced by turning it into a person. We imagine a terrifying individual gripping a helpless narrator, and the idea becomes something concrete that we can see in our mind's eye.

Personification pushes back the boundaries that would inevitably limit any discussion of an abstract idea or an object. Human beings can be given physical appearance, character, personality, life history, dialogue and idiosyncrasies; the list is endless and all these elements make it easier for us to engage with the concept.

## Reification

This is similar to personification in that relates to employing something tangible or 'solid' to present either a person or an abstract or intangible idea. It is similar to personification, but instead of using a person, the writer makes use of a thing with similar qualities. 'Reification' derives from the Latin word 'res', meaning 'a thing'.

An example from T. S. Eliot's 'The Love Song of J. Alfred Prufrock' exemplifies this:

> I should have been a pair of ragged claws
> Scuttling across the floors of silent seas.

This process often occurs in everyday life. Perhaps you have heard of people suffering from a disease who will mentally turn the illness into a thing in order to cope with it better. Patients with a crippling disease, for example, will sometimes imagine it as an object. Some see it as a black shape that has long tentacles and sharp claws, which grip the victim painfully, seldom releasing its hold of them. Images like this, while they are unpleasant, do help us to make something that is essentially abstract become more tangible and therefore easier to handle.

Like personification, reification can give a writer enormous scope in terms of description. The thing can have a physical appearance and characteristics, which bring it to life in a way that means we can see it more clearly and respond to it more meaningfully. It is another way of giving abstract concepts concrete meaning.

## Hyperbole

Hyperbole is the use of a figure of speech that relies on exaggeration or overstatement to emphasise the importance or, conversely the insignificance, of something. The effects of this on a text can vary and it may be employed in order to be:

- genuine;
- comic; or
- ironic.

**Comic** and **ironic** use of hyperbole can be seen in Alexander Pope's *The Rape of the Lock*. The poem is inspired by an incident in which Lord Petre removes a lock of hair from the head of its owner, Miss Arabella Fermor. A great deal of ill-will is caused by this, and the aim of poem is to reunite the families by making them laugh.

The narrator tells of the man's longing for the lock of hair and Pope's mastery of the mock heroic style is evident in lines such as those that follow, in which the hyperbole is emboldened:

> For this, **ere Phoebus rose**, he had **implored**
> **Propitious Heaven, and every power adored**:

The grandeur of both language and concept contrasts sharply and comically with the trivial object of his desire. A line such as 'What dire offence from am'rous causes springs' could easily introduce an epic love story or come from a truly epic poem. This use of exaggeration relies on the contrast of the grandeur of style with the triviality of content, and the effect is both comic and ironic:

- *comic* – because of the discrepancy between style and content; and
- *ironic* – because of the way in which it highlights the folly of human nature.

**Genuine** use of hyperbole can be seen in Marvell's 'To His Coy Mistress':

> I would
> Love you **ten years before the Flood**:
> And you should, if you please, refuse
> **Till the conversion of the Jews.**
> My vegetable love should grow
> **Vaster than empires, and more slow.**
> An hundred years should go to praise
> Thine eyes, and on thy forehead gaze.
> **Two hundred to adore each breast:**
> **But thirty thousand to the rest.**
> **An age at least to every part,**
> And **the last age should show your heart.**
> For, Lady, you deserve this state;
> **Nor would I love at lower rate.**

Emboldened are the words and phrases of hyperbole at work in the poem. The narrator uses gross exaggeration to convince his coy mistress that, had he all the time in the world, he would indulge her by courting her for long periods of time.

**Genuine** use of hyperbole is also apparent in Shakespeare's *Antony and Cleopatra*:

> His **legs bestrid the ocean**: his **rear'd arm**
> **Crested the world**: his **voice was propertied**
> **As all the tuned spheres**, and that to friends;
> But when he meant to **quail and shake the orb,**
> **He was as rattling thunder.**

Later we read that:

> **in his livery**
> **Walk'd crowns and crownets; realms and islands were**
> **As plates dropp'd from his pocket.**

The words and phrases of hyperbole at work in this poem are emboldened, and we can see that the tone of Shakespeare's hyperbole is quite different from that of Marvell. Cleopatra is utterly in awe of her Antony. She sees him as a god, and to her he takes on superhuman dimensions. Here the imagery is of a man who lets 'realms and islands' fall 'from his pocket'. The hyperbole is not comic, nor is it ironic, but rather a reflection of the esteem in which she holds her lover.

## Symbolism

Symbolism is a powerful and effective device. It is the use of an object to stand for something else, often something more abstract. Well-known examples include a rainbow that symbolises hope, a dove that stands for peace, and a horseshoe for good luck. There are numerous others, which have woven themselves into the fabric of our daily lives and which we happily accept in everyday language.

Sometimes there is a known connection between the symbol and that to which it refers; for example, we know why the dove symbolises peace. After the biblical

Flood, a dove was sent from Noah's ark and returned with an olive branch in its beak as a sign that God's anger at a wicked world had passed. It signifies the quiet after the storm. Take away that connection and there is nothing inherent in a dove that says, 'peace' to us. The dove has *become* a symbol of peace because someone significant chose to use it as such, and it is commonly accepted as a symbol of peace by a particular culture.

However, it is important to remember that symbolism is in fact culture-specific. In the West, the colour black is commonly held to be a symbol of death. It is a popular colour at funerals and Victorians edged their condolence cards with black. Black armbands were worn as a symbol of death, and widow's weeds (black dresses) were worn for long periods following a husband's passing. Interestingly, if one ventures further east, the colour that is commonly believed to signify death is white. Mourners are expected to wear white at funerals, and funereal customs all operate around white where those of the West are based on black.

What is important is that symbols are a powerful language in any linguistic community and an inevitable part of the way in which we try to talk about our feelings. Understanding symbolism in literature relates to thinking in a certain way; looking for meaning in everyday objects. For example in Thomas Hardy's 'At Castle Boterel' the narrator 'look[s] behind at the fading byway', which symbolises his dimly remembered past life. In Ursula Fanthorpe's 'Family Entertainment' the narrator mentions the ladies wearing 'floral dresses and sandals'. These items do not in themselves *mean* propriety and social correctness but in the context of the poem, they *suggest* or *connote* it.

In Virginia Woolf's *To The Lighthouse*, the eponymous structure is distant, austere, built upon rock, stark and straight. It stands in water, which suggests fluidity and flux. Water could be seen to represent the feminine and the lighthouse the masculine (the obviously phallic form leaves little room for doubt). The lighthouse becomes a symbol of the eternal and immutable.

Some symbols are less 'representational'. Consider the 'no entry' traffic sign. There seems to be little connection between a white horizontal line through a red circle and no access to traffic. But it doesn't matter; what does matter is that we all *know* what the symbol means in our culture, therefore it *works* (usually).

There is a constant striving in every writer to find new and personal ways of conveying his/her thoughts and feelings about the world. When a writer turns to simile, metaphor, imagery in general and symbolism, among other devices, it is a sign of this striving. He or she needs to find another *dimension* in which to tell us his/her story. It is a similar idea to that of a *parallel universe* in a way, and this *lateral thinking* is discussed in detail in Chapter 5.

Vital clues as to meaning are frequently missed because candidates fail to recognise symbols at work in a text. The category that suffers most from this neglect is that of Christian symbolism, and there is a guide to this and to other patterns of symbol use in the reference section in Chapter 15.

## Conventions

This refers to customary practices in literature; what it is usual to do in certain literary circumstances. The *sonnet* offers us a good example of the conventions of form. It is customary for it to have fourteen lines and a rhyme scheme that follows one of two particular patterns. There is usually a change in course after either eight or twelve lines, and convention also states that sonnets are love poems.

There are numerous conventions existing in all forms of literature. Essential to the art of practical criticism is familiarity with these conventions, and the ability to recognise and comment in a meaningful way on the ways in which texts deviate from these, suggesting reasons why.

There is, for example, a customary diction for verse; language that it is usual to use when writing poetry. We are quite accustomed to this variety of language and we expect it when we read poetry. When poets choose to deviate from this norm and use diction that is unexpected in the context of verse, this deviation demands analysis and comment. Nothing in good literature is ever random, and the breaking of conventions, be it in the diction, form or any other aspect of literature, must be carefully considered.

A poet might choose to write about a trivial theme in language that is elevated, such as in mock-heroic verse, exemplified in Pope's *The Rape of the Lock*. As discussed earlier, this deals with the theft of a woman's curl, but it presents the actions and repercussions in lofty terms. Pope's intention is to ridicule society's folly and pride, and he does this is in a light-hearted and playful way through his diction. Brian Patten does the opposite, but also defies convention, in 'Dead Thick', when the English teacher discusses educational achievement and the learning process using colloquial and mundane language. This contradiction between diction and content is an example of deviation from convention and it can have dramatic effects on the reader's response to the text. It says much about the writer's *attitude* to the subject.

For a fuller discussion of diction and convention you should read the analysis of the two versions of 'They Flee From Me That Sometime Did Me Seek', in Chapter 12.

## Sound

### Rhyme

Rhyme is perhaps one of poetry's most noticeable properties and it plays a significant role in establishing the *aural* nature of a poem, in other words what it *sounds* like. As with rhythm, it is a key component in determining the *musical* features of verse. Rhyme refers to the likeness between sounds, particularly noticeable at the end of lines.

Certain forms of poetry – for example, the sonnet and rhyming couplets – will dictate the pattern of rhyme, which will pertain throughout the poem. Although rhyme is normally considered to be the easiest of the many features of literature to be analysed, its use is sometimes subtle, and the student needs to be alerted to the presence of rhyme in all its forms.

### End rhyme

This simply refers to rhyme that occurs at the *end* of a line of poetry and it is this position we most frequently consider when we discuss this element of analysis.

It is essential to think about the *effect* that different types of rhyme have on the writing, both in terms of *that line and the whole piece.*

Depending on the precise type of rhyme, end rhyme will produce a feeling of completion, resolution or satisfaction, or indeed the opposite. For details see below.

### Internal rhyme

This, as its name suggests, is rhyme that occurs *within* a line of verse. Rhyme within lines of poetry will:

- enhance the pace at which the poem moves; and
- emphasise the words that rhyme.

Hilaire Belloc's 'Tarantella':

> Do you remember an Inn,
> Miranda?
> Do you remember an Inn?
> And the **tedding** and the **spreading**
> Of the straw for a **bedding**,
> And the **fleas** that **tease** in the High **Pyrenees**,

Notice how the pace of the verse *quickens* at the site of internal rhyme. The poem begins slowly and somewhat pensively. The first three lines are unhurried; rather meandering with their language of recollection such as, 'Do you remember', which is repeated for emphasis and the line breaks slowing it down further. Suddenly the pace increases with the internal rhyme of 'tedding' and 'spreading', which is echoed in the end rhyme of 'bedding'.

This occurs again immediately with the 'fleas that tease in the High Pyrenees', giving the verse a speed and vivacity that we do not see in the first three lines. Notice the way in which the emphasis seems naturally to fall upon the rhymed words.

So what has this to do with the meaning? It could be said to mirror the way in which our thoughts seem to gather speed when we reflect on past events. This process often begins slowly and then seems to quicken as we 'grasshopper' from one thing to another. The repetition of the 'edding' sound also gives the verse a sense of continuity. The sound seems to go on and on, suggesting almost a list of the things that the narrator can remember about Miranda and their past together.

## Types of rhyme

### Masculine rhyme

This term refers to rhyme in which the *last* syllable of the rhyme is stressed, as in 'before/adore' and 'expect/reject'. This pattern of rhyme is more emphatic and conspicuous and it highlights the rhymed words. This is well illustrated in William Blake's 'The Poison Tree':

> I was angry with my **friend**:
> I told my wrath, my wrath did **end**.

> I was angry with my **foe**:
> I told it not, my wrath did **grow**.

Masculine rhyme includes the rhyming of monosyllabic words, which are inevitably stressed, and this is where much of the emphasis comes from. 'Friend' and 'end' are typical examples. It is important to remember that *rhyme links the ideas of the rhymed words*, so, bearing this in mind, if we consider 'friend' and 'end' in the context of 'The Poison Tree', we can soon see that rhyme has provided a vital clue to the *meaning*. Blake is saying that when he tells his anger to his 'friend', experience has taught him that it will 'end', but when he does not do this with his 'foe' his anger will 'grow'. If we now take the ideas that are represented by the pairs 'friend/end' and 'foe/grow' we can see that *the whole meaning of the poem is encapsulated in the rhymed words*.

It is essential to remember that all the features of text, which are our tools of analysis, exist merely to enhance and support the *meaning* of the text. You must always *ensure that your discussion illustrates this point*. Remember the questions, '*Why* has the writer done that here?' and '*What effect* does it have upon the text?' You should be seeking constantly to *relate the 'how' to the 'what'*, or the style to the content.

## Feminine rhyme

Feminine rhyme refers to rhyme in which the last syllable is unstressed – for example, 'aching/breaking' and 'hollow/follow'. Because that last syllable is unstressed the effect that is created suggests a certain 'fading' or 'vanishing'. The end is less certain, more vague and unknown. There is sometimes a feeling of slight uneasiness, as in Wilfred Owen's 'Strange Meeting':

> Courage was mine, and I had **mys**tery,
> Wisdom was mine, and I had **mas**tery;

While the language itself in this example creates a sense of uncertainty there is also a feeling of vagueness that comes through the feminine rhyme. The last syllables seem to evaporate and the atmosphere is the more ethereal or intangible because of this.

Feminine rhyme gives a text a generally gentler, 'wispier' feel. It is less hard, less emphatic and this fading away tends to add softness to the tone.

## Half rhyme

Half rhyme, also known as para-rhyme, is rhyme that is in a way incomplete or imperfect. The paired words rhyme *up to a point* but not entirely, and this can create a certain discomfort. The rhyme is not quite satisfactory; loose ends have not really been tied up as pleasingly as they are with full rhyme. There is a feeling of unease and we feel perhaps a little troubled.

The characteristic of half rhyme is the matching of the consonants but with the dissimilarity of the vowels on either side of them. This gives the words a certain 'looseness' quite different from the 'tightness' and unity that comes from full rhyme.

Owen's 'Strange Meeting' once more provides an example:

> It seemed that out of battle I e**scaped**
> Down some profound dull tunnel, long since **scooped**

> Through granites which titanic wars had **groined**.
> Yet also there encumbered sleepers **gro**aned,

Here Owen's imagery vividly creates a sense of the horror of war, but this feeling is enhanced by the half rhyme or consonance because we are left with a rhyme that is not precise, somewhat discordant. It upsets the unity of the poem and its awkwardness makes us uncomfortable. It is an appropriate tool with which to draw a picture of war as a destroyer of harmony and unity, and it is a method frequently used by poets to create a sense of fragmentation, which was so popular with the early-twentieth-century modernist writers. It speaks of a fractured and disordered world, which, like the rhyme, is not entirely 'at peace'.

### Eye rhyme

As the term would suggest, this happens when a word rhymes 'visually' on the page

> Come live with me and be my **love**
> And we shall all the pleasures **prove**

Although when we *look* at them the words rhyme, in this example the *sound* effect is that of **imperfect rhyme**, because again the rhyme is incomplete and the feeling is one of discordance and disruption. The only harmony created by eye rhyme is visual; it unites the verse *visually* on the page.

## Alliteration

Alliteration is the name given to the repetition of consonant *sounds* (not letters) at the beginning of two or more words and as such it is an aspect of aural imagery discussed earlier. A distinction needs to be made between letters and sounds; alliteration exists even when the consonants are different, provided that their *sounds* are alike – for example, in Charles Dickens's 'feathered phenomenon' in *A Christmas Carol*. The 'f' *sound* of 'feathered' is reiterated in '**ph**enomenon'.

Poetry is written to be read aloud and it is important that you do not overlook its aural aspects, which are always extremely significant. Alliteration is perhaps one of the most easily identifiable devices, but remember that you will be given no credit whatever for merely spotting it. You have to be able to say something about:

- *Why* the writer has used it; and
- The *effect* that it has on the text.

Alliteration tends to *emphasise* the words to which it is applied. These words are highlighted and our attention is drawn to them automatically.

Alliterated words are *linked together by sound* just as rhymed words are joined by rhyme. It is worth seeing what happens when you consider the *meanings* of the alliterated, and therefore linked, words. Look at Owen's 'Arms and the Boy':

> Lend him to stroke these **blind, blunt bullet-heads**

The narrator talks of the innocence of youth and of the way in which it is exploited for the purposes of war. The alliteration in this line has some interesting effects on the verse.

First, consider the *connection* between the alliterated words. We have links made between 'blind', 'blunt' and 'bullet-heads'. The first two words are obviously adjectives for the noun 'bullet-heads' so in that sense they are linked already, but notice how they both have identical first *and second* consonant sounds, linking them even more strongly to one another. Owen tells us that the bullet-heads are blind, in other words they cannot see their target; it is perhaps an ironic twist on Cupid and his blindness: 'All's fair in love and war'? Because they cannot see they cannot *discern* and so they have the frightening potential to strike randomly. 'Blunt' also suggests a lack of feeling, a dullness or absence of sensitivity. They are made of metal, cold and lifeless. The bullet-heads have no sense of the damage they are doing. They are senseless, obedient only to the orders of the soldiers who discharge them. The bullets are unquestioning; they are aimed and they perform mindlessly the task they were created to carry out. Owen says that they 'long to nuzzle in the hearts of lads'. The word 'nuzzle', with its associations of warmth and cosiness, is an interesting contrast to the feeling we have just discussed.

Then it is helpful to look at the *sound* of the alliterated words. 'Bullet-heads' is the third word to begin with 'b', and this letter is interesting in itself. Notice how the 'l' that came next to the 'b' in 'blind' and 'blunt' is only one letter away in 'bullet'. 'B' and 'p' are known as 'plosive' consonants, which means that they 'explode' or 'burst' because they are in fact the result of a small explosion of air from the lips as they are spoken. They add a harsh, *explosive* quality to the language and therefore, *in this context* they are an eminently suitable choice, because we are discussing bullets *and* because the plosive 'b' and 'p' are harsh. Remember that we are always seeking to *link the 'how' with the 'what'. Always try to relate the style to the subject matter.*

It is essential that you analyse language *in the context of the whole text.* You could take almost any example of language use, put it into another context and derive a very different meaning from it. Every element of analysis must be seen *in context.* It is by doing this that you will discover the subtler meanings at work in any text.

While some exponents of practical criticism reject the idea of analysing the sounds of individual letters it seems to be a natural thing to do when considering such features of text as sound. Common sense suggests that the sounds of individual letters can greatly enhance the overall effect of the text on the reader, particularly if the text is poetry.

Here are some basic guidelines.

## Consonants

Without venturing into the deep and somewhat treacherous waters of linguistics, let us keep our discussion extremely simple and for our purposes assume that consonants fall into two main categories:

- **hard**, which predictably give the text a harsh, severe feel; and
- **soft**, which create a sense of softness or tenderness.

The **hard** consonants are: b, c, d, g, k, p, q, s, t, x, z and the **soft** consonants are: c, f, g, h, j, l, m, n, ph, s, sh, z.

It *is* correct that some consonants appear in both lists, and there is a reason for this. It was established earlier that it is necessary always to analyse language *in context*. The reason why 'g', 's' and 'z' can shift between the two consonant groups is that the harshness or softness of these two sounds depends to a large extent upon the *context*. By 'context' I mean:

- the other letters around them in the same word;
- the other words around them in the same text; and
- meaning.

No word can *ever* be looked at in complete isolation; neither can the writer or the reader. Language is a *collaborative* affair:

- the letters collaborate with the words;
- the words collaborate with the rest of the text; and
- readers collaborate with the writer.

These are the strands that go to make up the woven material, and all the strands are needed for the fabric to hold together.

The letter 's' can sound soft, gentle and mystical, as it does in 'Silver' by Walter de la Mare:

> Slowly, silently, now the moon
> Walks the night in her silver shoon;
> This way, and that, she peers and sees
> Silver fruit upon silver trees;

*Why* does this sound so soothing? Because we are listening to the 's' sounds *in the context of each word and the whole poem*. 'Slowly' has an unmistakably gentle feel to it because of the denotative meaning of the *word*, but we also sense this softness through the meaning of *the whole poem*. 'Slowly' implies gently; the word means 'without haste', and this suggests a certain softness. The poem is about the moon, which is personified as a woman with a silver touch. She is described as moving almost imperceptibly through the night leaving a sterling trail in her wake. This creates a sense of delicacy and magic.

So there we have it; *sound*, *word* and *text* have *collaborated* to create meaning.

Owen produces a different effect in 'Dulce et Decorum Est' using the same letter sound:

> His hanging face, like a devil's sick of sin;

The poet is describing a gruesome scene in which a dead soldier's face is looking up from the wagon into which his body has been 'flung'. The previous line describes his 'white eyes writhing in his face' and the consonance on 's' in the following line seems to *hiss* at us Owen's disgust at the war and at what it does to people. How extreme an image this is; can a devil ever really be 'sick of sin'? The 'sin' of war seems to the narrator to be so profound that even a devil can stomach it no more. Notice the monosyllabic 'sick' and 'sin', which add a heaviness and an emphasis to the line. Combine this weight with the hissing 's' and this sinister feeling is quite different from the gentle delicacy of 'Silver'.

Again, we have considered the *sound* of a word *in the context of its meaning* and *in the context of the text as a whole*. Again, *sound*, *word* and *text* have *collaborated* to create meaning.

The sound of a letter must *never* be considered in isolation. Always look at the denotative meaning of the word, and indeed its connotative meaning also. (This will be discussed in detail in Chapter 5.) As well as the meanings of the word, the meaning of the whole text has to be taken into account. Only then will a meaning be derived that can be shown to be present throughout the text *at all levels*.

The other consonants that can shift between the hard and soft groups are 'c' and 'g', and this is because they rely on the vowel that *follows* for their texture. 'C' is hard when it comes before 'a', as in 'cat'; 'o', as in 'cot'; and 'u', as in 'cut'. It is soft before 'i', as in 'cinder'; and 'e', as in 'ceiling'. The same applies to 'g'. You might like to try this out now with some examples of your own.

The consonant 'h' is called an 'aspirate', coming from the Latin word meaning 'breathe' and it tends to give an airy, 'breathy' feel to a word. The letters 's' and 'h' together reminds us of the 'sh' that we sound when we want silence, and its effect is just that; it makes the piece feel somewhat hushed.

## Vowels

Vowels are the letters a, e, i, o and u, and for our purposes we could say that they also fall into two groups: **short** and **long**.

**Short** vowels are: 'a' as in 'cap'; 'e' as in 'red'; 'i' as in 'pin'; 'o' as in 'hop'; and 'u' as in 'cut'. Short vowels tend to speed up a piece of writing, precisely because they *are* short and therefore take less time to pronounce. For the same reason; they can give the text a harsher, brusquer feeling than long vowels; they are firmer and heavier and can, *depending on the context*, create emphasis.

Owen demonstrates the use of short vowel sounds at the end of lines to create such an effect in 'Anthem for Doomed Youth':

> What passing bells for these who die as cattle?
> Only the monstrous anger of the guns.
> Only the stuttering rifles' rapid rattle
> Can patter out their hasty orisons.

The short vowels in cattle/guns and rattle/orisons shorten the lines, quicken the pace and create a sense of rapid harshness, highly pertinent to the content of the poem which is about the way that war offers to the young men who die by it its own ghastly version of an Edwardian funeral. As has been said before, *examine the 'how' and relate it to the 'what'.* In this poem, Owen is angry, and the texture of the language is suitably sharp and abrasive. It is *appropriate* that the narrator's language should be like this. The short vowel sounds enhance the meaning in the text. Remember that *style reflects and reinforces content*.

**Long** vowels are: 'a' as in 'cape'; 'e' as in 'reed'; 'i' as in 'pine'; 'o' as in 'hope'; and 'u' as in 'cute'.

Do you remember learning to read at school? Perhaps you recall a teacher telling you that 'The Magic "E"' made the vowel 'say its name'. We call the first letter of the alphabet 'a' and the sound of the letter when you say its 'name' is the *same* sound it makes when it is *long*. Compare 'cap' and 'cape' and you will hear that the 'a' in 'cap' is much shorter than the same letter in 'cape'. The first is a short vowel sound, the second long. The same rule applies for all the other vowels.

Long vowels tend to slow down a piece of writing precisely because they *are* long, and therefore take more time to pronounce. They can give the text a softer, gentler feeling than short vowels, for the same reason; they are more fluid and lighter and can, *depending on the context*, create a more thoughtful mood.

Marvell's 'To His Coy Mistress' creates a sense of this prolonged, slow thoughtfulness by his use of long vowel sounds at the ends of the lines:

> Had we but world enough, and time,
> This coyness, Lady, were no crime.
> We would sit down, and think which way
> To walk, and pass our long love's day.

The long vowels in time/crime and way/day draw out the lines, slow the pace and create a sense of smooth persuasion, highly pertinent to the content of the poem which is about a young man trying to seduce the object of his desire into losing her virginity to him. As has been said before, *examine the 'how' and relate it to the 'what'.* At the beginning of the poem, where these lines appear, his approach is still comparatively flattering and gentle, the texture of his language smooth. The long vowel sounds enhance the meaning at this point in the text.

## Assonance

This term refers to the repetition of vowel sounds, where alliteration is the repetition of consonantal sounds.

Keats' 'Ode on a Grecian Urn' exemplifies this well:

> Thou still unravish'd bride of quietness,
> Thou foster-child of silence and slow time,

The effect this has on a text is to emphasise and unify the relevant words. Keats is enchanted by the motionless urn and its faultless beauty, and words he uses, such as 'bride', 'quietness', 'child', 'silence' and 'time' all reflect this. Assonance works here because it *unites* the words to which it is applied and *emphasises* their meaning.

## Consonance

Related to assonance is the technique known as consonance, which refers to the repetition of the same consonant sound on either side of different vowels in two words; for example, 'grieve' and 'grove'. Consonance is also given the term 'half-rhyme' when it is a substitute for rhyme and, *depending on the context*, it can suggest a certain lack of harmony. Look back at the example from Owen's 'Strange Meeting' under 'Half rhyme' (see pages 44–5), which offers a good example of consonance used in this way.

Things do not feel entirely comfortable because the rhyme is 'not quite right'; there is an unease between the two words – little concord or unity. As ever, it is essential to examine the *context* and decide whether this interpretation of a writer's use of consonance 'fits' the other features of the text and its meaning.

## Onomatopoeia

First, learn to spell this word correctly. This device occurs when a writer uses a word that *sounds like* the noise that it describes. Everyday language is full of such examples – 'cuckoo' and 'crash' being common. The word 'cuckoo' sounds like the noise that the bird makes, and the word 'crash' imitates the noise that something makes when it breaks or knocks against something else. You only have to look at the bubbles in cartoon strips to see numerous examples of onomatopoeia: remember 'wham!' 'smash!' and 'crunch!'?

The effect of using this device is obvious; it *brings sound to the writing* in a very real way. The reader does not have to imagine the sound; he or she can *hear* it as he/she reads. Let us revisit Owen's 'Anthem for Doomed Youth'. The 'rifles' rapid rattle' offers us a clear and effective example of onomatopoeia in action; the words 'rapid rattle' *imitate the sound* a rifle makes. The language seems to *bring sound into the text*.

Onomatopoeia is a powerful device that can add a great deal of texture to a text. The aural contribution it makes enhances a piece of writing because it brings to it another dimension and, given that poetry is meant to be read aloud, it is not difficult to appreciate the quality of what it has to offer literature.

## Repetition and accumulation

Repetition is a simple and reasonably straightforward device that occurs when a word or synonym, phrase or line is repeated. The most obvious effect it has on a text is that of emphasis. Our attention is drawn to repeated features and they are in a sense underlined to heighten their significance within the writing.

It is worth looking at *what* is repeated and asking yourself the essential questions, '*Why* has the writer repeated this word or phrase?' and '*What effect* does it have on the text?' Like all literary devices, repetition comes under the 'how' heading, and you must ask yourself constantly: 'In what ways does the 'how' reflect or enhance the 'what'?' Look at these lines from Hardy's 'The Voice':

> Woman much missed, how you **call to me, call to me**,
> Saying that now you are not as you were.

The repetition of 'call to me' in the poem's first line creates a sense of this calling happening several times, and this is central to the meaning of the poem. The narrator speaks of continually hearing 'the voice' of his beloved. It seems to echo through his life and evokes a sense of yearning in him.

Look at the *effect* of the repetition; it does echo (that, after all, is what an echo is – repetition) and the effect is a deep longing for the lost woman – a desire that will not go away, just as the words 'call to me' will not go away. It also influences the rhythm, adding a lilting effect to the line.

William Blake uses repetition in a potent way in 'London':

> In **every** cry of **every** Man,
> In **every** Infant's cry of fear,

> In **every** voice, in **every** ban,
> The mind-forg'd manacles I hear.

In this poem Blake sets out to express his concern at seeing the marks of restraint on the minds and imaginations of the capital's inhabitants. He feels that reason and perhaps its embodiment, the law, impose destructive controls on the very souls of humankind, and his somewhat revolutionary poetry openly questions the effect of this on individuals.

The *effect* of this repetition is that the reader's attention is drawn naturally to the word 'every'. Having established this, we need to ask, '*Why* has Blake done this?' The answer is surely that in repeating the word 'every' he emphasises the fact that each single 'cry', 'voice' and 'ban' of 'every Man' speaks to him of chains and constraints. What he is saying is that the evidence for his case is to be found in 'every cry of every Man'. His proof is everywhere. The repetition gives the poem a certain monotony and predictability, and this is what Blake feels that reason and the law have done to humankind; they have taken away people's spirit of freedom and individuality. *Again we have related the 'how' to the 'what'.*

Repetition can be used to considerable effect when a writer is trying to construct an argument. In 'To His Coy Mistress', Marvell uses what we might call **accumulation**, which is similar to repetition, but simply means that what is repeated is similar but not identical to the original:

> **An hundred years** should go to praise
> Thine eyes, and on thy forehead gaze.
> **Two hundred** to adore each breast:
> But **thirty thousand** to the rest.
> **An age** at least to every part,
> And the **last age** should show your heart.
> For, Lady, you deserve this state;
> Nor would I love at lower rate.

The accumulation here consists of the similar words and phrases marked in bold type. At this point in the poem Marvell is trying to assure the object of his desire that had they time, he would offer her praise and adoration in direct proportion to her worth. Note the **hyperbole** in respect of this; each breast would demand two hundred years' praise. The narrator can afford to be this generous with the time that he *would* give her because he has no intention of waiting so long to fulfil his desire for her.

The accumulation consists of several similar (but not identical) words or phrases, all of which support his argument. The fact that the language is slightly *different* perhaps helps his assertion even more; he has a *variety* of examples instead of a single one to further reinforce his argument.

## Dialogue

You may be surprised to see this among a chapter on the tools of analysis, but a consideration of the speech in a text can be a useful and productive exercise. *Why* do writers include direct speech in a text? Dialogue fulfils many functions, some of which are listed below.

### Creates character

The **character** that uses Standard English in a text often comes across as one who conforms. Upholding the rules of formal speech suggests that this is a character who also obeys the laws of good behaviour. If he or she uses Standard English and does not conform then there are interesting incompatibilities, which can serve to make the character all the more intriguing. Perhaps the person is outwardly a conformist but inwardly a rebel.

If the language used is non-standard, then perhaps the writer is trying to tell us that this person comes from a background that is lower down the social scale. Characters such as this have a very natural, honest feel, particularly if they are given a regional dialect or an accent. Sometimes the writer wants us to sympathise with these less sophisticated, and therefore by implication more innocent, characters.

### Dialect and accent

You will need to look closely to distinguish between *dialect* and *accent*. Dialect relates to *grammatical rules* and *vocabulary*, whereas accent is concerned with the way that words are *pronounced*.

### Dialect

- *Grammar*   The child who protests, 'I ain't done nothing' is using a non-standard dialect as he/she is not following the grammatical rules of Standard English, which would demand, 'I haven't done anything'.
- *Vocabulary*   Dialect is responsible for the wide and interesting variety of words from different parts of Britain that can be used for the same thing. An example of this is the Standard English word 'sandwich'. Regional variations include 'butty', 'cob' and 'sarnie', among others.

### Accent

Accent relates to the way that words are *pronounced*. If a person comes from an area north of an imaginary line that runs roughly from east to west across Britain he will pronounce the word 'bath' with an 'a' sound that imitates the 'a' in the word 'cap'. If, however, he or she comes from south of that line the word 'bath' will be pronounced with an 'a' sound similar to the 'a' in the word 'pardon'.

Accent, particularly in Britain, carries with it associations of social class and status, and these must be considered when a character in literature is given a particular accent. If a writer deliberately attributes a less prestigious accent to a character, it has been done for a *reason*, and that accent is intended to help draw that character more finely. The same applies, of course, to a character given an obviously high-status accent by a writer.

The *issues* around accents tend to be those of power, status, conformity and naturalness. The *more prestigious* (usually known as Received Pronunciation) accent of the south of England smacks of more power, higher status, greater conformity and, being less natural, more sophisticated; while the less prestigious (usually regional) accent of other parts of England suggests less power, lower status, less conformity and being closer to nature, and less sophisticated.

These are, of course, gross simplifications of a somewhat complex issue, but as a rough guideline they are somewhere to start.

## Communicates personality

**Personality** is easily communicated through dialogue but you need to *read closely* and ask yourself:

- How would I describe the *language* used by this character? What sort of *vocabulary* does he/she use? The way in which you describe the language is likely to be similar to the description you would give to the character.
- How does the language *move*? Is it fluent and confident, or halting and uncertain? Is it brisk and bubbly, or slow and steady?
- To what extent does one character *dominate* the dialogue? If a character dominates a dialogue he or she is generally the more powerful personality.

The character's language will inevitably be a *reflection of his or her personality.*

## Alters the mood quickly

Dialogue can change the tone of a piece of writing very quickly. A writer does not need lengthy descriptions to modify the **mood**; he or she simply makes a character speak and the whole feel of the piece can change in a moment. If this change is very sudden it can have a dramatic effect on the piece as a whole, and you will need to be aware of this.

Dialogue can also illustrate significant contrasts between characters, and a discussion of the contrasting styles and content of speech can prove fruitful to an analysis of the text as a whole.

## Creates a sense of immediacy – the here and now

Dialogue can give a text a sense of the action taking place **now**. It brings immediacy to the writing, far more than reported speech can ever do. We have a feeling that we are witnessing what someone is actually saying, giving us a sense that it is all taking place *in the present.*

## Gives the text a sense of reality and life

To hear the *actual* words spoken by a character provides us with information about them that we could never hope to glean from a third party's version of what they said without long descriptions in the narrative. Dialogue can bring a text to **life** and give it a sense of being **real**, even though we know that it isn't. We hear 'real' people speak; we hear the actual words that they say, and this gives the text a soul and a certain vivacity. You probably have a sense of this already when someone recounts a conversation they had. Consider how much more 'real' it feels if you know *exactly what* was said and *the way* in which it was said rather than hearing it merely as reported speech.

## Can transmit the themes of the text

Always look for the evidence of the text's central meaning in the dialogue and this will include the existence of its **themes**. Writers often give their characters lines that reveal themes and meaning. Remember that these appear in all elements of a text; the threads are all woven together.

## Metre

Metre needs to be considered briefly before we embark on a discussion of rhythm. The two words do not mean the same thing but they are connected. Although Advanced level examining boards do not require candidates to have a detailed knowledge of metre, you should be aware of its existence and of the ways in which it *relates* to rhythm. Undergraduates need to acquire a clear understanding of this concept.

All language contains natural rhythms, in that some syllables are emphasised and some are not. Any native speaker will have an inherent ability to locate these places of emphasis accurately; for example, when you see the word 'elephant' you know that the stress goes on the first 'e'. All a writer does is to use these naturally occurring rhythms in artificial ways to enhance the mood and meaning of his/her message. When a poet does this he or she is using metre. Metre is simply a rhythm the poet has chosen to use and repeat throughout the stanza or poem, and if a poem is to be described as being written in metre, there must be evidence of this being sustained. There will be variations in the metre according to the subject of the poem and the effect that the writer is trying to create.

Metre, then, is the idea that each line of poetry should follow a consistent and exact *pattern*. It is believed that this helps to unify the text and hold it together. This pattern is simply the arrangement of stressed and unstressed syllables that are characterised by the symbols / and ~ respectively. When the metre of a poem is followed doggedly we get the typical nursery-rhyme rhythm:

> Up Jack got and home did trot as fast as he could caper;
>
> /　~　/　~　/　~　/　~　/　~　/　~　//
>
> He went to bed to mend his head with vinegar and brown paper.
>
> ~　/　~　/　~　/　~　/　~　/　~　~　/　~　//

This effect is also present in limericks. The pattern is clear to see, and the way it is read aloud reflects *absolute adherence to it throughout*. This is what helps to give nursery rhymes their childish feel; this rather 'sing-along' quality provides a firm, unshakeable shape and we can all join in because we *know* that shape; the pattern becomes familiar. It is predictable and safe and it holds the piece together.

For a more detailed analysis of different metrical forms and their effects, refer to the Reference Section at the end of the book.

## Rhythm

First, learn to *spell this word correctly*. You will not endear yourself to any examiner if you show that you are unable to spell basic critical terms accurately.

We touched briefly on rhythm in the section on form and structure, but it is a somewhat complex textual feature and needs much fuller consideration. It is something that perplexes many students and yet it is essential that you develop a *feel* for this aspect of any text.

While metre is concerned with established patterns in poetry – the number of syllables and the stressed and unstressed syllables in a line – rhythm refers to *the way in which we read aloud* a line of poetry (either right out loud or in our head). It is related to the poem's *movement – the way in which it progresses.* The rhythm need not necessarily follow the metre as it does in nursery rhymes, and indeed it can be very productive to look closely at lines in which it is clear that the rhythm has *departed* from the precise pattern of the metre.

A well-known example from Shakespeare's *Hamlet* might help here:

To be or not to be; that is the question.

The metre of Shakespeare's verse is *iambic pentameter*. This pattern is characterised by five 'feet', each of two syllables, consisting of an unstressed syllable followed by a stressed one. They are marked like this: ~ (light) and / (heavy). This is unquestionably the most common pattern for much of English poetry. Look again at Hamlet's line above and try to work out the metre for it.

This is the precise pattern that iambic pentameter follows:

To be or not to be; that is the question.

~ /   ~ /   ~ /;   ~   /   ~   /~

But were we to apply that pattern of stresses to the line when we read it, we should find emphasis where instinctively we know that it should not be. If we stick to the metre in Hamlet's line above we have a stress on 'is' and none on 'that'. Looking at the sense of the line, that is almost ridiculous; Hamlet has just identified the burning issue for himself – the issue of life or death. The play is full of Hamlet's questions and now he comes to the point when he feels the need to reason his way towards answering *the* big question, 'Should I kill myself or not?' The emphasis *has* to be on '*that*'. So the pattern of the stresses would need to be something like this:

~ / ~ / ~ /; / ~ ~ / ~

Look at where the rhythm *departs* from the established pattern and ask yourself these questions:

- *Why* has the writer done that here?
- *What effect* does it have on the text?

Let us consider the answers:

- *Why* has the writer done that here? Because in *breaking away* from the pattern of stresses, Shakespeare *highlights* that part of the text.
- *What effect* does it have on the text? He breaks the flow, disturbs the arrangement, weakens the unity and our attention is drawn to it. It is simply a case of our focusing on something that is *different*. That should not be a strange concept to us; it happens all the time. We tend to look more closely at things and people when they fail to conform to the 'norm'.

What we need to do is *establish the norm* and then *examine where the text deviates from it*. Ask yourself:

- *What* is the established pattern?
- *Where* does it change?
- *Why* does it change?
- *What effect* does the change have upon the text?

The last question has really been answered, but it is essential to be clear about it. The break in the pattern draws attention to the text *at that spot*. This digression then forces us to look at the content *at that point* and analyse the *connection between the content and the form*, or the 'what' and the 'how'. Once we have done that in the example above, it becomes clear that Shakespeare departed from the pattern to highlight the fact that Hamlet was in the process of identifying a key issue. It is a 'eureka moment' for him; he has established what should be the focus of his attention. To achieve this, the emphasis *has* to be on '*that*'.

You have only to think of limericks and children's nursery rhymes to be aware of the difference that rhythm makes to poetry. Indeed, rhythm is a key element of both of these forms of poetry, and it is rhythm that helps us to remember them so well. How else would such large numbers of people be able to recall lines of poetry they have not heard since early childhood?

Rhythm is used to good effect when small children learn their multiplication tables. Remember 'once two is two, two twos are four, three twos are six'? There is something about the movement that this musical quality creates that has a significant impact on us.

## Types of metrical feet

### Iambic foot      ~ /      ~ /
The pattern is ~ / as in 'return' or 'forgive', in other words a light syllable followed by a heavy one. This is the most common metrical foot in English poetry and is also referred to as an iamb.

Iambic pentameter, which is made up of five iambs or five iambic feet, is the most frequently used metre. A simple sum tells us that five iambs in a line will give us ten beats.

Iambic pentameter is thought to be the metre that most closely resembles human speech and it is partly for this reason that it is so commonly used. This feature also makes it eminently suitable for drama or, rather more accurately, dramatic verse such as in Shakespeare's plays.

### Trochaic foot      / ~      / ~
This pattern is / ~ as in 'hollow' and 'empty'; in other words, a heavy syllable followed by a light one. This can create a solemn mood, as the line commences with a stressed syllable.

### Dactylic foot      / ~ ~      / ~ ~
The pattern for this is / ~ ~ as in 'elephant' and 'heavily'. Again, the effect may be sombre as the stressed syllable comes first.

**Anapestic foot**  ~ ~ /   ~ ~ /

The ~ ~ / pattern of this metre as in 'intervene' and 'supersede' can add an air of excitement or movement to a text. There may be a suggestion of galloping horses or rumbling over railway sleepers.

It is usual to find that whole poems are written in one of these metrical forms, though at times an author might combine two types of metre, employing one of these as well:

- A **spondaic foot**, with this pattern: / /;
- A **pyrrhic foot**, which has this pattern: ~ ~ ; or
- An **amphibrach foot**, which has this pattern: ~ / ~ .

The effect of mixing two metres is to break any possible monotony that might have occurred through the use of a single metrical pattern throughout a text.

The other consideration is the number of feet in a line:

Monometer = one foot/unit of metre per line
Dimeter    = two feet/units of metre per line
Trimeter   = three feet/units of metre per line
Tetrameter = four feet/units of metre per line
Pentameter = five feet/units of metre per line
Hexameter  = six feet/units of metre per line
Heptameter = seven feet/units of metre per line
Octameter  = eight feet/units of metre per line.

In this way we arrive at terms such as 'iambic pentameter' which simply means five feet (pentameter) of iambs (~ /). These terms have *no intrinsic value in themselves*; they are merely a way of describing the metre concisely and precisely.

However, it is essential to remember that no matter how detailed and analytical your discussion of metre, it will have little relevance to your response unless it relates to the *effect* that such devices have upon the text. Always ask yourself, '*Why* has the writer used this metre? *What effect* does it have on the poem?' Your essay should explain the ways in which the metre contributes to the atmosphere and meaning of the text, and it is quite appropriate to use emotive language in describing this. For example, 'Iambic pentametre enhances the calm, serene feeling in the verse' or 'The use of anapestic trimetres adds a sense of relentlessness and excitement to the poem'.

Always examine moments of *change* in the metre. Where does this happen and *what effect* is produced? Remember that nothing in good literature is random. It has changed for a reason, and in changing the metre, the poet is trying to draw the reader's attention to the meaning *at that point* in the poem.

Finally, never comment on metre just for the sake of it; it can be a valuable key to meaning but it is not an element of analysis to be discussed *without* consideration of the *contribution* it makes to a text.

## Punctuation

Punctuation might appear to be a rather dull and irrelevant aspect of language to be discussing in approaches to practical criticism, but it is a much overlooked element of analysis which, if considered carefully, can provide some valuable insights into meaning.

You will be aware, of course, of the function of punctuation, which is to create pauses that enable writers to group words in meaningful ways. Just like any other element of analysis, it is there for a reason; **nothing is random**. Punctuation has a lot to do with pacing and pausing, which is why it is included in the section on rhythm. It helps a writer to add drama to a text.

To review punctuation briefly:

(a) The *more forceful* pauses come from end punctuation, such as full stops, exclamation marks and question marks. These pauses are very definite and dramatic.
(b) The *less forceful* pauses come from mid-sentence punctuation, such as commas, semi-colons and colons. These pauses are less definite and lighter.

Pauses in literature are more than merely places in the text where you can take a literal or mental breath before continuing; they are *spaces* for you to examine. Pauses caused by punctuation can create drama. In disturbing the natural flow of a piece of writing, a writer draws attention to the place where this disturbance occurs. It is your job as a close reader to be aware of these digressions from the norm and to ask yourself, '*Why* has the writer done this here? *What effect* does it have on the text?'

In theatre, the pause has tremendous dramatic effect on performance and it often either heralds some action of great importance or tells the audience that one has just occurred. It is known as a 'dramatic pause'. Pauses in drama create tension through anticipation and also through a sense of agitation.

The opening exchange in Act 2, Scene 2 of *Macbeth*, between Macbeth and his wife creates a thrill of excitement and a sense of fear at the murder that they have just committed.

| | |
|---|---|
| *Lady Macbeth* | Did you not speak? |
| *Macbeth* | When? |
| *Lady Macbeth* | Now. |
| *Macbeth* | As I descended? |
| *Lady Macbeth* | Ay. |
| *Macbeth* | Hark! – who lies i'th' second chamber? |
| *Lady Macbeth* | Donalbain. |

Pauses are used to considerable effect at the *end* of lines.

Notice how:

- The lines are fractured, broken into small segments, often one-word lines. The continuity has gone and there is a jerky, panicky feel in the air. It does not take much imagination to hear the breathlessness in their voices and see their eyes' dilated pupils.
- Most lines end in a question mark, suggesting panic, fear and a need for reassurance. They are experiencing a mixture of emotions, but none of them has anything to do with peace of mind. The constant questioning creates a sense of uncertainty and drama.

## Caesura

A pause that occurs *within* a line is called a caesura, and this can also be used to considerable effect. Consider this extract from Marvell's 'To His Coy Mistress':

> Had we but world enough,/ and time,/
> This coyness,/ Lady,/ were no crime.//
> . . . . . . . . . . . . .
> Thou by the Indian Ganges' side
> Shouldst rubies find:/ I by the tide
> Of Humber would complain.// I would
> Love you ten years before the Flood:/
> And you should,/ if you please,/ refuse
> Till the conversion of the Jews.//
> . . . . . . . . . . . .

The / denotes a light pause and // highlights a more pronounced delay. Notice how the caesuras break the continuity of the piece and slow it down. Relating the 'how' to the 'what', Marvell's intention is clear to see here. His argument in this section of the poem is that *if* he had 'ages' in which to woo this woman, he gladly would. He is trying to create the impression of dramatically extended periods of time, and of the slowness of its passing. What better way than to slow the pace so that the style mirrors the content or the 'how' reflects the 'what'?

Consider the extract from John Milton's 'Paradise Lost':

| 997 | While thus he spake, th'angelic squadron bright |
| | Turned fiery red, sharp'ning in moonèd horns |
| | Their phalanx, and began to hem him round |
| 980 | With ported spears, as thick as when a field |
| | Of Ceres ripe for harvest waving bends |
| | Her bearded grove of ears, which way the wind |
| | Sways them; the careful ploughman doubting stands |
| | Lest on the threshing floor his hopeful sheaves |
| 985 | Prove chaff. On th'other side Satan alarmed |
| | Collecting all his might dilated stood, |
| | Like Teneriffe or Atlas unremoved: |
| | His stature reached the sky, and on his crest |
| | Sat Horror plumed; nor wanted in his grasp |
| 990 | What seemed both spear and shield: now dreadful deeds |

The first appearance of caesura in this extract, in line 985:

> Prove chaff. On th'other side Satan alarmed

creates a great deal of drama, partly because it comes after several lines of enjambment. The verse flows over eight line breaks (notice there is no end stop from line 977–984) and the breach is a sudden one that effectively splits the verse in two and heralds the appearance of Satan. The subject is, up to this point, 'th'angelic squadron'; at the full stop after 'chaff', we suddenly encounter 'th'other side' where Satan is 'alarmed'. The pause enforced by the full stop, together with the new breath needed for the next sentence produce that brief discontinuity which is a suitable marker for the contrast in content that follows.

Caesura and enjambment often occur together as writers manipulate rhythm to reflect meaning.

## Other features of text

### Archaism

This term refers to the use of outmoded language to create an 'other worldly' feel. Virginia Woolf's use of it in *To the Lighthouse* exemplifies this:

> And when he came to the sea, it was quite dark grey and the water heaved up from below, and smelt putrid. Then he went and stood by it and said,
>
> > 'Flounder, flounder, in the sea,
> > Come I pray thee, here to me;
> > For my wife, good Ilsabil,
> > Wills not as I'd have her will'.

When the diction of a text is far removed from that of everyday language, so is the atmosphere that is created by that writing. Quite simply, we tend to choose mundane language to describe the mundane, and elevated diction to discuss what is special and different, or to reflect our attempts to make it so.

The use of archaic diction can have the effect of transporting the reader to another world in another time.

### Sympathetic background

This refers to the way in which writers create a background for their characters that is sympathetic to them, or that mirrors their actions or feelings. Shakespeare does this clearly in the opening scene of *Macbeth*, when the Witches meet on the desolate heath. Thunder and lightning rage in the heavens, creating the same disorder above as the Witches are about create on earth. The storm acts as a fitting backdrop to their character and behaviour.

Similarly, in Act 4 of *King Lear*, the reclining figure of Lear asleep on his bed, the sound of soft music, the presence of a physician and restorative language of the Christ-like Cordelia, all combine to *sympathise* with the action of reconciliation and healing at this point in the play.

In this way there is a harmony and continuity between character and background, and the feelings and responses created in the audience are intensified because our experience of them is more complete and all encompassing.

### Unusual juxtapositions and binary opposites

You may not have heard of either of these terms before but the concepts are quite straightforward. The word 'juxtaposition' means placing something alongside something else, and in literary terms this refers to what happens when a writer positions two or more unusual or unexpected words or ideas near each other.

In Philip Larkin's 'The Explosion' we see an example of this:

In the sun the slagheap slept

'Sun' and 'slagheap' are quite distinct from each other in both their visual appearance and in the associations we make with them. Juxtaposing the two images by placing them so close together creates a dramatic effect on the reader; it is the bringing together of two binary opposites – light, associated with 'sun'; and dark, connected with 'slagheap'. The first image is pure and natural, a source of healing and strength; the second is somewhat dirty and man-made, connected with disasters and death.

The effect of juxtaposition is to enhance both of the elements that are juxtaposed. Imagine that you held next to one another a sheet of black paper and one of white. The black would look blacker and the white, whiter. By bringing together two such different elements you emphasise the qualities of each and the contrast between them seems all the more stark.

## Pronouns

The issue of pronouns is included under 'Unusual juxtapositions' because a writer's use of personal pronouns in juxtaposition can tell the reader a great deal about his/her attitude to the subject. If, for example, a writer uses 'we', a sense of unity is created; two individuals are joined together by the use of the single (first person plural) pronoun. If, on the other hand, he or she chooses to refer to two people as 'she'/'he' or 'I'/'you', then a separation of the two individuals is suggested. This type of juxtaposition, achieved by placing two different pronouns near each other, highlights their separateness and their differences, drawing attention to the fact that they are represented individually and not as a single entity.

Sometimes it is possible that a writer might refer to two individuals as 'they' or 'we' at one point in the text and then as 'he' and 'she' or 's/he'/'I' at another. If this happens, your job is to think about this change. *Why* are these two people referred to as one at one particular point in the text, and then as two separate individuals at another? An analysis of the places where a text *digresses* from its established pattern/s can provide the reader with meaningful explanations and interpretations.

Remember always to look carefully at pronouns; a great deal of valuable insight into meaning may be gained from a consideration of pronoun use, and its value in the process of critical appreciation should not be underestimated. Many essential insights have been overlooked by students because they have not read the text closely enough or thought carefully about this element of analysis.

## Paradox

Paradox is a statement that is seemingly absurd or contradictory. However, it is usually the case that, on closer inspection, it is *not*.

Shakespeare offers us a clear example of this in Act 1, Scene 1 of *Macbeth*, when the Witches declare that 'fair is foul and foul is fair'. Given that 'foul' and 'fair' are, quite obviously opposites, the statement, at first hearing, is somewhat confusing. However, if we consider it *in the context of the whole text* (which we must always do), there is a meaning that starts to emerge.

In this paradox, the Witches are suggesting that all is not what it seems. What appears to be 'fair' is in fact 'foul', and what seems 'foul' is really 'fair'. Is this so? At the beginning of the play Macbeth is the perfect hero; brave in battle and loyal to his king. He is undoubtedly 'fair'. This 'fair' man, however, later betrays his king, murdering him and several others. What appeared 'fair' at the start becomes 'foul' later.

Notice the way in which Shakespeare also *links* the two words 'foul' and 'fair' by alliteration. This heightens the effect of the paradox, because two such opposite words have been connected by the alliterated 'f' *as well as* by the verb 'to be'.

So the paradox is explained. It is perhaps surprising but *not* as contradictory and absurd as was first thought. To summarise the function of paradox in a text:

- It intrigues and surprises the reader;
- It draws the reader further into the text in an effort to reconcile the contradiction;
- It often encapsulates deep, unexpected truths and complex ideas which are beneath the surface; and
- It frequently contains important issues which are essential to the meaning of the text as a whole.

Another example, from John Donne's 'Holy Sonnets', illustrates these functions well:

> One short sleepe past, wee wake eternally,
> And death shall be no more, Death thou shalt die.

Donne's narrator spends much of this fourteen-line sonnet trying to defy death, which he personifies. The poem is a direct address to 'Death' (the person, hence the capital 'd') and a challenge to 'his' power over human beings. The climax of the sonnet is the last two lines in which the narrator threatens 'Death' itself with death.

If we think of death in terms of victory, then, once we recover from the surprise at the paradox in the last line, we can see that Donne's narrator is waging war on death and telling 'him' that 'Death' itself will be conquered; in other words, that which is the ultimate destroyer of human kind will itself be destroyed.

## Allusions

You need to be aware that there will be times when a writer *alludes* to something outside the text. This means that he or she refers, sometimes briefly or indirectly, to an idea that is different or separate from the subject of the piece. There might be religious allusions or subtle references to another piece of literature, or to another genre of writing. This is *not* the same thing as symbolism. The writer is *creating an interesting or enlightening connection* between the text and another aspect of life or type of literature. This serves to make the text richer and more complex.

A narrator facing his/her own mortality or in the depths of despair may allude to Hamlet's famous soliloquy beginning, 'To be or not to be' in order to give his writing a dramatic and tragic texture. Alluding to something, in this example presumably 'greater' in literary stature than the author's writings *enhances* and *enriches* his/her own text.

## Narrator

The word 'narrator' simply refers to the person who is telling the story. It is *'the voice' of the author or poet*. Students frequently confuse the writer with the narrator, and it is important to remember that *they are not the same*.

I might write a poem about the loss of my dog and choose to write it *as if I were a five-year-old boy*. I am the poet, but *the narrator is a five-year-old boy* and as such he will see the world very differently from me. When we respond to literature we are responding to *the narrator's version of the truth* and every narrator will see the world from his/her own, individual *viewpoint*.

Perhaps the most common is the **omniscient narrator**, who sees all. 'Omniscient' comes from two Latin words meaning 'all knowing'. This narration is in the third person – 'he' or 'she' – and the narrator seems to be able to see into the minds of *all* the characters.

Usually we are unaware of a narrator as an actual character or persona. He or she is normally quite 'transparent' and tells the story without passing judgements or commenting on the actions of the characters within the text. This sort of impersonal narrator does *not intrude* upon the text in any way and there is *no narratorial presence*. These narrators add a certain realism to a text, as the focus is on the action of the characters, not on the reactions of the narrator. William Golding, among countless others, offers us examples of this type of narrator.

Sometimes a narrator does intrude upon the text and we *are* aware of him or her as an actual character or persona. He or she is *not* 'transparent' in that he/she passes judgements and comments on the actions of the characters within the text. In this case we sense a *narratorial presence*. These narrators add another 'layer' to the text because we have to take into account *their* characters *as well as those in the actual text*. In some cases, narrators such as these actually *become another character*. We have to get to know this character because we must remember that the action of the text is in fact 'filtered' by the narrator who will, if he/she is intrusive, point out the significance of his/her responses to the actions of the characters and offer us as readers *his/her interpretations* of what is happening, along with his/her *moral judgements* on it.

In brief, then, the **omniscient narrator**:

- sees everything;
- sees into the minds of all the characters;
- is impersonal;
- can be a character him/herself;
- 'filters' what happens; and
- can be present/absent and therefore is intrusive/unintrusive.

The **third person narrator** (a frequent choice of writers, such as George Eliot, for example) can elect to see into the mind of one particular character *more* than any other. This provides an interesting combination of the depth of insight associated with the first-person narrator (see below) and the breadth of view we connect with the omniscient narrator. The dual potential of this type of narration can present the reader with a conflict to resolve because while we inevitably sympathise with someone whom we know well, we also gain insights into the less pleasant aspects of their character. It is often hard to know how to respond, and we are frequently torn in two very different directions.

**Multiple narrators** (as in Emily Brontë's *Wuthering Heights*) are less common. These tend to share in the narration, with one narrator relating certain events that the others perhaps did not witness. It is essential to remember the discussion about viewpoint when dealing with multiple narration; literature is not *really* concerned with *reality*, but with writers' *versions* of it. *Literature is a construct; it is not reality itself.* Narrators bring their own layers of 'pseudo' reality to a text, and we, as readers, must be aware of this 'layering' effect, particularly when it comes to multiple narrators.

Sometimes a text is written using a **first-person narrator**. When this occurs, the first person or 'I' narrates events in such a way that he or she could be seen as the central character. We are told what he/she has experienced so that he/she is, to some extent, *in* the story but *also telling it*. Sir Arthur Conan Doyle used this technique in his 'Sherlock Holmes' stories, in which Dr Watson is narrator as well as a key character. In 'The Empty House', Watson acknowledges his part as narrator:

> Let me say to that public which has shown some interest in those glimpses which I have occasionally given them of the thoughts and actions of a very remarkable man that they are not to blame me if I have not shared my knowledge with them, for I should have considered it my first duty to have done so had I not been barred by a positive prohibition from his own lips. . . .

Here we see not only Watson talking to us, the reader, but also confiding in us that Holmes has forbidden him to talk to us about him! Can you see how the text is building up 'layers'? Although Watson is a character in the stories he is also the one who is telling them, and we must take into account his character when we read because this has been woven into the fabric of the text. Narrator has blended with narrative.

This 'blending' occurs in a slightly different way in Dickens's *A Christmas Carol*. In the first paragraph of Chapter 1 the narrator comments:

> You will, therefore, permit me to repeat emphatically that Marley was as dead as a door-nail.

Here we see the narrator directly addressing us, the reader, while commenting upon the action, but this narrator remains *outside* this action; he is *not* part of what is going on in the novel, and indeed he disappears as a character by the end of the third paragraph of the first chapter. After that point the storyteller is replaced by a standard third-person narrator and we do not hear of him again. He 'blends' into the background soon after he has set himself up as the narrator and by the fourth paragraph he is nowhere to be seen.

It might be helpful to look at narrators and language in similar ways. The function of both is surely to communicate. A narrator can be seen as a window through which we view the world the writer wants us to see. Language is a means of expressing what the author wants to say about that world; it is also in a way a window because it shows us what the writer wants us to see.

Now these windows can be made of plain, clear glass. They can be unadorned, insignificant and easy to see through. If they are this plain, you might not even notice they are there because your attention is drawn to what is on the other side and not to the windows themselves. This happens when the narrator is invisible and when language is plain. We look *through* the window and past it to what is being referred to by the writer. There is only one thing to look at – the 'what'.

Alternatively, these windows may be made of stained glass. They can be decorated, interesting and difficult to see through. If they are adorned in this way you will be very aware of them because your attention is drawn to the windows themselves before you look at what is beyond. This is what happens when the narrator is present and when language is ornate. We look *at* the window before we look past it to what is being described by the writer. There is more to look at than simply the 'what'; in this case we have to consider the 'how' *as well as* the 'what', and this is a far more complicated process.

You might be saying, 'Give me a nice, clear window any day', but I suggest that you would be missing out on a great deal of beauty, pleasure and fun by going for the easy option. Keep looking *through* the window in order to see what the writer wants to share with you, but enjoy looking *at* the beauty of the stained glass as you do it.

The element of narrator is an important one in practical criticism of any genre because it is of vital significance to the way in which the text has been 'crafted'. **Remember that nothing in good literature is ever random.**

## Stream of consciousness

It has long been accepted that human thought is an undisciplined affair, and the stream of consciousness technique is one that serves to replicate this rather haphazard process on the page. You have only to recall a sleepless night in which your mind hops or flows, depending on the speed, to one subject after another, continually changing direction. One thought seems to flow into another, one idea to give birth to another, and so on. Human beings tend not to think in straight lines. Stream of consciousness is a writer's way of recording the somewhat chaotic business of someone's thoughts and feelings, and it is therefore much to do with the *internal life* of a character – perhaps a little like the frantic paddling of the swan's feet under the surface while it glides gracefully on the top of the water.

Until late in the nineteenth century, a third person narrator was usually the one to disclose the psychological life of a character, but towards the end of the nineteenth and beginning of the twentieth century, writers became more interested in the mental processes of their characters. Sigmund Freud was writing on psychoanalysis, and the modern movement in literature saw a growing interest in the intricacies and complexities of the human psyche.

The stream of consciousness technique is not always easy to follow, because writers can choose to 'stream' in and out of the minds of various characters, often without clear indications to the reader of exactly when this is happening. The reader has to be alert and constantly vigilant, and ask him/herself from time to time, 'Whose mind am I in now?' or even, 'Is this narrative or this character's thoughts?' Some writers will choose to enter the mind of one character only, while others, such as Virginia Woolf, will wander at will into the consciousness of more than one character. The effect is intriguing, and the reader experiences powerful insights into the minds and hearts of whichever character the writer chooses to 'stream' into, but it often greatly complicates the reading process.

An example from James Joyce's *Ulysses* should illustrate this point:

> Hark! Shut your obstropolos. Pflaap! Pflaap! Blase on. There she goes. Brigade! Bout ship. Mount street way. Cut up. Pflaap! Tally ho. You not come? Run, skelter, race. Pflaap!

Not the easiest of texts to follow. The effect of the stream of consciousness is a certain fluidity (it's not called a 'stream' for nothing) and a closeness to the characters. The distance and objectivity of the traditional nineteenth-century novel is absent.

## First person soliloquy

A soliloquy is the speech of an actor who appears either alone upon the stage or in isolation and speaks aloud his thoughts and feelings. Because of his isolation, physical or otherwise, it is convention to believe what he says; there is no one about to either impress or deceive.

Shakespeare's soliloquies often appear at either the beginning or the end of a scene, but they do also appear in other parts of Shakespearian plays. Edmund opens Act 1, Scene 2 in *King Lear* in his address to Nature, and Macbeth introduces Act 1, Scene 7 of *Macbeth* by agonising over his intended murder of the king, and there are numerous other examples.

Soliloquies fall into two categories:

- private; and
- public.

A **private** soliloquy is similar to our eavesdropping on a character who is revealing his/her private thoughts and feelings by speaking them aloud. The character is not overtly and 'deliberately' sharing the innermost workings of his/ her mind with the audience but we, the audience, are conscious of witnessing the self-questioning that is going on in the character's mind.

This is no more clear than in *Hamlet*, when Hamlet himself is questioning his own courage and society's perception of it. He asks *himself*:

> Am I a coward?
> Who calls me villain? Breaks my pate across?
> Plucks off my beard, and blows it in my face?

What is important to note here is Hamlet's confusion and his striving to find answers to what is bewildering him. The questions he asks are directed towards *himself* and *not* to you or me in the audience.

A **public** soliloquy is quite different; this is clearly addressed to the audience and it is not always, but often, the villain of the piece who uses this device to share his thoughts, feelings and often his plans openly with us. If it is the villain who is divulging his wicked intentions, it can feel somewhat uncomfortable for him to take us into his confidence in this way. Sympathies are such that we often don't *want* to know what evil he is planning; it feels as if we are colluding with him.

Consider Edmund's speech as he opens Act 1, Scene 2 of *King Lear*. He is Gloucester's illegitimate son and he dedicates himself to nature because society has turned its back on him. He cannot accept his low status in the world on the grounds of illegitimacy and determines to overthrow his legitimate brother Edgar and seize his land:

> Thou, nature, art my goddess; to thy law
> My services are bound. Wherefore should I
> Stand in the plague of custom, and permit
> The curiosity of nations to deprive me,
> For that I am some twelve or fourteen moonshines
> Lag of a brother? Why bastard? wherefore base?
> When my dimensions are as well compact,
> My mind as generous, and my shape as true,
> As honest madam's issue? Why brand they us
> With base? With baseness? bastardy? base, base?

Later in the speech:

> Well, then,
> Legitimate Edgar, I must have your land.
> Our father's love is to the bastard Edmund
> As to the legitimate; fine word 'legitimate'!
> Well, my legitimate, if this letter speed
> And my invention thrive, Edmund the base
> Shall top the legitimate. I grow; I prosper.
> Now, gods, stand up for bastards!

Edmund discloses everything to the audience: we hear of his adherence to the laws of nature as opposed to the laws of man, of his determination not to allow himself to feel inferior because society sees him thus, of his decision to take his legitimate brother's land, and finally of his determination to thrive with the help of the gods.

There is no doubt whatever that Edmund is a villain, but generations of students have asked why he is so irresistibly attractive. In this soliloquy we detect a delight in evil, a relish in exacting revenge upon a condemning society, and this evil intent certainly has an appeal. It is not a coincidence that generations of audiences have fallen for the villain of the piece; we *know* he is wrong but he has a fiery spirit that many find attractive.

When discussing a soliloquy you should consider two points:

- What dramatic effect does it have upon the play?
- In what ways does it reflect what you know about the character?

## Word order

The term, rather obviously, refers to the order in which a writer uses words, and this can greatly influence the effect that a text has on its readers. There are normal patterns of word order that are part of everyday speech, and writers of all three genres often break these conventions intentionally in order to create poetic effects and emphasise particular words.

Positions of emphasis are:

- beginning/end of a line;
- beginning/end of a poem; and
- before/after a pause.

It is always worthwhile considering word order because it often identifies key concepts in the text.

Look at this example of Edmund's speech from *King Lear*:

> Thou, nature, art my **goddess**; to thy law
> My services are **bound**. Wherefore should I . . .

Notice the way in which Shakespeare has arranged the words – immediately before a pause – so that 'goddess' and 'bound' are highlighted. Our focus rests on Edmund's dedication of himself to the laws of Nature, as opposed to those of humankind, which motivate him to make Nature his 'goddess'. Because of this devotion he is, indeed, 'bound' to her, and this contract is a key element in what drives and motivates him during the rest of the play.

## Dramatic irony

Dramatic irony occurs when we, the reader or the audience, know more than the other characters in the novel or on the stage. Its purpose is to draw attention to the gap that exists between what characters think they know and what is really the case. It is often the result of other characters not knowing all the facts or failing to perceive the complicated nature of a situation. In satire this can serve to illustrate folly, or it can demonstrate a character's failure to understand or perceive the truth.

Whatever the purpose, dramatic irony places the reader or audience in a superior position to that of the characters because it gives him/her an almost omniscient perspective of the truth. The reader/audience can see *everything* from a detached position; we know what the characters know and what they don't. We can see that life is complex and that most individuals' view of the world is incomplete and imperfect.

There is an example of this in Act 1, Scene 2 of Shakespeare's *King Lear*. As the scene opens we witness Edmund, Gloucester's illegitimate son, allying himself to the forces of nature in a bid to overthrow his legitimate brother and seize from him all the material benefits that his legitimacy has bestowed on him. Gloucester then enters the stage and sees Edmund [*ostentatiously*] pocketing a letter. Unknown to Gloucester, Edmund has written this letter, supposedly from Edgar to him, expressing his intention to take his inheritance from his father before he dies.

Having read the letter, Gloucester then explodes in Edmund's direction with, 'abominable villain. Where is he?' We see the father calling the innocent son a villain and asking the real villainous one where he is. We, the all-knowing audience, must resist the urge to call out in true pantomime fashion, 'He's in front of you!'; the dramatic irony has engaged us closely with the action of the play. A few lines later, Gloucester exhorts Edmund to, 'Find out this villain, Edmund'. Here we see with shocking clarity that all that stands between Gloucester and the truth is one comma. The effect of this technique here, particularly with the use of that vital comma, is to highlight the smallness of the gap that sometimes stands between what we think we know and what we really know. The breach in this instance underlines Gloucester's ignorance about the true nature of his children, and his ability to be duped into seriously misjudging both of them. The use of dramatic irony has engaged our critical faculties so we are more involved in the judgement of such characters; we know what they don't know, so we are in a position to assess the extent of their blindness and folly.

## Approaches to drama

Apart from the actors on stage, there are, especially since the development of electronics, endless possibilities when it comes to sound effects, and we have all experienced the power of music to alter mood.

However, it is important to remember the way in which some drama was staged *originally*, particularly Shakespeare – in daylight on a bare stage. We *should* take into account things such as modern theatrical equipment but it is also necessary to look at the *intended* dramatic experience and thereby appreciate the text as an historical story of change. In this way it is possible to consider drama's changing sociocultural role, but to do this we need to look at it on two levels at the same time. We must ask ourselves, 'What *was* the dramatic intention *when this was written*?' and 'How might this *differ* in the *twenty-first century*?' In this way we can see the drama in two sociocultural contexts at the same time and derive multiple layers of meaning and significance from it.

What is essential to remember in the study of drama is that what you have in front of you in the form of a book, is in fact a play*script* and that *it is written to be performed* and this element of performance is one that should be foremost in your mind *at all times* as you study drama. Keep asking yourself, 'What would this look like, sound like, feel like *on the stage*?'; 'How would the audience *of the time* respond?' and 'How would *I* respond if I were watching it *now*?'

There are important considerations that need to be taken into account when analysing and appreciating drama, which are not relevant to other genres. You should think about the following features:

- the grouping and positioning of characters on the stage and their relationships;
- the centre of power or dominance;
- the presentation of themes;

- identifying crisis moments (moments of dramatic change and personal development);
- staging and movement; and
- the question of offstage/onstage.

Chapter 10 contains an analysis of modern drama in which these issues are addressed.

## Unique qualities of drama

Just as failure to recognise that poetry is written to be read aloud impoverishes our appreciation of it and its aural qualities, failing to recognise the element of performance in drama means that we ignore some of its most significant qualities. The genre of drama has extra dimensions, such as:

- public;
- visual element;
- immediacy;
- enforced pace;
- layers of interpretation;
- actual sound;
- tangibility;
- movement;
- acts and scenes; and
- continuous dialogue.

### Public

Perhaps one of the features of drama that distinguishes it most strikingly from prose and poetry is its public nature. Prose and poetry *may* be read or performed aloud, but more often these two genres are enjoyed in private. Drama, however, is a public affair and therefore a social activity. A public performance means that we gather with other people in the audience to share our experience of it, and the fact that we seldom watch drama in isolation means that our experience of it is usually, inevitably, influenced by those around us. At no time is this clearer than in pantomime, with the audience's group response of cheering on the hero or hissing at the villain.

### Visual element

Perhaps one of the most striking differences between drama and the other two genres is the visual quality it offers; we watch the action taking place before our very eyes. A stage direction on the page that merely reads 'kneels' takes on enormous significance on the stage when an actor interprets the word as an action. There is great force in witnessing something with our own eyes; actions speak louder than words.

### Immediacy

Arguably, one of drama's most important unique qualities is its immediacy. When we see a play acted out in front of us, it is happening *here and now*, despite the date of its conception in the mind of the playwright, or its first appearance in print. This immediacy has a powerful effect on those who witness it. The conflict (which is at the heart of all drama) is happening *now*, before our eyes and we watch, forming opinions, making judgements, sympathising with or distancing ourselves from the characters, according to our personal responses. It has an immediate effect on our thoughts and feelings; we feel part of the action. It is, to varying degrees, a version of 'real life' played out in front of us, and with which we engage.

Because drama on stage is live, it is always subject to change. It is not fixed and life is breathed into it by acting out the script. You might respond differently to the same play, acted by the same cast on two separate occasions because there are several variables:

- *The actor* may feel differently. Perhaps he or she has a personal problem on Tuesday that he/she did not have on Monday and this causes his/her performance to be flatter (or perhaps more animated) than it was on the previous night. An actor's response to his/her role will inevitably affect *your* response to that character.
- *You* may feel differently. It could be that you have a problem, or that you know something on Tuesday that you did not know on Monday, which influences the way in which *you* respond to the performance.
- *The director* may have changed some aspect of performance between Monday's and Tuesday's shows. Maybe he or she has decided to emphasise something different in Tuesday's performance that was not so obvious on Monday. This will affect *your* response to the play.

There are numerous features in drama that influence the overall effect of the production and there is no guarantee that all these elements will remain absolutely constant in every performance.

### Enforced pace

The energy that live drama has inevitably enforces a certain pace upon the text. When we watch a stage performance of a play, the director and actors impose their own pace on the text and this is one of the things that engages us so effectively. We cannot put down the book or re-read a section, or linger over particular words or phrases as we do when we read a text and, in a sense, this may also be a disadvantage, particularly if the content or style is complex.

We have to keep up with the performance and at times, inevitably, understanding will be incomplete, but it is interesting to see how much of a complex text we can still grasp by means of all the other elements that are at our disposal in live drama. The pieces of the puzzle we miss in terms of a detailed understanding of the text itself can be made up, at least in part, by aspects such as tone of voice, facial expression, gesture, interaction between characters, sound, lighting and so on.

### Layers of interpretation

Much of the tone of voice and physical movement made by actors on the stage is in the hands of the director who has already interpreted the text before he or she directs the cast. The direction offered to the actors is a *result* of the meaning that the director has derived from the text. As with poetry, the choice of a tone of voice in which to read it is to have already interpreted a meaning, because the choice of tone of voice reflects that interpretation.

In this sense, we are perhaps one layer removed from the playwright's meaning, because the director has decided his/her own meaning *before* we watch the play. We merely watch his/her interpretation of the script; we do not interpret it ourselves. However, I would suggest that we can still respond to it, and this is the key to our helping to make meaning.

## Actual sound

Although the element of sound is present in all literature, particularly poetry, we never in fact *hear* that sound outside our own heads. Of course, the techniques of onomatopoeia, alliteration, assonance, consonance, repetition and so on all add greatly to the sound quality of a piece of writing, but it is only in staged drama that that sound is externalised.

Techniques employed by writers are given life in live drama, and the effect of certain sounds in our ears cannot be underestimated. Neither indeed can 'the sound of silence', and this also needs to be considered. Silence is an empty space in dialogue but it is not 'nothing'. You will know from examples in real life when a silence has spoken most eloquently; it can be dramatic and thought-provoking. Listen for what is *not* said in a silence; its effect can sometimes be to entice the audience to fill in the gap. We tend to try to imagine what is going on in the head of the character who does not speak, or, if the silence is caused merely by a lack of people on the stage, that moment of stillness can have an enormous dramatic impact on an audience. It is often at moments like this that we really see the power of theatre to entrance a large group of people.

As with silence, emptiness should not be ignored. We need also to look at the times when physical objects and people are absent from the stage. Emptiness on stage can be dramatic; perhaps it follows the departing sweep of an exiting monarch, or the nervous scrambling of a peasant. Savour the moment of the empty stage as you must the silence, then be aware of what comes in to fill it; this could create a dramatic contrast.

Emptiness on stage has a photographic quality. We are often impressed by photography that portrays the dramatic, the bleak and lonely – the footballer on the pitch of an empty stadium, the solitary tree on the heath. Look for these icons on the stage; they are powerful carriers of meaning in live drama.

There is a wide range of possible interpretations open to directors and actors that can all be expressed in the way that actors deliver their lines. We are treated to a tremendous range of tones of voice: quiet whispers, dramatic climaxes, challenging questions, roars of indignation and many more. We see bustling crowds, intimate groups, couples united or apart, solitary figures and empty stages. None of these variations can be represented adequately in print.

## Tangibility

Despite the power of the human imagination to interpret words and create mental pictures from them, nothing quite replaces actually seeing the thing itself. In a sense, 'the word is made flesh' and many of the uncertainties we may have had about a text when reading it are clarified in performance.

The stage direction that states, 'enter with sword' is immediately transformed into solid reality when the prop is there on the stage in the hands of a character. All that object represents is brought home to us in an instant, and the stage direction tucked away in brackets somewhere on the page suddenly becomes a lethal strip of metal on the stage – a tangible symbol of destruction.

## Movement

Movement of actors on the page is given scant attention in most scripts. You may have a stage direction that reads, 'kneels' or 'exit', but much of this aspect is left to the discretion of the director and cast. *How* does the character exit, *how* does he/she kneel? Because the visual element of drama is so central to its impact on an audience, the aspect of physical movement is one that needs to be considered carefully.

Much can be communicated by the imperious sweep of a king as he exits, or the loving embrace of an admirer as he or she enfolds the object of his/her desire. The body language used by actors on stage is a signal every bit as powerful as it is in everyday life, and perhaps more so, because with drama we are actively looking for clues to a character's thoughts, feelings and reactions to other characters. The movements made on stage add another layer of meaning and therefore a greater richness to a written text.

Let us not, however, forget the opposite of movement – stillness. A character frozen on stage can be just as dramatic, or even more than the one who lunges and swirls. Sometimes it is in the *contrast* between these two opposites that the director can speak most eloquently. Moments of stillness must be looked at sensitively as they can add considerable drama to a scene. The audience is sometimes intrigued by this lack of movement and ask themselves, 'Why doesn't he do something?' or 'Why is she so still?', thereby enhancing our involvement in the performance. If the stillness is sudden, after a great deal of activity, the effect is all the more dramatic.

What any script does is to offer up endless possibilities for interpretation, and where there is ambiguity in the text, the director's choice of movement at that point functions as an interpretative act. Again, in movement, as in so many other aspects of drama, the director helps to create meaning. One director's choice of movement to accompany either a line of speech or a stage direction may differ greatly from another's; what results is two different interpretations of the same material.

## Acts and scenes

Perhaps one of the most obvious distinguishing features of drama is its separation into acts and scenes that break up the action in much the same way as chapters do in novels. When Shakespeare was writing, the convention was five acts. This gradually reduced to three, and modern dramas often have only two or are written as merely a succession of scenes in one act.

The purpose of a scene is to identify a piece of action that occurs in one place over a continuous unit of time. When this action moves elsewhere or the playwright wants to signify a break in time, the scene ends and another begins.

Where fast scene-changing occurs, there can be a sense of events spiralling out of a character's control. The pace is heightened and such rapid ongoing movement can leave an audience almost breathless. While short scenes are effective for the portrayal of action, including battles, longer ones help the dramatist to develop ideas, characters, feelings and relationships.

You must ask yourself how the play is divided into acts and scenes, and what effects these breaks have on the text and on its performance on the stage.

### Continuous dialogue

It is only in drama that dialogue is sustained for such a considerable length of time. This imposes a certain strain on an audience. We cannot stop the production or, as was said earlier, put down the book or re-read a difficult section. Attention needs to be sustained if we are to understand and appreciate the text in action. Unlike a video, in a live performance we cannot rewind the tape. Continuous dialogue is one of the features of drama that most mimics real life, because surely it is through a person's actual speech and actions and the responses of others to them that we form opinions about them as we watch them acting out their lives in front of us.

The three sources of information about a character that we receive from any text are all bombarding us at the same time at a considerable speed. These are, of course:

- what a character does;
- what a character says;
- what other characters say about him/her.

Much can be communicated through dialogue that is difficult to put into print. Dialect, accent, pitch and tone are all powerful carriers of meaning. We know from real life how much information about a person can be gleaned from merely listening to his/her voice. For example,

- gender;
- age;
- place of birth/breeding;
- social class;
- level of education;
- level of intelligence;
- mood;
- attitude;
- character; and
- personality.

There may be more that you have thought of, and certainly 'character' and 'personality' could be scrutinised more closely.

### Approaches to texts – some schools of literary criticism

It can be argued that no text really comes to life until it is read; that it is not until someone *interprets* it that it *means* anything; up to that point it is merely a collection of words on a page. Interpretation is an inevitable part of reading; whenever we read a text we are trying to derive meaning from it. What is interesting in this process is the number of different meanings a reader can find in a text, depending upon the critical approach he or she uses.

Literary criticism is the term given to the theory of interpreting literature. There are numerous theories in this field and therefore a wide variety of possible approaches to literary texts. While it is not possible in a book of this nature to explore each school in detail, the following brief summaries of some of the better-known approaches might help to introduce you to the range of thinking in this area.

It is important that you read widely from this range of approaches at undergraduate level, and A-level students will find this complements their study of the literature. It will help you to find new questions to ask of texts, and new ways in which to interpret them. You will find it useful to read the text *before* you read any critical work on it. This way you will have formulated some of your own responses and are then in a better position to appreciate and evaluate the views of others.

### Marxist theory

This rests on the notion that all our thinking and behaviour is the product of our social conditions and it argues that literary works can be understood and appreciated in terms of social and economic factors. Social and cultural contexts are extremely important when using this theory, because it maintains that these are the only significant influences upon us. Marxism is concerned with the issues of domination, subordination and power relations. It holds that social class is defined by the ownership of the means of production, which also determines who has power. Exploitation is a common theme, as is the notion of who speaks, who is listened to and what they say.

### Semiotic theory

This is built upon the idea of signs and it works on the premise that there are signifiers and signifieds. The signifier is a *sign* of the signified. A simple example is the *word* 'cat' (a signifier) *standing for* (or being a *sign* of) the concept of a furry domestic animal with four legs, which we know as a cat (the signified). Ambiguity exists when the gap between the signifier and the signified leaves room for doubt – when we are not sure to what signified the signifier is referring. It is in this gap that we, as interpreters, must strive to make meaning, and it is here that we encounter the range of possible meanings that constitute responses to that ambiguity. You might find it helpful to look again at Vernon Scannell's, 'A Case of Murder', which was discussed in Chapter 3, and at the numerous signifiers he uses to signify the cat.

Semioticians believe that there exists a gap between *all* signifiers and their signifieds – that signifiers and signifieds are never firmly connected and therefore language is always an inadequate means of representing the world.

### Psychoanalytic theory

Psychoanalytic critical theory gives us another set of meanings. It owes its existence to the findings of Sigmund Freud and works on the need to identify and explain the presence of sexuality in a text, on the grounds that sexuality is a significant constituent of the human psyche and therefore of every product of it, such as literature. It acknowledges the presence of the writer's unconscious mind at work in a text, sometimes betraying hidden desires.

However, it goes further than merely searching for phallic symbols. It can be divided into four types, depending on its focus. It can look at the author, the contents of the work, its structure or its reader. It works on the premise that all texts have a sub-text and that what is not said is as important as what *is*. It looks at ambiguity, overemphasis, or avoidance – gaps – things that do not quite fit together – in other words, the unconscious of the text itself, to provide crucial clues to its meanings.

## Feminist theory

Feminism provides us with an approach involving the notion that all thinking is creating – that if we *think* and *speak* about men and women in certain ways, they will be seen to *be* like that. Therefore it is concerned with the presentation of women in literary texts, which is perhaps best observed by a consideration of them in terms of their interaction with men. This can also give rise to some interesting reflections on the portrayal of men in literature. As with Marxism, the concepts of power, control and ownership are central, as is that of exploitation. There is controversy over some feminists' view that modes of writing may be differentiated by gender – that there are masculine and feminine sentences and forms of expression.

## New historicism

This involves looking at works of literature in their political and historical context because they are seen as products of their time. The theory argues that, in order to interpret a text fully and accurately, one must understand the time in which it was created. This offers the opportunity to consider the interpretation of texts in a context not merely of past events, but more importantly of power, control, authority and ideology.

## Deconstruction

Deconstruction argues that language is an inadequate method of imposing order on the world, and that writers cannot organise and express their experience effectively or accurately using words. It is sceptical about the way society is ordered in binary pairs such as black and white, good and evil, male and female, maintaining that life is more complicated than this, and that these systems do not express adequately its complex nature. The traditional objection to it was that, far from appreciating what a text says, it seems to suggest that it cannot say anything that is either meaningful or conclusive. This might appear to be a negative approach, but as deconstruction believes that there is no conclusive meaning attributable to a text, discussion enjoys a certain freedom and often results in the consideration of lively, if rather implausible, possibilities.

## Focus on the question

Practical criticism of poetry – Seamus Heaney's 'The Wife's Tale'. Imagine that you have just opened your examination paper and the question that faces you is:

'The Wife's Tale' presents the relationship of marriage from the point of view of the wife bringing lunch to her husband and his workers.

Read through the poem several times until you have the feel of it, and then write about it as fully as you can.   (AQA (AEB) June 1992)

### The Wife's Tale

When I had spread it all on linen cloth
Under the hedge, I called them over.
The hum and gulp of the thresher ran down
And the big belt slewed to a standstill, straw
Hanging undelivered in the jaws.
There was such quiet that I heard their boots
Crunching the stubble twenty yards away.

He lay down and said "Give these fellows theirs,
I'm in no hurry," plucking the grass in handfuls
And tossing it in the air. "That looks well."
(He nodded at my white cloth on the grass.)
"I declare a woman could lay out a field
Though boys like us have little call for cloths."
He winked, then watched me as I poured a cup
And buttered the thick slices that he likes.
"It's threshing better than I thought, and mind
It's good clean seed. Away over there and look."
Always this inspection has to be made
Even when I don't know what to look for.

But I ran my hand in the half-filled bags
Hooked to the slots. It was hard as shot,
Innumerable and cool. The bags gaped

Where the chutes ran back to the stilled drum
And the forks were stuck at angles in the ground
As javelins might mark lost battlefields.
I moved between them back across the stubble.
They lay in the ring of their own crusts and dregs
Smoking and saying nothing. "There's good yield,
Isn't there?" – as proud as if he were the land itself –
"Enough for crushing and for sowing both."
And that was it. I'd come and he had shown me
So I belonged no further to the work.
I gathered cups and folded up the cloth
And went. But they still kept their ease
Spread out, unbuttoned, grateful, under the trees.

Seamus Heaney

The first step is to do a focusing exercise on the question:

'The Wife's Tale' presents **the relationship of marriage from the point of view of the wife** bringing lunch to her husband and his workers.

Read through the poem several times until you have the feel of it, and then **write about it as fully as you can**. Key points to note are:

- the relationship is seen from *the point of view of the wife*;
- you are asked to *write about it . . . . fully*; and
- *personal response* is important (*until you have the feel of it* and *as fully as you can*).

## Informed personal response

To see the process of practical criticism in simple terms, we could say that it is a fascinating blend of:

- **analysis**;
- **interaction**; and
- **creation**.

Taking 'The Wife's Tale' as our example, let us now go through the stages that any candidate would need to, in order to produce a concise and well-expressed response.

### Analysis

Your first task when faced with a text for appreciation is to *read it closely* and this is done with *analysis* in mind. Every word is thought about and the *reason for its presence* is considered. You ask yourself, '*What* does this word *mean* and *why* has the writer used it here?'

## Interaction

When understanding has been established, you then move on to another form of interaction with the text. Your own thought processes start to move you towards *responding* to it. This is when it is important that you 'make the text your own'. This might seem a rather obscure and ambiguous thing to say, and it is something to which literature specialists frequently refer. What it means is that the student in a sense 'absorbs' the text, 'soaks it in' and *mixes a part of him/herself with it.*

To illustrate the point a little more clearly, let me use the example of a child who is doing a project – for example, on cricket. You would soon be able to distinguish between the work of a child who has looked up the subject in an encyclopaedia or on the Internet and copied the text verbatim, and that of the pupil who consults a reference source and *uses* this material to write his *own* account of the sport.

The first example would constitute 'an informed response' and one can safely predict that it would be bland, impersonal and 'dead'. The second would represent 'an informed *personal* response' and this would be more interesting, personal and lively.

## Creation

Examiners are looking for the *second* type of response from you. They need to see some evidence in your essay that you have *mixed a part of yourself with the text.* This 'mixing' is where **creativity** comes in and this process requires (remember the 4 Cs?):

- **calmness**;
- **confidence**;
- **concentration**; and
- **continued close reading**.

# Methodology

## Read closely and think

Long before you even pick up your pen to write there is a great deal of important work to be done in preparation. Remember the analogy of building a house? Before you start to lay a single brick you must excavate the land and lay down solid foundations for your structure.

You are 'digging away at the soil' when you start to analyse a piece of literature. You break the surface of the ground and enter the muddy world of the text. In scraping away at the soil you reveal truths about it and also establish your boundaries: 'How far can I go with this idea?' or 'Does this idea link in with any of the others?' The preparation you do for your essay helps you to draw out the shape of your building and to decide in what direction you want to go in order to construct it.

It is important to remember that this pre-construction preparation starts *as soon as you begin to read the text*.

Reading for practical criticism is *different* from reading for pleasure; it must be active and, after your initial reading, you should approach the process with a pencil in your hand so that you can record your responses to the text as you read.

It is essential to read *closely* and *dynamically*, searching for meaning and *helping to construct it* from your own *interaction* with the text. In a sense, the text is dead without the reader; it is merely words on a page. It is you and I, when we read, who respond to the writer, breathe life into a poem and make it *mean* something.

You must bring to this process *your own knowledge and experience*, gained from past encounters with poetry, *and your own experience of life* that are likely to be more numerous and fruitful than you imagine at first. This is one of the reasons why wide reading is so important. Your aim should be to increase the number and widen the nature of the experiences you have with literature so that your stock of these is enriched.

You need to move through the poem with some sense of direction, looking for patterns, recurring language, imagery, ideas or associations, which give us clues as to the meaning within the poem.

With this poem it is relatively easy to establish that it is a description of a wife bringing a meal to her husband and his workers in the field as they labour, but an account of this alone would lack a grasp of any larger meanings. Much literature is, on the surface, about everyday life, almost trivial events which, on first reading, lack serious 'weight', and candidates frequently fail to do more than re-describe what the poet has already written, offering what is little more than a narrative version of the poetic original. How do we avoid this?

What we need to look for are the **issues** within the poem. We seek to do far more than rewrite a poet's description in prose. We must search out the *larger idea at work* in his/her writing. It is this issue, concept or argument that pervades all aspects of the work. This is the poem's *driving force*, and once we have identified this we can see how the poem 'works' as a crafted piece of writing.

Your *very first* reading of a text should be with the purpose of answering that simple question, '*What is the text about*?' This should become clear as you read, but if you find this stage of the process difficult it may help to jot down briefly the key points in terms of the 'what' (or content) as you go.

You may find it helpful to ask yourself some basic questions, such as:

- **What** is happening? This establishes the main action.
- To **whom** is it happening? This tells you who are the main protagonists.
- **Why** is it happening? This leads you towards finding explanations if there are any.
- **When** is it happening? This puts it in context; for example, it establishes whether the narrator is reflecting on the past or looking to the future. Is it the recent or distant past? Is it imminent or far into the future? Is it happening now? It might also help to establish an historical context, which is very important to an appreciation of any text.
- **Where** is it happening? Again, this helps to put the text in context, as the setting of any text has a significant bearing on it.

- **How** is it happening? This will tell you about the feelings in the work, which are vital clues to meaning.

These are the initial questions that need to be asked on any fact-finding mission. Answers to these questions are *not the end of the road*, however; they are merely *the first steps on your journey of discovery* into any text.

- Subsequent readings should be undertaken with an ever-closer analysis of significant features in mind. Keep asking yourself, '**What is happening?**' and '**What are the feelings I can sense?**' Briefly note down *alongside the relevant sections* of the text a word that represents the *emotions* you sense – for example, 'wistful', 'nostalgic', 'angry', 'bitter' and so on. At this point you are trying to identify the *tone* of the writing.
- You should expect to read the piece set for study *several times* during your course and at least *twice thoroughly* in the examination. Subsequent readings in the exam might take the form of scanning for specific details. Do not be misled into thinking that you can hope to gain a thorough understanding of any text *without this much close reading*. Remember that *the quality of your writing will only be as good as the quality of your reading and thinking*.

## Summarise the central conflict/s

It could be argued that in all literature there is an element of **conflict**, a tension that must be resolved, and identifying the nature of this can be central to fathoming the deeper meaning of the poem. The final stage of a drama is referred to as the 'resolution', the stage during which the conflict in the work is in some way resolved. Remember that conflict can be signified by a writer using opposites, oxymorons, differences and pairs of words such as references to light/dark, old/young, happy/sad, past/present and so on.

These references are not always obvious; sometimes they operate on a connotative level. (See discussion on connotations on pages 85–7.)

## What? Who? Why? When? Where? How?

Start to look for signs of *conflict* and note these carefully. Ask yourself:

- **What** is this conflict?
- **Who** is involved?
- **Why** is it there?
- **When** is it taking place?
- **Where** is it?
- **How** is it being acted out?

Let us look at Seamus Heaney's 'The Wife's Tale' and try to identify any early signs of conflict or opposition. Read the poem through carefully *at least twice* '*until you have the feel of it*'. Now read it again, searching for the essential **tension** or **conflict** discussed above. Where there is opposition there are going to be two elements that **contrast**, pairs of characteristics or qualities – for example, black/white, happy/sad, old/young. Look for this and identify any pairs you see.

---

*Box 5.1*  **CONFLICT ANNOTATIONS**

**CONFLICT: 'I'/'THEY'**
           **MASCULINE/FEMININE**
           **DOMINANCE/SUBSERVIENCE**

*I/them*        *masculine/feminine*

When I had spread it all on linen cloth
Under the hedge, I called them over.
The hum and gulp of the thresher ran down     *dominance*
And the big belt slewed to a standstill, straw
Hanging undelivered in the jaws.      5

*masculine/feminine*
       There was such quiet than I heard their boots
       Crunching the stubble twenty yards away.

He lay down and said "Give these fellows theirs,
I'm in no hurry," plucking grass in handfuls     *dominance*

*masculine/feminine*
       And tossing it in the air, "That looks well."    10
       (He nodded at my white cloth on the grass.)
       "I declare a woman could lay out a field
       Though boys like us have little call for cloths."
       He winked, then watched me as I poured a cup

*I/them*
       And buttered the thick slices that he likes.    15
       "It's threshing better than I thought, and mind
       It's good clean seed. Away over there and look"
       Always this inspection has to be made
       Even when I don't know what to look for.
But I ran my hand in the half-filled bags    20
Hooked to the slots. It was hard as shot,
Innumerable and cool. The bags gaped
Where the chutes ran back to the stilled drum
And forks were stuck at angles in the ground
As javelins might mark lost battlefields.    25
I moved between them back across the stubble.

*I/them*   ——— They lay in the ring of their own crusts and dregs
Smoking and saying nothing. "There's good yield,
Isn't there?" – as proud as if he were the land itself –

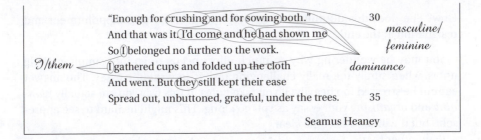

"Enough for crushing and for sowing both."        30
And that was it. I'd come and he had shown me
So I belonged no further to the work.
I gathered cups and folded up the cloth
And went. But they still kept their ease
Spread out, unbuttoned, grateful, under the trees.   35

*masculine/
feminine*

*dominance*

*I/them*

## Annotating a text

There is no definitive way in which to annotate a text set for study, but there is a method that is thorough, timesaving and constructive, and that is the method which will be discussed here.

Look at the annotations to 'The Wife's Tale' and notice how:

- All the significant references have been *circled*;
- The circles are *linked to a note* in the margin;
- This note explains *why they are important*; and
- Lines come from this marginal note to *other examples of the same point*.

You will see that three areas of conflict have been addressed, and that there are several references for each aspect. We identified:

(i)   **Separation** as seen in the 'I'/'we' split;
(ii)  **Gender** differences in her 'linen cloth' and his 'crunching'; and
(iii) **Dominance** because:

    (a)   we hear his words but only her thoughts; and
    (b)   they each dominate in their own sphere.

Let us return to our key questions. What answers do we have?

**What?** We know that the conflict is within the relationship and that it is to do with the three areas outlined above.

**Who?** We can see that the conflict is between the husband and the wife.

**Why?** Answers to this question are not so easy at this stage. In a sense, the response to *what?* above is helpful, but it might not provide us with the whole picture *yet*. Perhaps we have more analysis to do before we can answer that question fully.

**When?** It would seem to be in the recent past but after the husband and wife have been married for some time. In terms of history, it is set at a time of traditional roles for men and women.

**Where?** It takes place in a rural context and the implications of the setting must be considered carefully. She is taking lunch to her husband and his workers in the field.

**How?** She does this dutifully, lovingly yet with a sense of disappointment and resignation at the end.

You may be wondering why so much effort needs to go into simply making notes, when surely the really challenging task is to write the essay. **The answer cannot be stressed too heavily**: if you take notes in this way you are actually *planning* and *organising* your essay as you go along. This might be hard to see at present, but it will soon become clear.

Remember that:

- It is *essential that you organise this stage of your study very carefully.* A little time spent at this stage will save you a great deal of valuable time and mental energy later.
- Vague notes scribbled in the margin with no explanations are of little use, as indeed are 'floating' notes which are not 'tied' to any part of the text. Remember that every point you make has to be substantiated by close textual reference, so comments and quotations should *always be linked*. Be sure to *anchor* a note or comment to the part of the text to which it refers *as you go along*. The comment in the margin should be *precise* and *concise* and it is worth thinking carefully about *what* you are going to write *as you write it*. This will save you valuable time and mental energy in an examination. Look at the annotation diagrams of 'The Wife's Tale' to see how this is done.
- Students often like to underline words or phrases that strike them as being significant, but without a note alongside this underlining you will have to return to that part of the text and read it *again* to discover *why* you underlined it. Doing this *as you go along* saves time and effort.

There are clearly elements of **tension** or **conflict**, but where do you go from here?

- To start with, we can see that a **separation** exists between the two. There is no mention of 'we' or 'us', no sense of being together or as one, only 'I' and 'them' in two distinct groups. Analysis of personal pronouns is important. There is a fuller discussion of this in Chapter 4, under 'Tools of Analysis – Features of Text'.
- The imagery used is heavily suffused with **gender**; she lays out her meal 'on linen cloth', suggesting soft, white fabric and a sense of femininity. He turns off the 'hum and gulp of the thresher' and the 'big belt slewed to a standstill' – aural and visual images of harsh, loud machinery, and therefore by implication, masculinity. The 'hum and gulp' and the 'crunching' all suggest masculine activity, without which there is 'such quiet'. The noise represents the masculine; absence of it the opposite – the feminine.
- Noise suggests aggression and **dominance**. Note that we hear *her* thoughts and *his* words; linguistically, he dominates in this scene.
- Woman as dominant in the *domestic* arena; man dominant in the *agricultural* – 'I called them over' – to eat the food *she* had prepared, whereas she is instructed to 'away over there and look' at *his* achievements in the field.

It is these greater meanings that we seek to identify in practical criticism and it is partly this search for meaning that makes the process a creative as well as an analytical one.

# Connotations

You may at this stage be wondering how and why I make this connection between 'linen cloth' and femininity, and this brings us to the issue of *meaning*.

There are two types of meaning with which we deal when we analyse pieces of literature:

- **Denotative meaning**; and
- **Connotative meaning**.

**Denotative meaning** is when a word 'stands as a name for' (*Concise Oxford Dictionary*) something else. We could say that the word 'black' **denotes** 'very dark, having no colour from the absorption of all or nearly all incident light' (*Concise Oxford Dictionary*). The denotative meaning of 'black' is the common, everyday, literal meaning that we all understand immediately.

**Connotative meaning** is to do with 'that which is implied by a word etc. in addition to its literal or primary meaning' (*Concise Oxford Dictionary*). We could say that the word 'black' **connotes** death, mourning, night, darkness, evil, the unknown and so on. Notice how in this area of meaning we go well beyond the literal and start to enter the world of powerful ideas and emotions.

What practical criticism seeks to do is to go *beyond* the **denotative** meanings of words into the more exciting, creative and personal world of **connotative** meanings. It is in *this* area that the reader helps to make meaning, by exploring the possible **connotations** that exist in writers' language and thereby exploring their *feelings and attitudes*.

Be prepared to *be bold* and to *take risks*. It is important to *try out* your ideas, to share them with others, to see if they work. Remember that practical criticism is a skill, and that the only way to acquire a skill is to *practise it* and, inevitably, sometimes get it wrong.

When you learn to drive a car your instructor does not teach you these skills in the comparative safety of a classroom. He or she takes you straight out on to the road and you learn to drive *by driving*. It's rather a dangerous business really and, in a sense, your instructor is taking a considerable risk (not all cars have dual controls), but it is the only way to learn. We need to take risks sometimes.

We actually deal with **connotative** meaning frequently in everyday life without realising it. If someone were to refer to 'a black day', we would know immediately what they meant. We are unlikely to infer that the day was literally black (in any **denotative** way); more probably we would understand that, for the speaker, the day involved deep unhappiness or gloom. Words that are used **connotatively** are powerful carriers of meaning, and they are some of the most valuable keys to uncovering the wider messages at work in a piece of writing.

# Emotion

We should always remember that poetry is essentially about *emotion* and it is in the area of **connotation** that we are most likely to engage with poets' *feelings*.

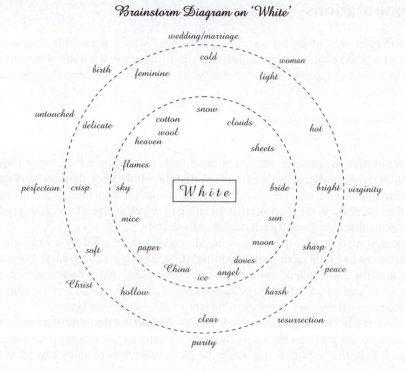

*Brainstorm Diagram on 'White'*

wedding/marriage
cold
birth    feminine    woman
light
untouched    snow
delicate    cotton    clouds    hot
wool
heaven    sheets
flames
perfection    crisp    sky    bride    bright    virginity
mice    sun
soft    paper    moon    sharp
doves
China    angel    peace
Christ    ice    harsh
hollow
clear    resurrection
purity

White

## Association

It might be helpful to consider this idea further, and play a game similar to the one that psychologists sometimes use – the word association game. Find a piece of paper and write the word 'white' in the centre of it. Then, without thinking too carefully about it, jot down whatever you associate with that word. This could be concepts, feelings, moods or things. Try to be spontaneous and think broadly about the word. Do this now.

Compare your diagram with the one shown here. You were asked to think *broadly* about the word, and this is important. *Lateral thinking* is not based on logic, and this exercise is designed to reinforce that fact. It involves thinking *around* an issue; looking at it from *wider* angles than perhaps we normally do. It is *not* 'straight-line thinking'.

Notice that the idea of weddings appears on the diagram. There is in fact no *logical* connection between these two words. 'White' does not '*mean*' wedding in the denotative sense, but we *connect* these two ideas because in our culture white has become a symbol of purity and it is deemed appropriate for the bride to wear it at her wedding. We simply *connect* the idea of wedding with that of white. This is how **connotation** works.

Notice in the diagram that the words are grouped roughly into three categories: things; feelings/descriptions; and associated ideas. If you look at the inner circle you will see that the items listed range from 'ice' to 'flames', and this has interesting implications for practical criticism. This exercise serves to illustrate that the range of meanings at our disposal in terms of **connotation** is considerably wider than the scope of **denotative** meanings. In **denotative** terms, 'white' can only mean one thing; when we consider its *associations*, the possibilities range from 'ice' to 'flames'! Who can say which **connotation** is 'right'? Ice *is* white and so are flames when they are very hot. What will direct us towards a more appropriate meaning is the *context* in which the word appears.

## Lateral thinking

It is with this same *open-mindedness* and *lateral* thinking that you need to approach texts for practical criticism. A close analysis of a writer's imagery will tell you about his or her thinking. The **connotations** that surround words are commonly shared by a culture and it is worth considering the author's culture in order to determine *how* he or she sees such things.

If we return to 'The Wife's Tale', we can perhaps see now that 'linen cloth' has **connotations** of femininity because if we use our visual imagination we can sense that soft, white fabric has a certain feminine quality about it, particularly when we compare it with the masculine 'boots', 'crunching' and 'stubble'. White linen sheets have also been a symbol of virginity in more traditional cultures – taken off the marriage bed after the first night and shown to the community as a sign that the bride was a virgin. In this context, the 'linen cloth' is a symbol of the wife's giving of herself to her husband.

She 'poured a cup' and 'buttered the thick slices that he likes'. This is a task *associated* with traditionally feminine behaviour, just as winking is in some sense, part of masculine conduct. She 'ran her hand' through the grain *suggests* a typically feminine action of caressing. What she felt was the masculine seed that was 'hard as shot'.

We need not worry at this stage where the poem is going, what will happen to these conflicts, or how it will develop. It is essential merely to identify the tension from the poem's opening lines, looking for contrasts, opposites, tensions, and pairs of words.

## Track the themes

Read through the poem with the areas of conflict outlined above firmly in your mind, and look for further evidence of them. How does the writer continue to weave this thread of conflict throughout the work?

Remember to use the approach discussed earlier. You should have headings in the margin:

'I'/'them'
'masculine'/'feminine'
'dominance'/'subservience'

and to these headings should be 'tied' by lines *all textual references that relate to that point*. **This is very important**. A great deal of time is saved in this way *and* you are more likely to produce an essay that bears the signs of organisation and planning which are such essential requirements to gain the higher grades.

Now we need to consider what happens to these themes. Where do they go? How are they developed? The elements of **I/them, masculine/feminine, dominance/subservience** identified in the first stanza can be seen recurring and being developed in subsequent stanzas.

- Stanza two – 'He'/'woman' (**masculine/feminine**) 'boys like us'/'a woman' (**dominance/subservience**; males outnumber females); and
- Stanza three – 'They'/'I', 'I went...'/'They still kept their ease' (**I/them**; separation of the wife from the men).

Now that you have identified some key conflicts, you can build on these as you work through the poem, looking for ways in which you can develop these ideas in subsequent stanzas. Notice how these elements are, to some extent, *blended together* in some of these examples. The **dominance** issue is alluded to in 'boys like us' (the **masculine/feminine** theme) because the men outnumber the lone 'woman'.

The concept of *separation* is clearly a major one. She is apart from the men ('**I**'/'**them**'). Her role and function as a wife is clearly differentiated from his (**masculine/feminine**) and generally he dominates, although there is evidence to suggest that she has the power in the domestic arena (**dominance/subservience**). See 'Developing the Themes'.

The first stanza presents to us something of a rural idyll (a brief description of a picturesque scene or incident in rural life); the farmer's wife taking lunch to her husband in the field. On closer inspection, however, contrasts are soon established that suggest conflicts, and this is borne out later in the poem. Beneath the surface of a man and a woman performing traditional roles in their marriage lie the traces of 'battlefields', although there are also signs that all is not conflict in their relationship and it is this that we move on to now.

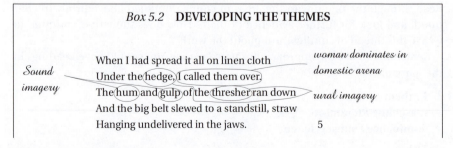

*Box 5.2*  **DEVELOPING THE THEMES**

sound imagery

> There was such quiet that I heard their boots
> Crunching the stubble twenty yards away.

Language of abandon/ease helping himself to Nature (a taker)

> He lay down and said "Give these fellows theirs,
> I'm in no hurry," plucking grass in handfuls
> And tossing it in the air. "That looks well."

rural imagery

10

> He nodded at my white cloth on the grass.
> "I declare a woman could lay out a field
> Though boys like us have little call for cloths."

'Though' highlights their differences – idiosyncrasies to which the other panders

conflict or acceptance

> He winked, then watched me as I poured a cup
> And buttered the thick slices that he likes.

15

> "It's threshing better than I thought, and mind
> It's good clean seed. Away over there and look."

man dominates in agricultural arena

> Always this inspection has to be made
> Even when I don't know what to look for.

masculine imagery

> But I ran my hand in the half-filled bags

20

> Hooked to the slots. It was hard as shot,

sensuous/sensual

> Innumerable and cool. The bags gaped

brotherhood in a closed circle, excluding her 'ring' = symbol of marriage

> Where the chutes ran back to the stilled drum
> And forks were stuck at angles in the ground

imagery of war

> As javelins might mark lost battlefields.

25

'back' suggests retreat in battle

> I moved between them, back across the stubble.

> They lay in the ring of their own crusts and dregs

post-coital/ post-prandial behaviour

> Smoking and saying nothing. "There's good yield,

post-coital/ post-prandial detritus

> Isn't there?" – as proud as if he were the land itself –

> "Enough for crushing and for sowing both."

30

> And that was it. I'd come and he had shown me

sexual connotations (dominance/fertilisation)

monosyllabic and final masculine language

> So I belonged no further to the work.
> I gathered cups and folded up the cloth

separation – she leaves them

> And went. But they still kept their ease
> Spread out, unbuttoned, grateful, under the trees.

35

Seamus Heaney

(First + last stanzas highlight woman as provider – the giver of food and herself?) Feminist reading; feminine gives, masculine takes

they continued as, no doubt, will this event – cyclical feeling

language slow and lazy – long vowel sounds – sense of ease

# Develop the themes elsewhere

We have established that all is not conflict between this husband and wife. Go through the poem now and highlight references to the feeling of *calm* that punctuates it. Focus on these areas:

- a feeling of abandon;
- a sense of mutual acceptance; and
- signs of indulging each other's idiosyncrasies.

These headings should go in the margin and *all textual references to them* should *be joined by a line*. There should be no 'floating quotations' or 'loose comments' in the margin.

We should be able to build on our initial discoveries as we look further into the poem.

> He lay down and said "Give these fellows theirs,
> I'm in no hurry", plucking grass in handfuls
> And tossing it in the air. "That looks well."
> (He nodded at my white cloth on the grass.)
> "I declare a woman could lay out a field
> Though boys like us have little call for cloths."
> He winked, then watched me as I poured a cup
> And buttered the thick slices that he likes.

The *feeling* in this extract is one of *calm* and relaxation:

- There is a sense of **abandon**; 'He lay down', 'I'm in no hurry', 'plucking grass in handfuls and tossing it in the air'.
- There is also a feeling of **mutual acceptance**, despite an acknowledgement of their differences. 'That looks well', the husband remarks, and nods at her white cloth, while he also differentiates between the sexes by pointing out that 'a woman could lay out a field/Though boys like us have little call for cloths'.
- There are also signs that each one **indulges the other's idiosyncrasies**. He winks and nods at her while she performs her traditionally feminine role, and she 'butters the thick slices that he likes'. They give to each other and this highlights not only their differences but also the way each accepts the other's.

> "It's threshing better than I thought, and mind
> It's good clean seed. Away over there and look."
> Always this inspection has to be made
> Even when I don't know what to look for.

This idea of mutual indulgence continues in the way that he orders her 'away over there and look' at the threshed seed. She almost confides in the reader that 'always this inspection has to be/Even when I don't know what to look for'. She indulges his need for her to approve of his efforts in much the same way as a child might ask a parent to witness a recent accomplishment: 'Mummy, look what I've drawn', and Mummy patiently replies, 'Lovely, darling', even though she cannot make out what on earth the drawing is about.

Use of the word 'always' *suggests* that this is a **recurring event** and we sense an acceptance of (and perhaps a little exasperation at) his behaviour as she obeys.

## Separateness

The acknowledgement of their **separateness** is evident again in the last stanza: 'They lay in the ring of their own crusts and dregs'. The circle is closed and excludes all those outside it. Note also that a 'ring' is a symbol of marriage; this man is locked into an exclusive relationship with his workers in the field; along with him, they actually form this 'ring'.

She explains that 'that was it' and this monosyllabic and somewhat blunt observation suggests that she knows only too well that she has performed her function and that now she must go. She has been as integrated in his world as she is going to be and she now 'belong[s] no further to the work'. She had 'come and he had shown me'; now she is no longer required. She obediently 'gather[s] cups and fold[s] up the cloth' and goes.

## Masculine, war-like elements

We considered the **masculine** and **war-like elements** in the text, so now you should look for those and underline and link them appropriately.

It is interesting to see that *alongside* this sense of calm and relaxation discussed earlier, there seems to *co-exist* a reference to **war** that is closely associated with **masculine imagery**. The pictures are phallic – 'javelins' and sharp 'forks' and we are told of 'lost battlefields'. How and why are they lost? Is it the battle between the sexes that has been fought and lost by the wife? Or are the battlefields 'lost' because the battle was in the past and is 'lost' to the present?

Students frequently ask whether these sorts of meanings do actually exist in pieces of literature, or whether teachers infuse texts with such interpretations. What is obvious is that practical criticism, critical appreciation or any such close analysis involves the reader in helping to create meaning. The conflict in 'The Wife's Tale' is undeniably there, as has been shown; it is the candidates' personal responses that differentiate precisely what they do with it.

Note that the 'forks were stuck at angles in the ground' and that 'she moved between them'. The masculine image suggests that the male has established himself as a dominant and immovable object around which the wife must navigate carefully and move accommodatingly. This idea appears again when, in stanza three, the men form a ring that she can only circumnavigate, not enter.

## Sensuous/sensual

The masculine imagery leads us on to a consideration of the **sensuous/sensual** in the piece so that should be the next target for annotation.

We can build further on the masculine/feminine issue in the poem by examining the **sensual** and **sensuous imagery**. It is hardly surprising that, in a poem about a marriage, the subject of sexuality creeps in. The poem starts with 'When I had spread it all on linen cloth', creating a sense of giving and of placing at the feet of the male a gift for his enjoyment. Although here it is the meal that is being offered, there are also **connotations** of the woman offering herself for his enjoyment. Sensuous imagery in 'buttered the thick slices' and, bordering on the sensual in her running her 'hand in the half-filled bags' progresses to the more overtly sexual description of seed (with its allusions to reproduction) being 'hard as shot'. The men lay among their 'own crusts and dregs', suggesting the left-overs from a feast and this post-coital mood is also created when we learn that they are 'smoking and saying nothing'.

References to 'crushing' or domination and 'sowing' or implanting seed also lead us to a sense of post-coital ease, enhanced by the long vowel sounds of 'ease', 'out', 'grateful' and 'trees'. The image of the men 'unbuttoned' and 'grateful' suggests that they have enjoyed being fed and are satisfied. The ease can be post-prandial (after a meal) *and* post-coital (after sex). In psychological terms, food and sex are closely linked. The woman is provider. She brings her food (and her self) and he enjoys it.

A feminist reading could develop this idea quite fruitfully, and at undergraduate level a variety of critical theories applied to this text would bring about some interesting interpretations. Marxist, semiotic, psychoanalytic and indeed any other critical theory all have interesting readings to offer the student of practical criticism, and undergraduates might find it useful to apply some of these to this poem.

## Marxist theory

This rests on the notion of power being in the hands of those who own the means of production. Social and cultural contexts are extremely important when using Marxist theory. In 'The Wife's Tale', this ownership is enjoyed by the husband in that his domain is the agricultural one. He holds the power in the field, where he owns the means of production. However, to some extent, the wife 'owns' the means of production in the domestic arena and therefore she has power there. She is producing the food and giving it to him. If we pursue this, though, we might find that ultimately the husband owns the kitchen as he probably owns the farm, so then perhaps he owns the means of production here as well. On the other hand, if we think of the means of production as being her traditionally feminine skills of cooking and baking, then she owns those and so has power in the domestic sphere.

However, an important issue in Marxist theory is that of exploitation; she is in a worker-to-owner relationship, and his 'affection' is charitable hypocrisy, rather like the company housing that wealthy nineteenth-century mill owners built near the mills for their workers. She rebels but this rebellion is quashed. A Marxist reading of the text would interpret her 'always this inspection has to be made' as an expression of her resentment. She does not own her skills; he 'buys' her labour.

## Semiotic theory

This is built on the idea of signs, and works on the premise that there are signifiers and signifieds. The signifier is a *sign* of the signified. As discussed earlier a simple example is the word 'cat' (a signifier) *standing for* (or being a *sign* for) the concept of a furry domestic animal with four legs that we know as a cat (the signified).

In 'The Wife's Tale', the signifiers are numerous: 'When I had spread it all on linen cloth' signifies a submission, a giving of self and of food, a laying before the man of all that she has to offer him. The 'linen cloth' is a *sign* of femininity, purity, something upon which to spread her wares.

The 'crusts and dregs' at the end *point to* or *signify* recent enjoyment of food and/or sex. They are signs that something has been consumed and these left-overs are all that remain. A detective would value such a find in an investigation because it is a sign that something has happened.

We could continue, but this is sufficient perhaps to help you to start the process and you should carry on with it now.

## Psychoanalytic theory

Psychoanalytic critical theory gives us another set of meanings. This approach works on the need to identify and explain the presence of sexuality in a text. The sensual and sensuous elements in the verse, such the bags of seed through which the wife 'ran [her] hand' and found them to be 'hard as shot/Innumerable and cool' connotes the same sorts of meaning as the 'forks were stuck at angles in the ground' and the 'javelins'. The phallic imagery of 'forks' and 'javelins' suggests that the wife manoeuvres carefully between these established objects, symbolising the way in which his sexual role dominates and hers is subordinate to it. He is proud of his seed and she is instructed to admire it. There are numerous other such references, which have already been discussed.

It is interesting to note the different readings that can come from one text when various schools of criticism are applied. For the purposes of A-level practical criticism we have probably gone far enough, although it is worthwhile reading some critical theory even at A-level. Some recommended reading for this is given at the end of the book.

## How does it end?

Where has the poem taken us? Through what territories of the wife's mind have we travelled? It is *her* story. Where does she stand at the end?

Introductions and conclusions are crucial components of any poem and the final section will, of course, establish the precise direction that the work has taken. What we see at the end of 'The Wife's Tale' is a group of men formed into an **exclusive** ring that doesn't include the wife. She has played her part in her traditionally **feminine** role and now belongs 'no further to the work'. She leaves them to 'their ease' and goes.

The coming together of this man and woman signifies much more than just the bringing of food. Both parties act out traditional gender roles and in that sense there is the **separateness** and **conflict** that we identified in stanza one, but this is not total and their **mutual indulgence** of each other's likes suggests an **acceptance** of the differences between them, and a desire to please.

There may have been **conflict** on those 'lost battlefields', but the poem ends on a note of **calm** and we sense that this **process will continue** for a long time to come. The natural, rural setting suggests a rhythm, a cyclical pattern of behaviour which, although not entirely satisfactory, will endure eternally. This is the way of things.

So, what has the ending achieved? It has:

- returned the reader to the beginning of the poem, inviting him or her to compare the two situations; and
- revealed the writer's thoughts and feelings about the event or experience that 'gave birth' to the poem.

## Summarise your response

We need to summarise concisely the ground we have covered in this poem. What are we left with at the end of it? Response suggests *feelings*, so focus on these too. Remember that poetry is about *emotion*. If we have not identified and responded to *that*, then we have neither understood nor appreciated it.

The poem moves towards separation and exclusion, with heavy emphasis on conflict, opposition and contrast, and yet there is also a sense of acceptance and mutual indulgence – derived, one could assume, from love, affection or loyalty. The narrator confides in us, the reader, sharing her feelings about the nature of the relationship with her husband. We hear *his words* but *her thoughts*, and we enter the world of their marriage through *her* perceptions of it; it is, after all, 'The Wife's Tale'.

So, how did we get here? We seem to have come a long way, and yet the process has been a simple one:

- The first step was that of close reading and thinking.
- Then we focused in the first stanza on the central conflict.
- The next step was to track this theme in the rest of the poem.
- We then looked at the ways in which this was developed elsewhere, alerted by a consideration of connotative meaning.
- Finally, we thought about the end and reflected upon our whole response to the poem.

What is essential in practical criticism is to search out **patterns** that replicate themselves elsewhere in the piece; repeated types of language, imagery, connotations, which weave themselves into the fabric of the work – and it *is* like a fabric. A piece of literature is *crafted*, rather like weaving a piece of material, by the working together of features such as language, meaning, rhythm, rhyme, tone, imagery and a number of other literary devices at the disposal of a good writer.

What we seek to do in practical criticism is to identify and track the individual threads, see *how* they interlace themselves into a **pattern** with other strands, and blend to form a woven piece of fabric, rich in colour and texture.

Thus far, the step-by-step guide to writing a practical criticism essay has followed the route of the analysis, and we are now ready to think about the actual writing process. What we have just done seems to have taken a long time, and you might be concerned that this will not be practical in the examination. Do not worry. Once you start to approach practical criticism in this way, the process will become quite natural to you and you will go through its various stages relatively quickly. When you are beginning to learn any new skill there are moments when you wonder if you will ever grasp even the basics, but it does happen. If you have learnt to drive a car you might well remember this feeling. New drivers apply considerable concentration to performing what experienced drivers do without thinking. A little way down the line you will wonder what all the fuss was about, and you will do it almost automatically.

## Sample essay – 'The Wife's Tale'

From the very title of this poem Heaney implies his intention of presenting a relationship of marriage from the wife's point of view: 'The Wife's Tale'. Close analysis reveals a work that functions on many levels. On the surface, from the outset, we are faced with a rural idyll and a representation of traditional gender roles within a marriage as a wife brings lunch to her husband and his workers in the fields. However, as the first stanza develops, conflicts are revealed which cast a different light on the scene before us. Heaney takes these issues on to explore some of the more complex aspects of the relationship of marriage.

Within the first sentence, the separation of the sexes, and thus the distance between these two individuals, is highlighted in the words of the female narrator: 'I called them over'. This notion is continued throughout the poem, where there are no mentions of 'us' or 'we', always 'I' and 'them'. The gender roles are clearly differentiated and the differences highlighted as the husband observes, "I declare a woman could lay out a field/Though boys like us have little call for cloths". These gender distinctions filter into the very imagery of the piece, as the woman spreads out her 'white' 'linen cloth', with all its connotations of feminine softness and purity. In contrast, the men are linked with the 'hum and gulp' of machinery, with its 'big belt' and 'straw/Hanging undelivered in the jaws'. The wife here is surrounded by 'such quiet', which is interrupted by the masculine noise of men's 'boots/Crunching the stubble'.

Noise and quietness also reflect the issue of domination that is present throughout the whole poem, because it is the men's noise which dominates and destroys the woman's quiet. Similarly, the work is structured in such a way as to present the wife's silent thought processes and the husband's words; he dominates linguistically in this way. He directs his wife to "give these fellows theirs" and "away over there and look", and she responds obligingly;

> . . . I poured a cup
> And buttered the thick slices that he likes.
>
> Always this inspection has to be made
> Even when I don't know what to look for.
> But I ran my hand in the half-filled bags

While this seems to show general male dominance, particularly in the agricultural realm, it also reveals a degree of female control within the restricted sphere of domesticity. Similarly, the conflict issue is shown to be only a part of this relationship. The first half of stanza two creates the atmosphere of calm abandon as 'He lay down . . . / . . . in no hurry, plucking grass in handfuls/And tossing it in the air'. With this goes the notion of mutual acceptance, with each indulging the other's idiosyncrasies, whether the wife's spreading of the cloth, "Though boys . . . have little call for cloths" or inspecting seed, 'even when I don't know what to look for'. The use of 'always' here suggests that this mutual indulgence and acceptance is a repeated pattern in their situation. Thus both difference and acceptance are highlighted here. Towards the end of the poem, however, we are reminded that these are 'lost battlefields', and that the men remain in an exclusive 'ring of their own'; the ring that traditionally symbolises marriage reflects here the union of the workers and the exclusion of women.

'And that was it' the wife states – a short, sharp, monosyllabic sentence that marks the dividing line, the end of her role. She has provided for the men and interacted in a limited way, and now she 'belong[s] no further to the work'. Is this the lost battle referred to in line 25, the battle to unite with men; or does Heaney refer to a battle fought in the past and thereby lost to the present? Whichever way it is viewed, the forks, tools of men's labour, become weapons at sharp angles around which she must navigate carefully and move accommodatingly. Thus men dominate here, an immovable, unbreakable force; a ring that women can only circumnavigate and never enter.

The sharp forks stuck firmly in the ground carry sexual overtones in this poem that employ a great deal of sensual and sensuous imagery, particularly if we consider the link traditionally made by psychology between sex and food. Here, a wife offers herself for her husband's enjoyment; to satisfy a hunger. Thus the sensuous imagery of 'buttered thick slices' gives way to the sensual imagery of the womanly caress of the seed with its reproductive connotations, and which is described as 'hard as shot'. Indeed, the poem ends with the men lying 'in the ring of their own crusts and dregs/Smoking and saying nothing'; following what may be viewed as their dominating sexual role 'crushing' and 'sowing', the men slip into post-coital 'ease'. The atmosphere of this is conjured using the long vowel sounds of words such as 'ease', 'out', 'grateful' and 'trees'.

Thus, by the end of the poem, it may be argued that both parties have acted out traditional, distinct gender roles, and in this sense the separateness and conflict suggested throughout is an important part of the poem's meaning. It is not, however, the whole meaning, for their mutual acceptance and indulgence reveals a desire to please. Similarly, the calmness of the beginning and ending of the work, along with its natural, rural setting suggest continuity, a natural cycle and an inevitability to the situation.

# ■ ⋈ **6** Writing an essay

Now that you have annotated the text with precise and concise marginal notes and linked these to all other similar references, you are in a position to move on to the next stage of the process, which is to decide what you are going to say in your essay, and how you are going to say it.

## Organising and planning your essay

Lecturers and teachers of English will refer frequently to the need for students to *organise and plan* their essays prior to writing. Less often will these students be given a precise definition of those terms. Students of all ages, and up to post-graduate level, complain that no one has ever really explained what is meant by these words. They know that these are processes that should be gone through in the writing of a good essay, but just *how* to do it is something of a mystery.

This is arguably the most important stage of the essay-writing process, and it is at *this* point that many students fail to do themselves justice. Examining boards' annual reports refer frequently to candidates' essays showing a lack of organisation and planning, and it is often this weakness that ensures that many students fail to achieve the higher grades. It must not be overlooked that the study of English literature at either Advanced or degree level also requires the ability to express an argument clearly and concisely. Candidates who make the study of good literature their business are themselves expected to be able to produce a well-written essay; organisation and planning are central to that skill.

## Organisation
### Don't be linear; be organised

Organisation is the process that your essay undergoes when you *arrange* the material you have in a particular *order*; when you bring to your findings some sort of *structure*. What you have on the page when you have fully annotated your text is a somewhat chaotic mass of marginal notes and lines, but these annotations, however fruitful and full of meaning, cannot instantly transform themselves into a structured essay. Your next job is therefore to *organise* these notes.

Let us return to the example of 'The Wife's Tale'. Look now at the 'Conflict Annotations' on page 82. Notice how, in the margins, are scattered references to themes that contain an element of conflict. All that is required is that the similar themes are gathered into small groups. For example, from under the heading 'conflict' emerge three smaller groups:

(i)     I/they annotations;
(ii)    masculine/feminine annotations; and
(iii)   dominance/subservience annotations

Grouping into similar themes will enable you to discuss the poem in an organised way and *not in a linear way*. What is linear? This means, quite simply, going through the text line by line in chronological order. While this might seem to be a logical way to approach a text, if you think carefully about this approach you will soon realise that this is the way chaos lies. Writers do *not* create literary works so that ideas are conveniently grouped together in stanzas or paragraphs; you have only to look at the annotations on conflict to see that. Themes are scattered, apparently at random, throughout the fabric of the text. What you are doing when you annotate a text is trying to track these themes and identify their *pattern*.

Imagine that someone has broken a string of coloured beads and that they are lying scattered about the floor. Some of the beads are red, some blue, some green, some yellow, but they are all lying where they landed, with their colours all mixed. You come along with a needle and a piece of thread, passing the needle through one red bead and then the next red bead and so on until all the red beads are together on the thread. Then you do the same for the blue, the green and the yellow.

When you came into the room and saw the beads on the floor you soon realised that they comprised groups of different colours; from amid the chaos on the floor emerged a *pattern* that you were able to identify and classify – red, blue, green and yellow. You established which group of beads was to be collected – say, red – and you searched the room until you found a bead of that colour. When you had found that red bead you continued looking for more red ones until you had them all safely on your thread. Then you repeated the process with the blue, the green and the yellow beads until all were back on the thread *in an organised way*.

You are going to do exactly the same thing with the themes and ideas in a text. *This process must be completed if you are to write a well-organised response to the question*. If you do not do this, your essay will be a disorganised affair in which you jump from one point to another, confusing the examiner and leaving him/her to wonder where your argument is leading. The answer to that question would be simple – round and round in circles.

Thread the elements of the themes together, in groups, in your essay just as you threaded all the red beads, then the blue and so on with your needle. If you are organising by colour when rethreading your necklace, or organising by theme when writing a practical criticism essay you must *put similar elements together*. Your necklace will not be organised if your first red bead is followed by a blue, which is followed by another red, then a green, then a yellow. Your essay will not be organised if your reference to the masculine/feminine conflict is followed by a discussion of the 'I'/'them' issue, which then goes back to the masculine/feminine idea *again*. Deal with each of the headings in the margin thoroughly and then move on to the next one. *The movement in an essay must always be forward* – not forward, then backward then forward again – just forward.

Quite simply, if your thoughts are organised, the examiner will be able to follow your argument. You might find another analogy helpful. Reading your essay is, for an examiner, similar to embarking on a journey. He/she does not know where he/she is going and is entirely in your hands. You lead him/her through your essay. Be sure that you lead him/her in a straight line – forward – and not, as was said before, round in circles. Make it easy for him/her to keep up with you; do not suddenly charge ahead and take a short cut that he/she cannot possibly know, or change direction and return to where you have just come from. You will confuse him/her and lose him/her; *lose the examiner and you lose marks.*

Let us look at the essay on 'The Wife's Tale' written by an English undergraduate. It is possible to trace precisely how this student chose to organise her material and link together similar ideas.

*Paragraph one*    This is the overview. The meaning of the title is discussed, and *linked* to this is the idea that the poem operates on two levels.

*Paragraph two*    The idea of the separation of masculine/feminine is handled *together with* the 'I'/'them' distinction, which is then *linked* with the visual and aural imagery that reflects these separations.

*Paragraph three*    Continues the sound theme and *links* this with the dominance/subservience idea. The dominance theme is then *connected with* the notion of acceptance/conflict.

*Paragraph four*    The conflict idea then *embraces* male/war imagery.

*Paragraph five*    Male imagery *leads into* a discussion of the sensual/sensuous.

*Paragraph six*    The conclusion *returns to* the central conflict/acceptance theme.

Notice that all the italicised words in the analysis above refer to ways of *joining together* similar ideas.

This, then, is how this essay has been *organised*. This is the way in which the student felt she could best include all the main points in her preparation and *group them together* to form a logical progression of ideas.

I hope you will agree with me that it is a well-organised and sensibly structured discussion.

## Planning

Now that you have *organised* your material into sensible sections for discussion, your next task is to *plan* the essay, which involves deciding:

(i)    the general **direction** of your argument;
(ii)    **which points** you want to discuss; and
(iii)    the **order** in which you want to discuss them.

Look again at the essay on 'The Wife's Tale'. A careful analysis of the essay structure will reveal the logic behind the essay plan.

*Paragraph one*    The title is discussed and then the theme of conflict, which is so central to the work.

| | |
|---|---|
| *Paragraph two* | Then she chooses to address one of the aspects of that conflict – the masculine/feminine split. Still on the theme of the conflict, she moves on to the 'I'/'them' issue. |
| *Paragraph three* | She introduces the sound imagery because she can use that to develop the conflict theme, to include a discussion of the dominance/subservience issue. Still dealing with the dominance theme, she then introduces the idea of acceptance as another aspect of the conflict issue. |
| *Paragraph four* | Still dealing with the central issue of conflict, she brings in the male/war imagery. |
| *Paragraph five* | The discussion of male/war imagery leads naturally into a consideration of the sensuous and sensual elements. |
| *Paragraph six* | The conclusion ties it all together. |

Perhaps the following diagram will help to consolidate this analysis. Notice that not only does the diagram illustrate the way in which the essay has been **planned** (what to say and how to say it) but it also identifies the method by which is has been **organised** (similar ideas grouped together).

So, we have organised our material and planned the essay. Where do we go from here?

# Writing

You are now ready to start thinking about actually writing your essay, and it would be useful to establish the elements you will have to address. Your essay should include:

(i) **Top and tail**
    (a) an introduction in the form of an overview (top), and
    (b) a conclusion (tail);
(ii) **Main body** of the essay using the three-step approach.

# Topping and tailing

## Topping

This is an important feature of any essay, and one that requires careful thought before pen is first put to paper. Some experienced examiners claim that they can predict the grade of an essay by evaluating the first seven words of it. This might sound alarming, unlikely or even shocking, but it is not far from the truth. Most experienced markers will have formed some idea of an essay's ultimate worth by the time they have read the first sentence or two.

This has obvious implications for the quality of that opening paragraph. What those first two or three sentences do is to establish a grade in an examiner's mind. This may well happen unconsciously, and it is known as 'an emergent mark'. This is not to say that this grade is written in stone and cannot change. Indeed, as an

# ANALYSIS OF ESSAY STRUCTURE

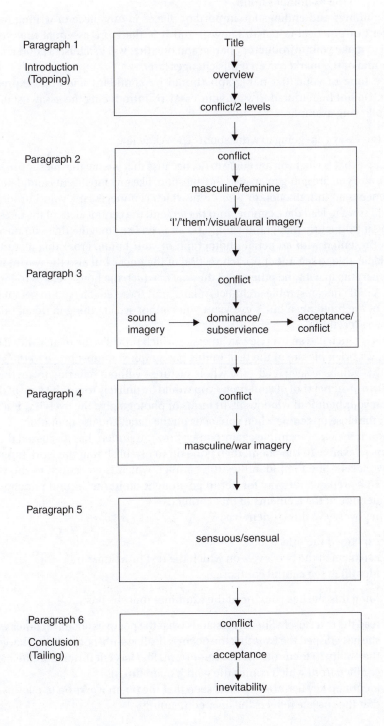

Paragraph 1

Introduction
(Topping)

Title
↓
overview
↓
conflict/2 levels

↓

Paragraph 2

conflict
↓
masculine/feminine
↓
'I'/'them'/visual/aural imagery

↓

Paragraph 3

conflict
↓
sound imagery → dominance/subservience → acceptance/conflict

↓

Paragraph 4

conflict
↓
masculine/war imagery

↓

Paragraph 5

sensuous/sensual

↓

Paragraph 6

Conclusion
(Tailing)

conflict
↓
acceptance
↓
inevitability

essay proceeds there is a real sense of its quality rising and falling in varying degrees, and these changes are reflected in the fluctuations in the grade that is forming in the examiner's mind.

Beginnings and endings are important places in any piece of writing (as any student of practical criticism knows!) and it is therefore essential that you try hard to make your introductory paragraph one that will establish a good grade in the mind of the marker, even if this changes later.

The **tone** of your first paragraph should be **confident** and your **expression clear**. Do **not** be tempted to start your essay by introducing the essay itself, as in the following example:

> In this essay I am going to write about 'The Wife's Tale'. . . .

Of course that is what you are going to do, because that is what the question *asks* you to do, and you are going to answer the question, like any intelligent candidate. This sentence is an introduction to *your essay*, which is unnecessary; your introduction should serve to lead the examiner into *the text* and the central ideas of the question.

The introductory paragraph should be an *overview*. Imagine that you have just been presented with an aerial photograph of your home. From this picture you would be able to see not only each section of the house but also the way in which each part fits in with the others and the way in which the house relates to the garden. Aerial shots resemble architects' plans, and these enable you to get an overview of the building, a bird's eye view. You cannot see anything in detail but you *can* see everything.

This is much like an overview in an essay, which provides the reader with a complete, yet brief, picture of the text. In this paragraph you must prove to the examiner that you have seen it all – the whole picture – without referring to anything in detail. In an aerial shot of your home you would be unlikely to see the vase of daffodils on your bedroom windowsill! In terms of photography, the overview is a 'long shot'; the close ups come when you focus on the detail and use quotation.

Look at the essay example again. Notice how the student has discussed the title and its relevance to the poem, then gone on to establish that the work functions on two levels. She then identifies the conflict, which is so central to the whole text. This prepares the way for her to go straight on in the second paragraph to consider one of the elements of that conflict.

In her overview, this student has:

(i)   explained the title;
(ii)  established the two levels on which the text functions; and
(iii) identified the central conflict.

In doing this she has convinced the examiner that she has:

(i)   read the text closely. She understands what the poem 'is about'; in other words, she has grasped the *issue* that the poem is dealing with, not just 'what happens'.
(ii)  the ability to focus on what is important. She has cut through to the central conflict, from which comes the work's main thrust.
(iii) identified key features. She has seen that the poem works on two levels, and that the surface reflects the deeper meaning.

## Tailing

Just as students are exhorted to write introductions, they are also encouraged to produce conclusions, but it is worth considering what exactly should go into this part of the essay.

It is important to remember that your conclusion is the last thing the examiner reads before he or she writes your mark on the examination paper, and as such this paragraph has as vital a part to play in your essay as the introduction, and is arguably even more important.

Quite simply, you want to leave the examiner feeling as happy as you can about your essay. You need to create a good impression in your conclusion because it is the last opportunity you have to do so. So often a strong essay merely fades away at the end because the conclusion was neglected, and it is important to remember that examiners are only human; they are likely to remember very clearly the last thing you said to them. So make that thing special. Go out with a bang, not a whimper.

What exactly *is* a conclusion? What does it do? Why do teachers and lecturers always insist upon it?

A conclusion is a tying up of loose ends. It is a rounding off, a shutting up, a saying goodbye, but most of all it is *a brief answer to the question*. Given that your performance in the examination is judged largely by your ability to answer the question, the conclusion to your essay is your last chance to do just that in a cogent and concise way and to convince the examiner that you have done what you were asked to do.

Look at the conclusion in the essay on 'The Wife's Tale'. The question asks the candidate to 'write about it as fully as you can'. This essay question is always a welcome one as it extends an open invitation to the candidate to address whatever aspects of the text he or she feels able to discuss effectively. In this sense it is a rather subjective task because what one candidate chooses to discuss might be of no interest whatever to another. But that is the task, and you may focus on whatever *you* are able to 'write about . . . . fully'.

What the student did was to answer the question by summarising briefly what her essay has discussed, but it is worth remembering that *just* providing a summary is not quite enough to convince the examiner entirely that you have answered the question. Try to *use some of the words of the actual question in your concluding paragraph*. This will encourage him/her to think that you have not strayed from the task and even if you *have* done this somewhere along the line, then returning so obviously to the question at the end might go some way to making up for this.

It has already been said that your movement in a practical criticism essay must always be *forward*; but perhaps the one exception to this rule is in the conclusion, where it is in your interest to *go back*, in a sense, to the question and *refer to it overtly in your answer*. This gives your essay a 'tight', disciplined feel and convinces the examiner that you are, right at the end of your answer, on course.

Your conclusion needs to be:

- **precise** (accurate);
- **concise** (succinct); and
- **cogent** (convincing).

The student's conclusion is all of these. What exactly does she do in her conclusion? It is clear that she:

(i) Refers to the question ('presenting a relationship of marriage from the wife's point of view');
(ii) Refers to her overview, where she mentions the two levels on which the poem operates ('it is not, however, the whole meaning'); and
(iii) Discusses each of her principal points concisely and precisely – difference and separation, conflict, acceptance.

Notice how she also draws in a final point in this paragraph on which she ends her essay – that of inevitability and the natural cycle of things. It is something that was mentioned in the overview but not discussed at length in the body of the writing. In closing, she chooses to place the action of the poem in context, and refers to the setting and atmosphere. In doing this she is able to bring in one final point that needs no further explanation. This is effective because she appears to have kept this little surprise up her sleeve for the end. This surprise element adds a greater finality and satisfaction to a discussion that is:

- **clear**;
- **concise**;
- **confident**;
- **conceptualised**; and
- **cogent**.

## The three-step approach

There is a simple guide to writing the main body of your essay, of which you will probably be well aware. The three-step approach is:

(i) **Statement** – make a point;
(ii) **Evidence** – provide quotation; and
(iii) **Development** – discuss and develop.

This is the standard pattern for all essays on literature and if you keep rigidly to this approach your essay will be structured clearly, substantiated soundly and well-developed. It is important to remember that **none of these stages should be neglected**.

### Step one

This should establish what it is you are discussing. Making the point at the start of the paragraph immediately establishes the subject matter and signposts the direction in which your essay is moving. When making the point you should be:

(i) **clear**; and
(ii) **concise**.

It must be **clear** so that the examiner knows exactly what it is you are trying to say; if this statement is ambiguous he or she will be confused. And it must be **concise** as this:

- helps the clarity and saves you time in an examination;
- enhances the quality of the expression, and good expression improves the general worth of the essay;
- adds a certain sharpness, a focus that gives it a keener sense of direction and makes it more convincing.

Examiners frequently remind students and teachers alike that English students are expected to have acquired the ability to express themselves clearly and concisely, and indeed they waste no time in pointing out that what often distinguishes a high grade from a mediocre one is the quality of the expression. It is a distinct area for assessment. Be in no doubt that if you fall down in this aspect you will lower your final mark.

Look at the second paragraph of the essay. Notice how she states quite clearly and forcefully at the *start* of that paragraph what it is to be about. Her point is the separation of the sexes and the distance between the husband and wife. In this way, the direction of the paragraph is firmly established and the point is clearly and unambiguously made at the outset.

## Step two

Few A-level or undergraduate students of English literature will have reached this stage of their education without being made aware of the need to substantiate each point made in an essay. For every claim made about a text, there must be *close textual reference*, as often as possible in the form of quotation. Everything you say must be rooted in the text.

Look again at the beginning of the second paragraph and notice how, after her initial statement about highlighting the 'separation of the sexes', the student *immediately* follows this with the *evidence* needed to support her claim; she writes, '*I* called *them* over'. The quotation is 'woven' into the fabric of her writing. It is **short**, **appropriate** and **embedded** in *her* text.

## Step three

This is the final but equally important stage in this process. Imagine what this essay would be like without the discussion and development offered by this step. The feeling of the writing would inevitably be disjointed, 'bitty' and undeveloped. It would read like a shopping list. Point, quotation, point, quotation and so on. Step three gives your work a 'well-rounded' feeling. There is a sense of fullness that is provided only by this stage in the process. This step shows that the candidate has *explored the ideas, played with them, and seen how far they can be stretched*. It is at *this* point that your response becomes a *personal* one. If you were only to make a point and provide evidence for it there would be little of *you* in the essay. Discussion and development is where you bring *yourself* into the process. It is the point at which *you interact* with the text and *create your response*, but this response can only come about when you have 'absorbed' the text and 'mixed' some of yourself with it.

Notice how the student chooses to *develop* her first statement about the separation of the sexes and the distance between the husband and wife; she quotes the use of 'I' and 'them' as opposed to 'us' or 'we'. A second piece of evidence is cited to support the same claim. She then goes on to *develop* this initial statement more fully by discussing the clearly differentiated gender roles and the differences between them. This *leads into* talk of the masculine/feminine imagery that is a *related* issue, but not quite the same one. This is then substantiated with numerous quotations.

The student is *exploring* the issue with which she began her paragraph – that of separation and distance. In her personal response she links *connected* but not identical issues. This is evidence of *organisation prior to writing*. After making her notes, she discovered that many issues were *connected* though distinct, and during the organisation and planning stages she decided precisely which ideas she would *link* with others.

She found a red bead and decided to look for all the other similar red ones. What we see in this essay is all the red beads threaded *next to* each other. She will *complete* the set of red beads *before* she threads the blue ones and all the others she found on the floor.

To track precisely how she has *developed* her ideas, let us note that she began with a statement about the separation of masculine and feminine. She then *went on* to discuss the 'I'/'them' issue, which she *linked with* a consideration of the imagery. Notice how this subtle 'moving' from one connected but not identical issue to another is in fact *developing* her initial statement. So we see that the third stage of discussion and development can incorporate the results of your organisation and planning.

## Expression

As has been said before, expression is a key ingredient of all good essays at any level, and there are two golden rules to follow in terms of how you express your ideas. Always try to be:

(i)   **clear**; and
(ii)  **concise**.

Let us consider the first requirement – to be **clear**. There are usually two reasons why a student's work lacks clarity:

(a)   **lack of organisation and planning**; and
(b)   **poor expression**.

**Lack of organisation and planning** gives a muddled feeling to your work. The ease with which we moved through the essay is impossible to create if you have failed to *organise and plan* your material before you start to write. Clarity comes with organisation and planning, because when you organise and plan you prepare a straightforward route through your essay for the examiner and he or she *will* reward this ease.

**Poor expression** is a real barrier to clarity. I can recall numerous occasions when students have submitted work that is riddled with poor expression. When challenged they have often given themselves comfort by replying, 'Well, *I* know what I mean'. There will be little comfort in that retort when they fail to achieve their desired grade in the examination because the examiner cannot understand what it is they are trying to say.

Checking your work for sense is an invaluable process and you should *always* do this before submitting it. However, it calls for a certain objectivity, and it is all too easy to ignore faults in our own expression because *we* know what we are trying to say. When writing coursework, a method that works well is to put away the finished rough draft of your essay when you feel that you have answered the question. Leave it somewhere where you cannot see it for at least twenty-four hours. When you look at it again it will be with fresh eyes and you will undoubtedly spot faults that you would not have seen when you were involved in its initial creation. Time gives us that valuable distance and helps us to look at our material more objectively. Try, then, to look at it as an examiner would and be alert to errors of expression. If *you* are in any doubt about the expression, be *sure* that the examiner will also be.

## Punctuation, spelling and sentence structure

Two of the commonest causes of poor expression are:

- **inaccurate punctuation and spelling**; and
- **faulty sentence structure**.

### Punctuation

**Inaccurate punctuation** is a major cause of misunderstanding in essay writing and it is essential to ensure that your material is accurately punctuated throughout. Remember that punctuation is a set of visual markers that distinguish the places where we pause when reading. Although you will not be reading the text set for practical criticism aloud in the examination room, there is always that inner voice we all hear when we read anything. Listen to the natural rhythms of it and it will indicate when to pause and when to stop.

### Full stops

These are *essential* in establishing the 'boundaries' of your sentence, and they must be used for that purpose. Particularly when dealing with complex ideas, it is important to delineate exactly where your sentence begins and ends. Frequently students substitute commas for full stops and it must be remembered that commas *do not* separate sentences; that is the role of the full stop. If you confuse commas with full stops you will ruin the sense of the sentence entirely and make your material difficult to understand.

## Capital letters

These must be used correctly because they act as signals to the reader. If one appears after a full stop we know that it heralds a new sentence. If you are at all doubtful about the function of capital letters then you should revise the rules.

## Commas

These *never* separate two sentences. Look at the following examples:

> *Right:*    The lane was wet; water trickled from every crevice.
> *Wrong:*    The lane was wet, water trickled from every crevice.

Alternatively, 'and' can be used as a conjunction:

> *Right:*    The lane was wet and water trickled from every crevice.

Or you can, split the sentence and make it into two:

> *Right:*    The lane was wet. Water trickled from every crevice.

## Inverted commas

*Single* inverted commas are used in the following circumstances:

- Around all quotations.
- Around all titles of texts for A-level students (universities will lay down their own regulations for punctuation of titles). Remember that, in a title, the first word and every succeeding 'main' word is capitalised.
- Around words and letters that are being discussed; for example, 'the assonance on the letter "u" in "hum and gulp" suggests a continuity or repeated pattern which is alluded to, however obliquely, in the poem's rural setting'.

*Double* inverted commas are commonly used to distinguish quoted dialogue, for example "I declare a woman could lay out a field".

## Spelling

Every year examiners report on candidates' performance in the previous examination, and every year there are comments about poor spelling. To *some* extent, spelling is a matter of chance; you are either good at it or you are not, but there is much that you can do to *improve* the quality of your spelling with a little motivation and effort.

Whatever the weaknesses in your spelling ability, it is important to try to spell correctly the words that occur *regularly* when discussing literature. Below is a list of frequently misspelt words that you should be able to spell correctly. The trouble spots in each word have been capitalised, so pay particular attention to this area of each word.

EmPHasise percEIve onomatOpOEIa alLiteration humoUr/humOrous emPathise argUMent and so on.

You might think that the odd incorrect spelling here and there is of little import-ance, and I do not suggest that it is the most important aspect of essay writing, but it *does* create a bad impression if common words are misspelt and, as has been said before, your aim is to create as *favourable* an impression as possible of the quality of your work.

## Sentence structure

**Faulty sentence structure** is a serious handicap to your expression at any level but it is a real disadvantage when doing practical criticism because it greatly impedes understanding. It can occur in two ways.

(i) It can arise from poor punctuation, so that a sentence goes over its proper boundary and wanders on into what is properly the territory of the next sen-tence. In this case the writer has failed to listen to the inner voice that tells him or her to stop at the fence. Straddling this boundary can cause signific-ant problems for the reader. It can be almost impossible to follow an essay that fails to observe the most basic rules of punctuation and you will *not* endear yourself to any examiner who has to try to work out where one sen-tence begins and the other ends. In fact, the examiner will not do this; he or she will quite possibly simply deem this sort of expression unintelligible and ignore it.

(ii) It can happen as a result of not being in control of a sentence because you have not thought out carefully *beforehand* just *what you are going to say and how you are going to say it*. It is always a good idea to let the inner voice 'speak' the sentence silently *before* you start to write it so that you know in advance the direction in which this sentence will take you. In this way you have some control over where you are going. If you just let the sentence evolve spontaneously as you write you will find yourself at the mercy of it, and may find that it gets out of hand and goes in a direction for which you were not prepared. This might sound like a strange thing to say, but it is true that words do have a habit of taking on a life of their own. Planning briefly in advance ensures that *you* stay in control.

Often, faulty sentence structure and wordy writing are a symptom of lack of con-fidence. Your lack of confidence is really only anxiety about your mark, and wordiness and vagueness is an unhelpful response to that concern. How can you become more confident? Train yourself: force yourself to be succinct and write sparely and barely. You need to be really disciplined to do this, but you will find that your confidence grows as your grades improve.

Think of learning to dive. Wordiness and lax sentence structure are the 'Oh, I can't', followed by the painful belly-flop response. It may take courage to dive in head-first but afterwards you realise that it is the right way, and that it actually hurts less. The reward is the sure feeling you get from completing a clear, concise essay.

## Enhancing the quality of the expression

How many times have you read something that is concise and succinct, and felt that the argument or point of view or feeling was well communicated and indeed convincing? Perhaps you have also read the work of your peers or of younger students and found it to be less cogent and somewhat rambling. However valid the argument, it is a fact that poorly written material is less 'sharp', less persuasive, and less impressive. Remember the song 'It ain't what ya say; it's the way that ya say it'? The next line of the song is, 'That's what gets results'!

The candidate who is able to express himself/herself concisely is perceived to be in control of the material; he/she gives the impression that he/she knows exactly what he/she wants to say because time and effort have been taken to think about it and plan it. The candidate is not exasperating the examiner by fumbling around for the best way to say it.

### Adding sharpness and focus

Connected to the point above is the idea of adding sharpness and focus to your work. A candidate who writes concisely gives the impression, quite rightly, that he/she has established the central argument, which constitutes an answer to the question, and that he/she is capable of communicating it succinctly. Again, it shows that the candidate is in control, not only of the argument but also of the language needed to express it concisely. It adds a certain 'tightness' to the work. The candidate who writes concisely appears to mean business. He/she suggests he/she has much to say, and knows that there is little time in which to say it. The focus is on the content of your argument because your concise language takes the examiner straight to its central thrust and he or she is not led all around the houses before he/she reaches the core of your discussion. The force that accompanies concise expression is in itself impressive and convincing.

### Saving valuable time

Time in examinations is something always in short supply, and *anything* that helps you to make the most of the time you have should be adopted as part of your approach to practical criticism.

Because this skill is practised on previously unseen material, time is in even shorter supply than in papers that examine candidates on knowledge of set texts. The time needed for close reading is considerable, and this will inevitably rob you of valuable moments later on. I am *not* suggesting for one moment that you skimp on the time needed for close reading; that is *not* to be reduced under any circumstances, but what you will need is the ability to express your response concisely so that the quality of your essay is not impaired by the need to spend a substantial length of time reading the texts.

## Vocabulary

It really is quite simple; it takes you five times as long to write five words as it does to write one, so try to extend your descriptive vocabulary to enable you to have at your mental fingertips a tool kit to help you to do the job of commenting upon previously unseen texts.

### How do I extend my vocabulary?

#### Reading

The simplest method of vocabulary extension is by **reading** a wide variety of literature. The better the quality of the text, the wider the vocabulary to which you are likely to be exposed. If you encounter a word you do not understand, look it up in a dictionary and then *try to use it*. Language that is not used is lost.

#### Thesaurus

Another method that works is to use a **thesaurus**. Many people automatically connect the author Roget with a thesaurus and they buy that version believing that it is the best because it is the most well-known. That may well be the case, but an easier type of thesaurus to use is the one that is laid out like a dictionary. Some come *with* a dictionary but either way, this type is easily accessible and therefore preferable; if a book is difficult to use, you won't use it.

As soon as you start to respond to the feelings in a piece of literature, you know that you are going to need a wide descriptive vocabulary with which to discuss them. Imagine reading your poem for the first time in the examination. Feelings of nostalgia begin to emerge. Straightaway, you know that you are going to need a *variety* of words with which to refer to this feeling. Imagine the response from the examiner if, *every* time you refer to the tone of the poem you use the word 'nostalgic'. For your language to be concise you need to have a vocabulary that is wide enough to find succinct alternatives to much-used words. If you were to look up 'nostalgia' in a thesaurus you might find the following offerings: longing, pining, reminiscence, yearning. 'Nostalgic' would give you: homesick, wistful, yearning.

A useful and extremely practical exercise is to write down a list of all the adjectives you can think of that describe feelings and tone. When you have done that, look up each word in a thesaurus and add the words you find there to your list as alternatives. *Practise* using these words in your essays or even in conversation; if we don't *use* language, we *lose* it. You will be expected to have acquired a descriptive vocabulary that is up to the task of practical criticism, and building this up is one of the skills that it is *essential* to acquire *before the exam*. Do not be tempted to leave this to the last minute; language acquisition quite simply does not take place in a mad rush. Just as we all did when we were children, we build up patterns of language use over long periods of time. It is *not* a matter for night-before-the-exam cramming, so start planning your programme of vocabulary development *now.*

## Practical criticism of poetry

Write a critical appreciation of 'To His Coy Mistress' by Andrew Marvell.

### To His Coy Mistress

Had we but world enough, and time,
This coyness, Lady, were no crime.
We would sit down, and think which way
To walk, and pass our long love's day.
Thou by the Indian Ganges' side
Shouldst rubies find: I by the tide
Of Humber would complain. I would
Love you ten years before the Flood:
And you should, if you please, refuse
Till the conversion of the Jews.
My vegetable love should grow
Vaster than empires, and more slow.
An hundred years should go to praise
Thine eyes, and on thy forehead gaze.
Two hundred to adore each breast:
But thirty thousand to the rest.
An age at least to every part,
And the last age should show your heart.
For, Lady, you deserve this state;
Nor would I love at lower rate.

But at my back I always hear
Time's wingèd chariot hurrying near:
And yonder all before us lie
Deserts of vast eternity.
Thy beauty shall no more be found;
Nor, in thy marble vault, shall sound
My echoing song: then worms shall try
That long preserved virginity:
And your quaint honour turn to dust;

And into ashes all my lust.
The grave's a fine and private place,
But none I think do there embrace.

Now therefore, while the youthful hue
Sits on thy skin like morning dew,
And while thy willing soul transpires
At every pore with instant fires,
Now let us sport us while we may;
And now, like amorous birds of prey,
Rather at once our time devour,
Than languish in his slow-chapt power.
Let us roll all our strength, and all
Our sweetness, up into one ball:
And tear our pleasures with rough strife,
Thorough the iron gates of life.
Thus, though we cannot make our sun
Stand still, yet we will make him run.

Andrew Marvell

# Read closely and think

The principal need of any practical criticism candidate is quite simply to make sense of the words on the page, so once again, *close reading* is essential. During your first reading of the poem your primary aim should be to *understand* at perhaps just a simple level *exactly what the poem is about.*

A useful tactic at this stage is to try to *summarise* the poem in two or three sentences. This will then serve you well as an *overview* paragraph, which can be used as the introduction to your essay.

In 'To His Coy Mistress', Marvell's narrator tries to explain to the object of his desire that, had they endless time, her reluctance to relinquish her virginity would be quite all right, and that he would indeed spend great lengths of time wooing her. However, he explains, this is not the case, and she should comply with his wish to consummate their relationship because time is passing quickly and if they fail to take the opportunity to enjoy such pleasures now they will miss out on them for ever.

In a rather basic sense then, this is what the poem *is about*. This overview does little more than establish meaning at a somewhat elementary level, but this is important, for the following reasons:

- It gives you a clear sense of direction for your forthcoming discussion;
- It provides you with a clear framework upon which to 'hang' any further development of ideas; and
- It keeps you focused on the essential meaning so you are less likely to stray from this into irrelevant realms of discussion.

# Summarise the central conflict/s

As was pointed out in the discussion on 'The Wife's Tale' in Chapter 5, it is essential to establish the nature of the *conflict* or *tension* that exists within a piece of writing, and this is invariably apparent in many of the aspects of a text discussed in Chapter 4 under 'Tools of analysis – features of text' (see page 20).

Read the poem carefully now and look for any signs of *conflict*. This tension can be reflected in any of the features discussed in Chapter 4, but for now just consider:

(i)   Form and structure; and
(ii)  Language.

In terms of the language, remember that *conflict* or *tension* can be represented by the presence of contrasts, differences, opposites, pairs of words, oxymorons, or even 'good' and 'bad' words. Make your conflict annotations on the poem now.

# Looking at form/structure

Notice the **form** or **structure** of the poem. How is it *put together* or *built*? Close reading should have disclosed to you that this poem is in fact *constructed* in three parts:

- **Part one** begins with '*Had we* but world enough, and time', in other words '*if* we had lots of time then your reluctance to sleep with me would not be a problem'.
- **Part two** opens with '*But* at my back...', which suggests that 'we don't have endless time because I can hear Time hard on my heels'.
- **Part three** starts with '*Therefore*...', suggesting that the narrator has the solution in terms of how they should handle the situation: 'We haven't got lots of time *so* you had better sleep with me now'.

  Briefly, then, the argument that the narrator sets out is this:

- *if* we had lots of time, I wouldn't rush you;
- *but* we don't; and
- *so* let's get on with it;

It is worth noting that the consummation of desire is an emotional, deeply instinctual affair, and yet this young man applies a very acceptable three-stage, logical argument to the task of seducing this young woman. Think about why the narrator adopts this approach. There will be a discussion of this later.

Back to the task of establishing the conflict. What is it?

- Surely *one* of the conflicts is the tension between *what would be ideal* in a perfect world and *what is necessary* in one that is like ours, less than perfect; and
- The *other* is, of course, the conflict between *the narrator* and '*his coy mistress*'. She is coy and wants to wait; he is bold and does not.

Here, then, we see an example of the ways in which the *style* or the '*how*' reflects the *content* or the '*what*'.

Look now at the sheet entitled 'Conflict Annotations' and compare your observations with this.

---

**Box 7.1   CONFLICT ANNOTATIONS**

**To His Coy Mistress**

*If (conditional tense – unreal)*

Had we but world enough, and time,
This coyness, Lady, were no crime.
We would sit down, and think which way
To walk, and pass our long love's day.
Thou by the Indian Ganges' side
Shouldst rubies find: I by the tide
Of Humber would complain. I would
Love you ten years before the Flood:
And you should, if you please, refuse
Till the conversion of the Jews.
My vegetable love should grow
Vaster than empires, and more slow.
An hundred years should go to praise
Thine eyes, and on thy forehead gaze.
Two hundred to adore each breast:
But thirty thousand to the rest.
An age at least to every part,
And the last age should show your heart.
For, Lady, you deserve this state;
Nor would I love at lower rate.

*But (present tense – real)*

But at my back I always hear
Time's wingèd chariot hurrying near:
And yonder all before us lie
Deserts of vast eternity.
Thy beauty shall no more be found;
Nor, in thy marble vault, shall sound
My echoing song: then worms shall try
That long preserved virginity:
And your quaint honour turn to dust;
And into ashes all my lust.
The grave's a fine and private place,
But none I think do there embrace.

Now therefore, while the youthful hue
Sits on thy skin like morning dew,
And while thy willing soul transpires

*unity/split (section 2)*

*Split (geographically)*

*Conflict (masculine/ feminine)*

*the ideal world*

*Conflict*

*Conflict*

*the real world*

*Conflict*

*split – 'I'/'your'*

*So*

*now – urgency (conflicting with her coyness)*

*separate/together*

---

At every pore with instant fires,

*now – urgency (conflicting with her coyness)*

Now let us sport us while we may;
And now, like amorous birds of prey,
Rather at once our time devour,
Than languish in his slow-chapt power.

*(imperative – urgent)*

Let us roll all our strength, and all
Our sweetness, up into one ball:
And tear our pleasures with rough strife,
Thorough the iron gates of life.
Thus, though we cannot make our sun
Stand still, yet we will make him run.

*Conflict (what is/ what will be)*

## Looking at language

The **language** is another element of analysis, which mirrors meaning. Notice how the poem begins with the narrator talking about himself and his mistress as 'we'; 'Had *we* but world enough, and time'. Gradually this 'we' disappears and is replaced with 'I' and 'you' or 'thou', suggesting a split in this togetherness and pointing to the conflict that exists between them – he does not want to wait; she does. Furthermore, he concludes that the only unity they will enjoy if she holds out against his amorous intentions is in death:

> And **your** quaint honour turn to **dust**;
> And into **ashes** all **my** lust.

If she stays separate from him sexually, he argues, they will be together only in the ashes and dust of death. Interestingly, notice the similarity and difference between 'ashes' and 'dust'. Both are alike in appearance and texture, but ash is the result of fire, as would be the case with his burnt-out passion, and dust is the effect of disuse, as with her virginity.

To focus on the central conflict in the poem, we looked closely at the 'But' with which the second section opens.

- This is where *one* aspect of the tension lies: 'if things were like this, all well and good, *but* they're not, so we must do something else'; and
- The *other* element of tension is that she wants one thing and he another.

These two aspects of conflict are enough for us to work on and develop.

## Track the themes

As part of close reading it is always important to look at the **tenses of verbs**. Notice that the **first section**, to do with 'if', is written exclusively in the **conditional tense**: 'were', 'we would', 'you *should*'. The conditional tense is about *unreality*; it's about things that do not exist. We say, 'If I were you . . .'? Of course I cannot be you, so whatever follows is bound to be *unreal, pure imagining*. The conditional tense goes with 'if', and it is always connected with what is *not*, or what *might* happen *if*.

The detailed descriptions of the lengths to which he would go *if* they had the time serve to prove to his mistress that he acknowledges she deserves such wooing, but is unable to honour her in this way simply because time is against them. Rather like a parent telling a child what extraordinary presents he would be bought *were* the parent to win the lottery. Somewhat reminiscent of the expression, 'talk is cheap', perhaps.

Still looking at the verb tenses, let us now consider the **second section**, the 'But' part. Suddenly the conditional tense disappears and is replaced by the far more *definite* and *immediate* **present tense**: 'But at my back I always hear'. A combination of the present tense and the adverb 'always' creates a sense of certainty. It is as if the long, meandering lines of 'conditional' wooing of the first stanza are sharply interrupted by a very 'present' obstacle – time.

Still focusing on verb tenses, let us look at the **third section** – the 'therefore' part. Notice that the whole segment is written in the **present tense** and 'now' appears three times. The combination of the present tense and 'now' suffuses the verse with a sense of *urgency*. It is also worth noting that some of the verbs are in the *imperative* form – that is, they are *commands* – '*let us* sport us while we may'; '*let us* roll all our strength'. The imperative form, the present tense and 'now' all work together to create a feeling of immediacy and a need to 'seize the day'.

## Emphatic verbs

Looking further into the last section, if we consider the final couplet, the doubt and suggestion of failure present in 'though we cannot make our sun/Stand still' is quickly and thoroughly erased by the use of the **emphatic** 'we *will*' as opposed to the plain future tense 'we *shall*'. Awareness of such subtle differences seems to be declining these days, and it is to the detriment of scholars of practical criticism, for it is awareness of subtleties such as this that helps students to read sensitively.

To explain clearly, the *plain future form* of the verb 'to be' is as follows:

I shall be
You will be
He/she/it will be
We shall be
You will be
They will be.

This form gives us a sense of merely what will happen in time to come. For example, 'If it is raining tomorrow we *shall* be taking the car'. This is really a prediction: 'if this is the case, then that will happen'.

To make this into an *emphatic* form you need to change it thus:

I will be
You shall be
He/she/it shall be

We will be
You shall be
They shall be.

The *emphatic* form of a verb changes the sense considerably. For example, 'He doesn't want us to take the car but we *will*.' This is less of a prediction and more of a statement of intent, even defiance.

Remember the Fairy Godmother in *Cinderella*, who told the heroine, 'You *shall* go to the ball'? That was more than a mere prediction; it was an emphatic promise, an assurance.

Look now at the sheet entitled 'Language Annotations'.

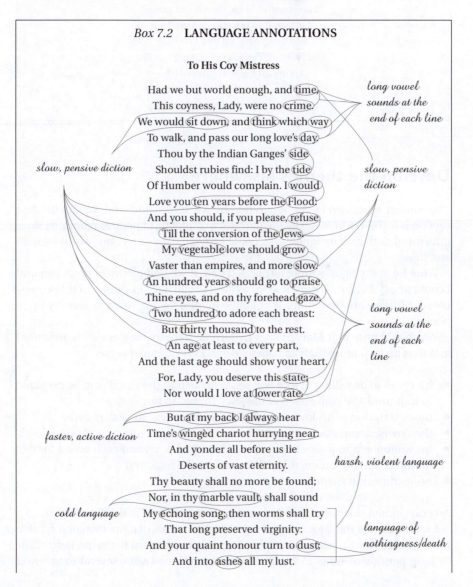

Box 7.2   **LANGUAGE ANNOTATIONS**

**To His Coy Mistress**

Had we but world enough, and time,
This coyness, Lady, were no crime.
We would sit down, and think which way
To walk, and pass our long love's day.
Thou by the Indian Ganges' side
Shouldst rubies find: I by the tide
Of Humber would complain. I would
Love you ten years before the Flood:
And you should, if you please, refuse
Till the conversion of the Jews.
My vegetable love should grow
Vaster than empires, and more slow.
An hundred years should go to praise
Thine eyes, and on thy forehead gaze;
Two hundred to adore each breast:
But thirty thousand to the rest.
An age at least to every part,
And the last age should show your heart.
For, Lady, you deserve this state;
Nor would I love at lower rate.
But at my back I always hear
Time's wingèd chariot hurrying near;
And yonder all before us lie
Deserts of vast eternity.
Thy beauty shall no more be found;
Nor, in thy marble vault, shall sound
My echoing song; then worms shall try
That long preserved virginity:
And your quaint honour turn to dust,
And into ashes all my lust.

*long vowel sounds at the end of each line*

*slow, pensive diction*

*slow, pensive diction*

*long vowel sounds at the end of each line*

*faster, active diction*

*harsh, violent language*

*cold language*

*language of nothingness/death*

Box 7.2    (Contd)

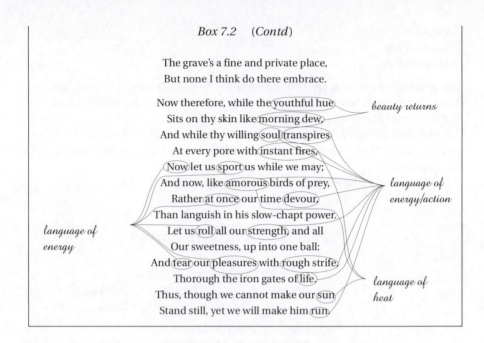

The grave's a fine and private place,
But none I think do there embrace.

Now therefore, while the youthful hue    *beauty returns*
Sits on thy skin like morning dew,
And while thy willing soul transpires
At every pore with instant fires,
Now let us sport us while we may;
And now, like amorous birds of prey,    *language of*
Rather at once our time devour,    *energy/action*
Than languish in his slow-chapt power.
*language of*    Let us roll all our strength, and all
*energy*    Our sweetness, up into one ball:
And tear our pleasures with rough strife,
Thorough the iron gates of life.    *language of*
Thus, though we cannot make our sun    *heat*
Stand still, yet we will make him run.

## Develop the themes elsewhere

The conflict expressed by the separation of 'we' into 'Thou' and 'you' in the first section is further developed by the narrator's catalogue of (almost painfully) slow, drawn-out activities in which they could indulge 'Had [they] but world enough and time'.

What he is saying in simple terms is, 'Look, if we had plenty of time, you and I could be off doing our own thing for as long as you like.' Examples of this 'conditional' (if) state are numerous. It might be helpful for you to try to identify them now.

We should note that Marvell uses **hyperbole** here to exaggerate his argument and thus make it more likely to convince her. Examples of this are:

- his claim to be willing to love her 'ten years before the Flood' and be prepared to wait until 'the conversion of the Jews' for her to respond;
- the description of his love as 'vegetable', which suggests slow growth;
- the slowness and extent of his love as in 'vaster than empires and more slow';
- his willingness to praise her eyes for a hundred years and each breast for two hundred, leaving a mere thirty thousand 'to the rest'; and
- his readiness to spend 'an age' on 'every part'.

An exaggerated slowness is created as the poem develops in this first section.

Examination of the language will reveal several words of more than one syllable (polysyllabic words), which have the effect of slowing down the verse. References to long periods of time and vast distances combined with several long vowel sounds both in the middle and at the ends of lines all serve to reduce the pace and draw it out.

Mid-line **linked and polysyllabic words** such as 'Indian Ganges', 'conversion' and 'vegetable' reduce the speed of the lines and create a lingering, languishing feel throughout the verse.

Look at the **end rhymes**: time/crime, way/day, side/tide, refuse/Jews, grow/slow, praise/gaze and state/rate. Virtually every rhyming couplet ends with a rhymed long vowel sound, but look also at the long vowels that occur *within* the lines: 'find', 'Thine', 'least', 'age', 'show', 'fine', 'private place'. Reference to 'Tools of analysis – features of text' in Chapter 4 (see pages 48–9) will remind you that the effect of long vowel sounds on the feel of a text is that of slowness. It seems more drawn-out and unhurried. Bearing in mind the theme of the poem (particularly in this first section) and that *our job in practical criticism is to relate the form to the content, or the how to the what*, can you see how successful this exercise has been?

**Punctuation** is an element that is frequently overlooked, but in ignoring this students often miss valuable insights into form and meaning. Look carefully at the first section of the poem and think about the poet's use of mid-line punctuation. The issue of punctuation was dealt with in some detail in Chapter 6, and you will remember the effects that commas, full stops, semi-colons and colons have on the speed and fluency of a text.

Looking at the first section of the poem, it becomes clear that the effect of mid-line commas and colons, and end-line full-stops, commas and semi-colons, is to halt the course of the lines and slow down the text in those places. **Caesura** (a pause within a line) serves to stem the natural progression of the verse and in this way we see punctuation *enhancing meaning*, as indeed do *all* other literary devices.

Remembering the initial conflict or tension that initiated our discussion, notice how the narrator and the object of his desire are *separated* in all these activities:

> **Thou** by the Indian Ganges' side
> Shouldst rubies find: **I** by the tide
> Of Humber would complain . . .

They are **separated by geography and context**. In these lines they even inhabit different countries. She is beside the exotic and colourful River Ganges finding rubies, and he is moping beside the grey and gloomy River Humber.

They are **separated by time**. The split is further enforced when he reassures her that he would love her 'ten years before the Flood' and she could refuse him 'Till the conversion of the Jews'. Vast periods of time stand between them here, as the Flood was documented in the Old Testament of the Bible, and the conversion of the Jews has not happened yet nor is there any sign that it will.

They are **separated by action and attitude**. He would love her and she would refuse him. He would want her and she would deny him.

The second, 'But' section sees this theme of conflict or separation develop further.

They are **separated by perceptions**. The segment begins with his taking control of the situation by explaining to her that *he feels* the pressure of time. It is 'at my back', he tells her. She, quite obviously, has no sense of this at all, hence 'this coyness':

> **Thy** beauty shall no more be found;
> Nor, in **thy** marble vault, shall sound
> **My** echoing song: then worms shall try
> That long preserved virginity:
> And **your** quaint honour turn to dust;
> And into ashes all **my** lust.

They are **separated sexually**. The 'marble vault' to which he refers is ostensibly her burial place after death, but it is also the empty female space in which his 'echoing song' of ecstasy will not be sounded. Notice that the qualities of marble are its coldness, hardness and purity, much like our reluctant heroine. A 'vault' is an empty (sometimes sacred) space where echoes sound. He knows that he will not fill her sacred void; but that 'Worms shall try that long preserved virginity' that he wants so much for himself.

They are **separated by motive**. He talks of her 'honour', and her 'coyness' is testimony to the purity of her feelings for him; he baldly declares his 'lust' for her and his wish to consummate their relationship as soon as possible.

Let us consider again our narrator's motives and methods. Lust, which he admits to, is much to do with emotions, and many would agree that it is not really a subject to be argued over on logical grounds. This narrator is driven by his feelings of sexual desire and it is clear that he is out to get what he wants by whatever means available to him. It is safe to assume that the object of his desire is an innocent and inexperienced young woman. In this poem we see him argue his way into her affections by use of a logical, well-structured, three-stage argument which, simply put, amounts to 'sleep with me or your virginity will be taken by the worms'. Man dominates the feelings of woman by means of masculine logic. This might have feminists reaching for their shotguns, because the suggestion is that only men can be logical and women can only be emotional. This is to miss the point entirely. *In the context of the period*, we see a man trying to seduce an innocent girl by the use of what is clearly an extremely unpleasant argument; it is a mixture of sexual games and outwitting the innocent. Look closely at these lines:

> Thy beauty shall no more be found;
> Nor, in thy marble vault, shall sound
> My echoing song: then worms shall try
> That long preserved virginity:
> And your quaint honour turn to dust;
> And into ashes all my lust.

He holds back nothing in drawing in the most vivid detail a picture of what will happen to her if she refuses his advances. When looked at in this light this poem becomes a rather sinister and threatening address 'to his coy mistress'.

The final 'therefore' section begins with references to 'thy' but this distinction soon vanishes and it is replaced by 'us', 'our' and 'we'. It is, of course, appropriate that the first person plural pronoun (we/us) is used in this last section, because it is here that our narrator shows the object of his desire exactly what he thinks they should be doing *together*.

It is the third and final part of his argument, 'if, but, therefore' and you can almost hear the vitality and enthusiasm in his voice as he tells her how they should 'seize the day' and take control *together*:

> **Now** let us sport **us** while **we** may;
> And **now**, like amorous birds of prey,
> Rather **at once our** time devour,
> Than languish in his slow-chapt power.

References to 'now' and 'at once' create a sense of urgency, and 'us' and 'we' enforce the unity that he wants to see between them. This is preferable to 'languish[ing] in his slow-chapt power'. Notice that when time is in control the verb lacks energy; they merely 'languish'.

This brings us to Marvell's development of the conflict. Remember that the nature of the conflict we established early in our discussion of this poem was that of tension between *what would be desirable* if things were different (the conditional – if) and *what is not possible* because things are as they are (the reality – but). The last section of the poem deals with the narrator's suggestions for reconciling this conflict – '*therefore*' – and the 'therefore' section is all about 'us' and *action*.

Notice the *language of energy* in this final part: 'transpires', 'instant fires', 'sport', 'amorous', 'at once', 'devour', 'roll', 'strength', 'tear', 'pleasures', 'rough strife', 'Thorough the iron gates of life' and 'make him run'. There is a vibrancy and vitality in this part of the poem that we see nowhere else. The verse seems to gather speed and we are caught up in its zest for life and fulfilment of desire. Compare this with the slowness of the first 'if' section, and perhaps in all this energy and warmth we have forgotten the cold and sinister nature of his threats in the second section!

Notice also that the language contains references to heat with 'fires', 'amorous' and 'sun'. This contrasts starkly with the coldness of the middle section when he talks about 'marble vault', 'echoing', 'dust' and 'ashes'.

However, it is still not enough to discuss these aspects of the 'how' without offering an explanation as to **why** they are there. **Why** does the narrator refer to cold in the middle section and heat in the last? The answer is clear: the middle section is a gloomy, inert and icy prediction of what will happen if she chooses to continue being coy; while the last section burns with the optimistic, vital and fiery vision of a future enriched with sexual passion.

You need to offer an explanation of a similar nature for the references to inactivity and inertia as opposed to those that create a feeling of vitality.

## How does it end?

As was said before in the discussion of 'The Wife's Tale', the introduction and conclusion of any poem are crucial components, and a careful consideration of the way in which a text concludes will help the student to establish precisely the direction it has taken.

What we see at the end of 'To His Coy Mistress' is the narrator painting a picture of life, vitality and the fulfilment of desire which is there to be shared by him and the object of his desire in a physical defiance of time. His vision of the future that is theirs for the taking if she will comply is one that is suffused with energy and in total contrast to the slow-moving opening section with its exaggerated rhetoric, which plays with time and distance on a huge scale.

The poem starts slowly with a sense of conflict and separation; it ends speedily with a feeling of unity and vigour. And what happened in between? The narrator presented a logical three-part argument to his potential lover in the hope of convincing her of the need to comply with his desire for sex:

- **if** we had time, then 'this coyness' would be fine;
- **but** we don't; and
- **therefore** we ought to get on with it now.

So, what has the ending achieved? It has:

- returned the reader to the beginning of the poem, inviting us to compare the two situations; and
- revealed the writer's thoughts and feelings about the situation or event that 'gave birth' to the poem – the need to take opportunities as they arise (or perhaps to gratify his sexual desire without delay!)

## Summarise your response

The poem moves towards unity and vitality with heavy emphasis on pleasure and a sense of cheating time by winning the battle against it. The narrator addresses the object of his desire directly and we are merely eavesdroppers. It is not possible to say that this poem is a conversation between the couple; we hear only *his* words. She is silent while he reasons his way to her heart and we cannot help but think that by the end of the poem he has put forward a very convincing case. It might have been a logical argument but it is presented with an almost irresistible verve and energy in the last section that is seductive in itself, and we are swept along with his enthusiasm for 'seizing the day'. The logical argument is presented emotionally and offers a very attractive alternative to passivity.

So, how did we get here? The process has been as straightforward as it was with 'The Wife's Tale'.

- The first step was that of **close reading and thinking**.
- Then we **focused** in the first section **on the central conflicts**.
- The next step was to **track this theme in the rest of the poem**.
- We then looked at the **ways in which this was developed elsewhere**.
- Finally we **thought about the end and we reflected on our whole response to the poem**.

# Sample essay – 'To His Coy Mistress'

The impetuous young narrator of Marvell's poem attempts to persuade 'his coy mistress' of the need to seize the opportunity to consummate their relationship. He makes it clear in the first stanza that if time were endless he would spend whole ages wooing her as she 'deserve[s]' and her reluctance to relinquish her virtue would be no problem. Reality, however, is very different, and this lover goes into gruesome detail in stanza two to explain the effects of the ravages of 'Time's wingèd chariot'. For this reason, in the final stanza, he entreats the object of his desire to enjoy the pleasures of their 'youthful' love while they can, before time catches them up and they lose out for ever.

From the title onwards we are aware that this is a piece addressed to a reluctant female. The fact that this mistress is described a 'coy' in the title suggests, by default, that the narrator is not, for why mention it if it were not a noteworthy point; one that sets her apart? Straight away Marvell uses the conditional tense, thereby alerting the reader to a conflict; 'had [they] . . . but world enough and time' there would be no 'crime' in spending time on wooing and playing. Again, however, there is an implied alternative truth. This is made evident in stanza two, which starts with 'But', that is to say the ideal outlined in stanza one is not the case. There is none of the uncertainty of the conditional here, rather, the narrator is definite, bringing both his addressee and the reader into the present reality with a great sense of immediacy; 'Time's wingèd chariot' is 'at [his] . . . back' and what is more, he is 'always' aware of it. As if propelled by the 'chariot hurrying near', the narrator propels his argument to the issue of immediate action in the final stanza. The imperative 'Now therefore' gives a sense of urgency and one might say an inevitability to his conclusion. The very structure of the text thus reflects the conflicts around which it revolves. Marvell's technique has been to outline the basics of logical argument; if . . . but . . . therefore. This gives the poem a tight structure and makes the text more persuasive as each point appears to be a logical, inevitable continuation of the previous one. The male narrator is thus able to use his education as a tool against his female counterpart, who is likely to have been denied such opportunities and is therefore given no voice in the poem.

This discourse is, thus, in many senses, a battle. First, there is the battle between the impetuous young man who remains ever aware of 'Time's wingèd chariot hurrying near' and 'his coy mistress' whose 'long preserved virginity' is a question of 'honour'. Then there is the battle of man and time, or the ideal and necessity, clearly encapsulated in the contrasting language used in the dream of the ideal, the brutal realisation of reality and the enthusiastic future plan of action. Marvell reflects the distance between the two parties in his narrator's changing use of 'I', 'me', 'you' and 'thou'. The couple's unity is evident at the outset, with the first two sentences referring to 'we' and 'our':

> Had we but world enough, and time...
> We would sit down, and think which way
> To walk, and pass our long love's day.

This is, however, quick to change as the two become separate, interrupting the sense of togetherness and highlighting the conflict between them. It is only in the final stanza – the conclusion – that they are reunited as 'us', no longer separated by continents and ages, as in the first stanza:

> ... Thou by the Indian Gange's side...
> ... I by the tide
> Of Humber... I would
> Love you ten years before the Flood:
> And you ... refuse
> Till the conversion of the Jews...

The narrator and the object of his desire are to become one as he urges her to 'roll all our strength, and all/Our sweetness, up into one ball'.

Thus we see how the lovers are separated by geography, context and time in stanza one, and this separation is further developed in stanza two. The narrator is clearly aware of 'Time's wingèd chariot' in a way that his mistress is not, thereby opening a gulf in their very perceptions of the situation. This is then brought into a more physical realm with the image of the woman being locked up in her own 'marble vault'. Indeed, this dense image functions on many levels literally to encapsulate their separation. First, there is the connotation of death – the ultimate separation. Then the qualities of marble, which are through this image attributed to the woman, namely the hard, cold purity for which the stone is renowned, serve to highlight the difference from her suitor, whose passion, impetuosity and burning optimism are reflected in references to 'ashes', 'lust', 'instant fires' and a challenge to the sun itself. Finally, the vault image serves as a reference to sexuality. This is *her* vault and as such may be seen as the female space which, cold and closed as it is, will not be 'penetrated' by the 'echoing song' of the male, but rather by worms traditionally linked to death, decay and stillness.

The penultimate couplet of stanza two acts as a summary of the points made in the argument thus far:

> And your quaint honour turn to dust;
> And into ashes all my lust.

First there is the split of the couple into 'your' and 'my', each even occupying a different line and separated by a comma. Then there is a belittling of the mistress's 'honour', seen as 'quaint', while her pursuer's 'lust', is enhanced by the use of 'all'. This brings us to the essential conflict between 'honour' and 'lust', and then finally to the images of 'dust' and 'ashes'. The mistress has already been likened to a cold place of death and this reference to 'dust' continues those connotations, adding to them the notion of disuse and decay. In stark contrast, the suitor's 'lust' burns to 'ashes' with their links to consuming fire, passion, light and heat.

The reuniting of the lovers in stanza three is presented by the persuasive narrator as the solution to the problem, and his enthusiastic vivacity and determination are very clearly reflected in the language. A sense of freshness and immediacy are conveyed with references to 'youthful hue' linked by rhyme to 'morning dew'. Similarly, we are faced with a call to action, to 'sport', 'devour', 'roll', 'tear' and finally 'run'. Thus, as well as a sense of heat referred to earlier, there is a notion of life, speed and enthusiasm. We have moved from a situation where man (or woman) is overcome by worms and death to the point where they are willing to take on the sun – the creator and measure of time and life itself:

> Thus, though we cannot make our sun
> Stand still, yet we will make him run.

With this final couplet, Marvell refers us back to the beginning of the argument and the first stanza of the poem. In doing so, he allows the slowness so carefully created in stanza one to function in juxtaposition to the speed of stanza three and vice versa, thereby highlighting the impact of each. The long vowel sounds used both in the end rhyme of stanza one – 'time'/'crime', 'way'/'day' and 'side'/'tide' – and mid-line in 'Lady', 'rubies' and 'empires' act to slow the pace, as does the use of polysyllabic words and punctuation in the middle of a line, as in:

> Vaster than empires, and more slow.

In contrast, the final stanza is made up of shorter words and sounds, and has far less mid-line punctuation:

> At every pore with instant fires,

Just as the negativity of the penultimate line of the poem is extinguished by the determination of the emphatic final line: 'yet we will make him run'.

So the positive tone of the final stanza overrides the slowness of the first, and the harsh, violent coldness of the second. This is indeed the tactic of the narrator as he tries to convince his love to surrender to him. Using logic in such an emotive situation would seem inappropriate, but the passion with which he argues is indeed persuasive, and the reader reaches the final line with a sense of triumph and determination to 'let love rule', which we can only assume is also conveyed to his silent, cold 'coy mistress'.

# ▨ 8 Practical criticism of modern prose

## Practical criticism of prose

What do you find interesting about the way Bruce Chatwin describes the last few weeks of Mary's pregnancy and the birth of the twins in this extract from the novel *On the Black Hill*? (AQA (AEB) June 1993)

One muggy evening – it was the first week in July – a clatter of wheel rims sounded in the lane, and Hughes the Carter drove up with Hannah and a pair of bundles. Amos was screwing a new hinge to the stable-door. He dropped the screwdriver and asked why she had come.

She answered gloomily, 'I belong by the bedside.'

A day or two later, Mary woke with an attack of nausea and throbbing pains that raced up and down her spine. As Amos left the bedroom, she clung to his arm and pleaded, 'Please ask her to go. I'd feel better if she'd go. I beg you. Or I'll – '

'No,' he said, lifting the latch. 'Mother belongs here. She must stay.'

All that month there was a heatwave. The wind blew from the east and the sky was a hard and cloudless blue. The pump ran dry. The mud cracked. Swarms of horseflies buzzed about the nettles, and the pains in Mary's spine grew worse. Night after night, she dreamed the same dream – of blood and nasturtiums.

She felt that her strength was draining away. She felt that something snapped inside; that the baby would be born deformed, or born dead, or that she herself would die. She wished she had died in India, for the poor. Propped up on pillows, she prayed to the Redeemer to take her life but – Lord! Lord! – to let him live.

Old Hannah spent the heat of the day in the kitchen, shivering under a black shawl, knitting – knitting very slowly – a pair of long white woollen socks. When Amos beat to death an adder that had been sunning itself by the porch, she curled her lip and said, 'That means a death in the family!'

The 15th of July was Mary's birthday; and because she was feeling a little better, she came downstairs and tried to make conversation with her mother-in-law. Hannah hooded her eyes and said, 'Read to me!'

'What shall I read, Mother?'

'The floral tributes.'

So Mary turned to the funeral columns of the *Hereford Times* and began:

'"The funeral of Miss Violet Gooch who died tragically last Thursday at the age of seventeen was held at St. Asaph's Church – "'

'I said the floral tributes.'

'Yes, Mother,' she corrected herself, and began again:

'"Wreath of arum lilies from Auntie Vi and Uncle Arthur. 'Nevermore!'... Wreath of yellow roses. 'With ever loving memory from Poppet, Winnie and Stanley....' Artificial wreath in glass case. 'With kind remembrance from the Hooson Emporium....' Bouquet of Gloire de Dijon roses. 'Sleep softly, my dearest. From Auntie Mavis, Mostyn Hotel, Llandrindod....' Bouquet of wild flowers 'Only good-night, Beloved, not farewell! Your loving sister, Cissie....'"'

'Well, go on!' Hannah had opened an eyelid. 'What's the matter with you? Go on! Finish it!'

'Yes Mother.... "The coffin, of beautifully polished oak with brass fittings, was made by Messrs Lloyd and Lloyd of Presteigne with the following inscription on the lid: 'A harp! A magnificent harp! With a broken string!'"'

'Ah!' the old woman said.

The preparations for Mary's confinement made Sam so jittery anyone would have thought that he, not his son, were the father. He was always thinking of ways to please her: indeed, his was the one face that made her smile. He spent the last of his savings commissioning a rocking cradle from Watkins the Coffin. It was painted red, with blue and white stripes, and had four carved finials in the form of songbirds.

'Father, you shouldn't have....' Mary clapped her hands, as he tried it out on the kitchen flags.

'And it's a coffin, not a cradle, she'll be needing,' Hannah mumbled, and went on with her knitting.

For over fifty years she had kept, from her bridal trousseau, a single unlaundered white cotton nightdress to wear with the white socks when they laid her out as a corpse. On August 1st, she turned the heel of the second sock, and, from then on, knitted slower and slower, sighing between the stitches and croaking, 'Not long now!'

Her skin, papery at the best of times, appeared to be transparent. Her breath came in cracked bursts, and she had difficulty moving her tongue. It was obvious to everyone but Amos that she had come to The Vision to die.

On the 8th of August the weather broke. Stacks of smoky, silver-lidded clouds piled up behind the hill. At six in the evening, Amos and Dai Morgan were scything the last of the oats. All the birds were silent in the stillness that precedes a storm. Thistledown floated upwards, and a shriek tore out across the valley.

The labour pains had begun. Upstairs in the bedroom, Mary lay writhing, moaning, kicking off the sheets and biting the pillow. Ruth Morgan tried to calm her. Sam was in the kitchen, boiling water. Hannah sat on the settle, and counted her stitches.

Amos saddled the cob and cantered over the hill, helter-skelter down the quarryman's tracks to Rhulen.

'Courage, man!' said Dr Bulmer, as he divided his forceps and slid each half down one of his riding-boots. Then, shoving a flask of ergot into one pocket, a bottle of chloroform into the other, he buttoned the collar of his mackintosh cape, and both men set their faces to the storm.

The rainwater hissed on the rooftiles as they tethered their horses to the garden fence.

Amos attempted to follow upstairs. The doctor pushed him back, and he dropped on to the rocking-chair as if he'd been hit on the chest.

'Please God it be a boy,' he moaned. 'An' I'll never touch her again.' He grabbed at Ruth Morgan's apron as she went by with a water-jug. 'Be she all right?' he pleaded, but she shook him off and told him not to be silly.

Twenty minutes later, the bedroom door opened and a voice boomed out:

'Any more newspaper? An oilskin? Anything'll do!'

'Be it a boy?'

'Two of them.'

That night, Hannah rounded off the toe of her second sock and, three days later, died.

## Read closely and think

As we have already established, the first step in the process of practical criticism should be simply to understand at a somewhat basic, uncomplicated level, what the piece is 'about'. When you have read it carefully once, try to *summarise* its most obvious and simple meaning in a brief overview of one short paragraph.

You might have come up with something like this: 'The extract describes the arrival of Hannah at the home of Mary and Amos. Hannah seems to be preparing for her own death while preparations are also being made for Mary's delivery. The text contains numerous references to life and death, and as Hannah leaves this world Mary's children enter it.'

There is no definitive summary at this stage, and there are several different ways in which you might have expressed it. All that matters now is that the most important issues are dealt with and you have a clear idea of what is happening.

Remembering *why* you summarise at this point should help you:

- It gives you a clear sense of direction for your forthcoming discussion;
- It provides you with a sound framework upon which to 'hang' further development of ideas; and
- It keeps you focused on the essential meaning so that you are less likely to stray from this into irrelevant areas of discussion.

## Summarise the central conflict/s

You now know that one of the first things to do is to try to establish the *nature of the conflict* that lies at the heart of the text and provides the substance for the final resolution. It is this conflict that is continually being worked on and worked out in a piece of literature. Sometimes it is subtle, and sometimes, as in this extract from *On the Black Hill*, less so.

Read the extract again and look for signs of *conflict*. Remember that these can manifest themselves in a number of quite simple ways. Search out words that oppose each other, opposite ideas, binary pairs. Chapter 4, 'Tools of analysis – features of Text', provides a number of areas for consideration of the presence of tension, but for now examine:

- Language; and
- Form and structure.

In terms of the **language**, remember that conflict or tension may be evident in the presence of contrasts, differences, oxymorons or even simply 'good' or 'bad' words. Now make your annotations on the conflict in the passage.

Compare your findings with the list below. None of the ideas has been developed yet; at this stage we are merely focusing on and developing the central theme of conflict.

- birth/death;
- black/white;
- heat/cold;
- coffin/cradle;
- wedding/funeral;
- black clouds/silver linings;
- mugginess/storm;
- silence/scream;
- action/inaction;
- birth/death.

How did your list compare with this one?

All that has been done here is that binary pairs or opposites have been identified, and in doing that we have identified and summarised the central conflict.

## Track the themes

Notice the **language** of the prose. It is important to remember that this is not an entire piece of literature, but merely an extract from a novel, so it is essential to consider it in that context. We do not have the whole picture, and *you must not be tempted to speculate on what might or might not be in the rest of the text.* All you have to deal with is what is in front of you in the examination, and even if you are familiar with the whole novel, *you must deal only with the extract. You will not be given marks for a discussion of content that is outside the extract.*

### Birth/death

The simplest way to start looking for conflict is to search out words that oppose each other. Quite simply, look for opposites. In paragraph six we see the juxtaposition of 'born dead'. At first glance this is merely a description of the birth of a child who is dead at the time of delivery. However, it is fruitful to look at this type of language in the light of our quest and consider the tension and conflict contained in those two words. You will soon discover how central these two words are to the extract, and how significant it is that they are juxtaposed in this way.

### Black/white

Look at paragraph seven. Hannah makes the gloomy prediction, 'That means a death in the family!', but we are already aware that Mary is about to give birth. There is a distinct tension here, again between life and death. In the same paragraph we learn that Hannah is 'shivering under a black shawl' and this would be unremarkable were it not for the fact that she does this in 'the heat of the day'. Thus far, then, we have the conflict of **life** and **death** and the tension between **heat** and **cold**. These two types of discord are not unconnected; do we not connect life with heat and death with cold? Life and death are juxtaposed, this time in temperature. Not only do we have the opposites of life and death, heat and cold, but also the paired colours, black and white. Although not overtly alluded to, there is evidence of some contrast in colour. The 'heat of the day' implies brightness and light, whereas Hannah shivers 'under a black shawl'.

### Coffin/cradle

Later in the passage we learn that Sam has commissioned Watkins the coffin-maker to produce a rocking cradle. Again, there is the tension between life and death – this time in the form of the product of man's labour. The man who makes the coffins and deals in death is also to construct a cradle for the new life that Mary is about to bring into the world. This juxtaposition is somewhat uncomfortable, and perhaps there is a feeling that the baby's new life should not be cradled by the work of hands that also deal in death.

### Wedding/funeral

Soon afterwards, we read that fifty years ago Hannah kept aside from her bridal trousseau a white cotton nightdress to wear with white socks when she was laid out as a corpse. Weddings signify new beginnings and hope for the future, but Hannah was looking to death even then. Once more, life and death are brought together, this time in clothing.

### Black clouds/silver linings

Chatwin describes the clouds as 'silver-lidded', and you need to take the time to visualise the imagery that a writer uses if it is to affect you in the way it is intended. Imagine in your mind's eye clouds that are 'silver-lidded'. The clouds are described as being 'smoky', suggesting a certain darkness in their appearance; if they are also 'silver-lidded', then the suggestion is that they are dark clouds with silver linings. Immediately we have another pair of opposites. The clouds themselves are gloomy and sombre but they are edged with brightness, suggesting that what is bleak is also tinged with joy. Again we see conflict, this time represented by colours in nature.

## Mugginess/storm

The first three words of the extract tell us that the weather is 'muggy' and we learn that there had been a heatwave for a month; Chatwin creates a sense of still warmth. Later, however, the birds stop singing and the air is silent before the storm. Suddenly 'a shriek tore out across the valley'. This dramatic contrast, this tension, shows nature reflecting the actions of mankind in a sympathetic background. The animals act out the stillness that is thought to characterise each foetus just before its birth. This stillness is torn, as is Mary, when her labour pains begin. Again we see a sharp contrast between mugginess and a storm, **inaction** and **action**, between **silence** and **noise** – a sort of death and life, once more represented by nature.

The last few lines of the extract present us with perhaps the starkest pair of contrasting elements; the twins are **born**, and Hannah **dies**.

What must be stressed here is that this list contains elements that are all connected by the idea of life and death, which is the central tension in the piece.

**Form and structure** are next for consideration. How is the piece put together? How has Chatwin constructed it? There is a detailed discussion of structure in Chapter 4, 'Tools of analysis – features of text'. As noted earlier, it is important to remember that the piece is only an extract from a novel and is by no means the whole text. This fact must inevitably have a bearing on the way in which we see it and on the manner in which we discuss its form and structure. You will be assessed on your ability to see the extract as just that – a part of the whole, and not as the whole story. You cannot know what happens in the rest of the novel, nor precisely how this extract fits into it. Simply look at the extract as a piece of work in its own right but also as a part of a bigger whole that you cannot truly know.

Look back at the list that outlines the precise nature of the conflict. Notice how the first pair is birth/death, and so is the last. The extract starts with reference to this particular conflict and Chatwin chooses to return to it later. Sandwiched between these two layers is a wide range of variations on the same theme. It is as if we have been taken on a short journey of exploration of this idea of life and death, but we return to the place from which we started. Why start and finish there? Perhaps because this is the main issue with which Chatwin wishes to deal – the inextricable link between life and death that characterises all existence. You might have heard the quotation, 'In the midst of life we are in death' or the adage, 'Death is part of life'. Even in the homely sayings that we all use at times, the presence of irony is unmistakable. Chatwin's passage starts with life and death and (quite literally), 'it all comes back to' life and death!

One of the clearest indicators of structure in literature is often the layout of the text on the page. You may already have noticed that the structure of this piece is very disjointed. There are few paragraphs of any real length, several being only one or two sentences long. As discussed in 'Tools of analysis – features of text', this fractured condition often creates an uneasy feeling. The smoothness and calm suggested by long sentences and ambling paragraphs is absent, and the movement of the text is jerky and uncomfortable. No sooner have we settled into one idea (represented by one paragraph) than we are torn away and propelled into another. These swift and rather brutal twists and turns in direction are reminiscent of the dodgems at the fair – hardly a calming experience!

Hence we see the structure of the piece endorsing the content. The feeling throughout is one of unease and discomfort, and this is reflected in the structure. In fact it is created in part *by* the structure. As has been said before, all the features of the text work together to produce the effect.

You may also have noticed the frequent appearance of Chatwin's motif of time. A time of day and almost a date are provided in both the first and last lines of the extract, and there are numerous such references throughout the text. This calendar acts as a framework upon which to hang the events leading up to the almost simultaneous births and death. We are made aware of time passing by Chatwin's continual references to it, 'a day or two later', 'on the 8th of August' and so on and, added to the uneasy 'jerkiness' of the fractured structure, a feeling of panic is not far away; we are propelled forward through time towards an inevitable conclusion accompanied by a significant loss of peace.

Closely connected to the countdown effect of references to time is the speed at which the piece moves. The short paragraphs and fractured structure create a faster pace that is easily detected in the brisk dialogue between Mary and Hannah from 'What shall I read, Mother?' onwards. This speed is counteracted later by sentences that are longer and slower, and there is a noticeable slowing of the pace after the two women's rapid exchange. The sense of speed is increased by Hannah's urging of Mary, 'Go on! Finish it!', by Amos's cantering 'helter-skelter' to fetch the doctor, and by the rapid movements of Dr Bulmer, 'shoving a flask of ergot into one pocket'. The pace increases towards the end of the extract as we hurtle in the direction of a climactic conclusion provided by the birth of the twins and the death of Hannah.

## Develop the themes elsewhere

In a sense, this section has already been dealt with to some extent under previous headings, because after we established the first sign of conflict, which was that of life against death, we then looked for other manifestations of tension that could be related to the main idea. It might be helpful to consider our list again:

- birth/death;
- black/white;
- heat/cold;
- coffin/cradle;
- wedding/funeral;
- black clouds/silver linings;
- mugginess/storm;
- silence/scream;
- action/inaction;
- birth/death.

We see Chatwin exploring this theme of the co-existence of life and death by interpreting it in a variety of ways. He does not *stray* from his principal theme, but he finds numerous ways of *playing it out and exploring it*. Here, then, we have successfully *tracked the main theme* and discovered how Chatwin *develops it* in different ways.

If we think for a moment about the duality of human life (and non-human, come to that) exemplified in this coexistence of life and death, we get a sense of 'two'. Opposites always come in pairs. Now look again at the extract and identify as many references to 'two' or 'pairs' as you can.

Below is a list for you to compare with yours:

a pair of bundles;
a day or two later;
a pair of long white woollen socks;
Lloyd and Lloyd;
the second sock;
forceps ... slid each half;
ergot into one pocket, a bottle of chloroform into the other;
both men;
two of them; and
second sock.

Now look at the sheet entitled 'Annotations on Conflict/Pairs'.

---

### Box 8.1   ANNOTATIONS ON CONFLICT/PAIRS

One muggy evening – it was the first week in July – a clatter of wheel rims sounded in the lane, and Hughes the Carter drove up with Hannah and a pair of bundles. Amos was screwing a new hinge to the stable-door. He dropped the screwdriver and asked why she had come.

*2 people arrive*

*pair of bundles*

5

She answered gloomily, 'I belong by the bedside.'

*pair of days*

A day or two later, Mary woke with an attack of nausea and throbbing pains that raced up and down her spine. As Amos left the bedroom, she clung to his arm and pleaded, 'Please ask her to go. I'd feel better if she'd go. I beg you. Or I'll –'

10

'No,' he said, lifting the latch. 'Mother belongs here. She must stay.'

All that month there was a heatwave. The wind blew from the east and the sky was a hard and cloudless blue. The pump ran dry. The mud cracked. Swarms of horseflies buzzed about the nettles, and the pains in Mary's spine grew worse. Night after night, she dreamed the same dream – of blood and nasturtiums.

15

She felt that her strength was draining away. She felt that something snapped inside; that the baby would be born deformed, or

*Box 8.1*    *(Contd)*

*juxta-*
*position*
*life/death*

born dead, or that she herself would die. She wished she had died
in India, for the poor. Propped up on pillows, she prayed to the    20
Redeemer to take her life but – Lord! Lord! – to let him live.

*death/*
*life*

*pair of*
*socks*

*heat/cold* Old Hannah spent the heat of the day in the kitchen, shivering
under a black shawl, knitting – knitting very slowly – a pair of long
white woollen socks. When Amos beat to death an adder that had
been sunning itself by the porch, she curled her lip and said,    25
'That means a death in the family!'

*2 women*
*together Mary*
*represents*
*birth Hannah*
*represents*
*death*

The 15th of July was Mary's birthday; and because she was feeling
a little better, she came downstairs and tried to make conversation with her mother-in-law. Hannah hooded her eyes and said,
'Read to me!'    30

'What shall I read, Mother?'

'The floral tributes.'

So Mary turned to the funeral columns of the *Hereford Times* and
began:

'"The funeral of Miss Violet Gooch who died tragically last Thurs-    35
day at the age of seventeen was held at St. Asaph's Church – "'

'I said the floral tributes.'

'Yes, Mother,' she corrected herself, and began again:

'"Wreath of arum lilies from Auntie Vi and Uncle Arthur.
'Nevermore!'... Wreath of yellow roses. 'With ever loving mem-    40
ory from Poppet, Winnie, and Stanley....' Artificial wreath in
glass case. 'With kind remembrance from the Hooson
Emporium....' Bouquet of Gloire de Dijon roses. 'Sleep softly,
my dearest. From Auntie Mavis, Mostyn Hotel, Llandrindod....'
Bouquet of wild flowers 'Only good-night, Beloved, not farewell!    45
Your loving sister, Cissie....'"'

'Well, go on!' Hannah had opened an eyelid. 'What's the matter
with you? Go on! Finish it!'

*pair*

'Yes, Mother.... "The coffin, of beautifully polished oak with
brass fittings, was made by Messrs Lloyd and Lloyd of Presteigne    50
with the following inscription on the lid: 'A harp! A magnificent
harp! With a broken string!'"'

'Ah!' the old woman said.

The preparations for Mary's confinement made Sam so jittery
anyone would have thought that he, not his son, were the father.    55
He was always thinking of ways to please her: indeed, his was
the one face that made her smile. He spent the last of his savings

birth/ death
commissioning a rocking cradle from Watkins the Coffin. It was painted red, with blue and white stripes, and had four carved finials in the form of songbirds.

60

'Father, you shouldn't have . . . . ' Mary clapped her hands, as he tried it out on the kitchen flags.

*death/birth*

'And it's a coffin, not a cradle, she'll be needing,' Hannah mumbled, and went on with her knitting.

For over fifty years she had kept, from her bridal trousseau, a single unlaundered white cotton nightdress to wear with the white socks when they laid her out as a corpse. On August 1st, she turned the heel of the second sock, and, from then on, knitted slower and slower, sighing between the stitches and croaking, 'Not long now!'

65

*pair of socks*

*pair of socks*

Her skin, papery at the best of times, appeared to be transparent. Her breath came in cracked bursts, and she had difficulty moving her tongue. It was obvious to everyone but Amos that she had come to The Vision to die.

70

*Vision suggests future — juxtaposed with death*

On the 8th of August the weather broke. Stacks of smoky, silver-lidded clouds piled up behind the hill. At six in the evening, Amos and Dai Morgan were scything the last of the oats. All the birds were silent in the stillness that precedes a storm. Thistledown floated upwards, and a shriek tore out across the valley.

75

*silence/ shriek*

*image of Grim Reaper (death)*

The labour pains had begun. Upstairs in the bedroom, Mary lay writhing, moaning, kicking off the sheets and biting the pillow. Ruth Morgan tried to calm her. Sam was in the kitchen, boiling water. Hannah sat on the settle, and counted her stitches.

80

*beginnings of labour (birth)*

*2 women — different states*

Amos saddled the cob and cantered over the hill, helter-skelter down the quarryman's tracks to Rhulen.

*pair of forceps*

*2 halves*

'Courage, man!' said Dr. Bulmer, as he divided his forceps and slid each half down one of his riding-boots. Then, shoving a flask of ergot into one pocket, a bottle of chloroform into the other, he buttoned the collar of his mackintosh cape, and both men set their faces to the storm.

85

*2 pockets*

*2 men*

The rainwater hissed on the rooftiles as they tethered their horses to the garden fence.

90

Amos attempted to follow upstairs. The doctor pushed him back, and he dropped on to the rocking-chair as if he'd been hit on the chest.

'Please God it be a boy,' he moaned. 'An' I'll never touch her again.' He grabbed at Ruth Morgan's apron as she went by with a water-jug. 'Be she all right?' he pleaded, but she shook him off and told him not to be silly.

95

Box 8.1    (Contd)

Twenty minutes later, the bedroom door opened and a voice
boomed out:                                                                               100

'Any more newspaper? An oilskin? Anything'll do!'

'Be it a boy?'

*twins*          'Two of them.'                                                        — *pair of socks*

That night, Hannah rounded off the toe of her second sock and,

          three days later, died.                                                   105

*life/death*               From *On the Black Hill* by Bruce Chatwin (Picador)

There are more, and subtler, examples, but these will suffice. Remember that **nothing in good literature is ever random**, so it is not a coincidence that numerous references to two or pairs appears in an extract that is about life and death, and the inextricable ties between these two states.

When Hannah's arrival at The Vision is described in the opening section of the extract she answers Amos's question about her being there with, 'I belong by the bedside'. Close reading unlocks the meaning of the text. Look carefully at the word 'belong': to 'belong' means 'to be the property of' or 'to be assigned to' or 'rightly placed or classified' (*Oxford Dictionary*). It is as if she knew that she *had* to be there; that she had something to do, something to achieve. She was a woman with a purpose, the precise nature of which is not obvious to us until later in the passage. There is a definite sense of accomplishment in the text, which you would do well to try to identify now. Then compare your findings with the notes below.

- The deaths referred to by Mary from this point are themselves a type of achievement. Death signifies a life lived, a race run, a battle fought.
- Hannah orders Mary to 'Finish it!' There is a sense of potential completion, fulfilment and satisfaction implied in her somewhat irate command. See the discussion of the penultimate line.
- Watkins the Coffin accomplishes his task of making a cradle for Mary and Amos. Something is finished; something has been completed.
- It seems that Hannah has spent almost a lifetime preparing for her own death. Fifty years ago, amid the joy of marriage, she made the first of her funeral arrangements. In the midst of life, Hannah has most certainly been in death. Her own passing at the end of the text comes as an accomplishment; her steady knitting has been the preparation at the latter end of her life. Finally she stops and the plan is fulfilled.
- 'Both men set their faces to the storm'. Amos and Dr Bulmer braced themselves to brave the elements that night. There is a sense of the two men battling with the storm to achieve a goal; Bulmer had to be fetched for Mary to deliver her baby safely. They were determined to succeed.
- Hannah finally 'rounded off the toe of her second sock and three days later, died'. The passage ends with her achieving what was almost a lifetime's ambition: to be prepared for death. She leaves this world having accomplished what

she set out to do fifty years before, and we almost breathe a sigh of relief, both with her and for her. Christ, as He hung on the cross, is reported to have said, 'It is finished', and we hear in these words the sense of accomplishment that comes from doing what we know we are meant to do. It is a fulfilment of destiny.

So, how do we connect these two ideas? Maybe you have done this already. We have established that Chatwin is dealing with the idea of existence being a paradoxical duality of life and death, and we find evidence of this sense of accomplishment. This accomplishment can be viewed as a race that has been run, a battle fought, and a life lived. Thus we see a clear connection between the process of life and the final act of death; the life we live as a means of achieving an end that is characterised in death.

Analysis of the language revealed that Chatwin has focused on binary pairs, numerous opposites that contrast with each other. In the second sentence of the passage we are told that Hannah arrives with 'a pair of bundles', and the frequent appearance of pairs or twos is a further exploration of the duality idea. Look again at the text and this time see how many references you can find to time and its passing. Do this with the book closed and then compare your notes with those below.

one muggy evening, the first week in July;
A day or two later;
All that month;
night after night;
the heat of the day;
knitting very slowly;
15th of July, birthday;
last Thursday, age;
Nevermore;
remembrance;
fifty years;
August 1st;
slower and slower, Not long now!;
8th of August;
six in the evening;
counted her stitches;
twenty minutes later;
That night; and
three days later.

You might like to look now at the sheet entitled 'Annotations on Time'.

## Box 8.2  ANNOTATIONS ON TIME

One muggy evening – it was the first week in July – a clatter of wheel
rims sounded in the lane, and Hughes the Carter drove up with
Hannah and a pair of bundles. Amos was screwing a new hinge to
the stable-door. He dropped the screwdriver and asked why she
had come.                                                                    5

She answered gloomily, 'I belong by the bedside'

A day or two later, Mary woke with an attack of nausea and throbbing pains that raced up and down her spine. As Amos left the
bedroom, she clung to his arm and pleaded, 'Please ask her to go.
I'd feel better if she'd go. I beg you. Or I'll – '                           10

'No,' he said, lifting the latch. 'Mother belongs here. She must stay.'

*effects
of time
and
drought*
All that month there was a heatwave. The wind blew from the
east and the sky was a hard and cloudless blue. The pump ran
dry. The mud cracked. Swarms of horseflies buzzed about the
nettles, and the pains in Mary's spine grew worse. Night after       15
night, she dreamed the same dream – of blood and nasturtiums.

She felt that her strength was draining away. She felt that something snapped inside; that the baby would be born deformed, or
born dead, or that she herself would die. She wished she had died
in India, for the poor. Propped up on pillows, she prayed to the     20
Redeemer to take her life but – Lord! Lord! – to let him live.

Old Hannah spent the heat of the day in the kitchen, shivering
under a black shawl, knitting – knitting very slowly – a pair of long    *speed*
white woollen socks. When Amos beat to death an adder that had
been sunning itself by the porch, she curled her lip and said,          25
'That means a death in the family!'

The 15th of July was Mary's birthday, and because she was feeling
a little better, she came downstairs and tried to make conversation with her mother-in-law. Hannah hooded her eyes and
said, 'Read to me!'                                                    30

'What shall I read, Mother?'

'The floral tributes.'

So Mary turned to the funeral columns of the *Hereford Times* and
began:

'"The funeral of Miss Violet Gooch who died tragically last      35
Thursday at the age of seventeen was held at St. Asaph's Church – "'

'I said the floral tributes.'

'Yes, Mother,' she corrected herself, and began again:

'"Wreath of arum lilies from Auntie Vi and Uncle Arthur. 'Nevermore'... Wreath of yellow roses. 'With ever loving memory from Poppet, Winnie, and Stanley....' Artificial wreath in glass case. 'With kind remembrance from the Hooson Emporium....' Bouquet of Gloire de Dijon roses. 'Sleep softly, my dearest. From Auntie Mavis, Mostyn Hotel, Llandrindod....' Bouquet of wild flowers 'Only good-night, Beloved, not farewell!' Your loving sister, Cissie....'"

'Well, go on!' Hannah had opened an eyelid. 'What's the matter with you? Go on! Finish it!'

'Yes, Mother.... "The coffin, of beautifully polished oak with brass fittings, was made by Messrs Lloyd and Lloyd of Presteigne with the following inscription on the lid: 'A harp! A magnificent harp! With a broken string!'"'

*prepar-*
*ation/*
*accom-*
*plishment*

'Ah!' the old woman said.

The preparations for Mary's confinement made Sam so jittery anyone would have thought that he, not his son, were the father. He was always thinking of ways to please her: indeed, his was the one face that made her smile. He spent the last of his savings commissioning a rocking cradle from Watkins the Coffin. It was painted red, with blue and white stripes, and had four carved finials in the form of songbirds.

'Father, you shouldn't have ....' Mary clapped her hands, as he tried it out on the kitchen flags.

'And it's a coffin, not a cradle, she'll be needing,' Hannah mumbled, and went on with her knitting.

*past*

*past*

For over fifty years she had kept, from her bridal trousseau, a single unlaundered white cotton nightdress to wear with the white socks when they laid her out as a corpse. On August 1st, she turned the heel of the second sock, and, from then on, knit-
*speed* ted slower and slower, sighing between the stitches and croak-
ing, 'Not long now.' *passage of time*

*future*
*date*

*like clock*
*ticking*
*(passage of time)*

Her skin, papery at the best of times, appeared to be transparent. Her breath came in cracked bursts, and she had difficulty moving her tongue. It was obvious to everyone but Amos that she had come to The Vision to die.

*date*

*time of day*

On the 8th of August the weather broke. Stacks of smoky, silver-lidded clouds piled up behind the hill. At six in the evening, Amos and Dai Morgan were scything the last of the oats. All the birds were silent in the stillness that precedes a storm. Thistledown floated upwards, and a shriek tore out across the valley.

*end of a*
*process*

*before the*
*storm*

40

45

50

55

60

65

70

75

Box 8.2   (Contd)

The labour pains had begun. Upstairs in the bedroom, Mary lay    80
writhing, moaning, kicking off the sheets and biting the pillow.
Ruth Morgan tried to calm her. Sam was in the kitchen, boiling    *clock ticking*
water. Hannah sat on the settle, and counted her stitches.

*speed*

Amos saddled the cob and cantered over the hill, helter-skelter
down the quarryman's tracks to Rhulen.    85

'Courage, man!' said Dr. Bulmer, as he divided his forceps and
slid each half down one of his riding-boots. Then, shoving a flask
of ergot into one pocket, a bottle of chloroform into the other, he
buttoned the collar of his mackintosh cape, and both men set
their faces to the storm.    90

The rainwater hissed on the rooftiles as they tethered their horses
to the garden fence.

Amos attempted to follow upstairs. The doctor pushed him back,
and he dropped on to the rocking-chair as if he'd been hit on the chest.

'Please God it be a boy,' he moaned. 'An' I'll never touch her    95
*future*   again.' He grabbed at Ruth Morgan's apron as she went by with a
water-jug. 'Be she all right?' he pleaded, but she shook him off
and told him not to be silly.

*passage*   Twenty minutes later, the bedroom door opened and a voice
*of time*   boomed out:    100

'Any more newspaper? An oilskin? Anything'll do!'

*end of*   'Be it a boy?'
*the day*
*(death)*   'Two of them.'

That night, Hannah rounded off the toe of her second sock and,
*passage*   three days later, died.    105
*of time*
From *On the Black Hill*  by Bruce Chatwin (Picador)

The numerous references to time are undeniable, but can we make any sense
of them and connect them to the themes we already have? We have already
addressed the issues of:

- life and death;
- the duality of existence; and
- the accomplishment of life and death;

Can we integrate the idea of time anywhere? There is a distinct sense of time passing in the extract, and it has a strong 'sense of passage'. During the second half of
the text this feeling is enhanced as Hannah 'counted her stitches', and numerous
references are made to periods of time and dates. The ticking suggested by Hannah's

clicking needles reminds us of a clock, and we can almost feel the sands of time draining away as Chatwin takes us nearer and nearer to Hannah's death.

The time element gives the piece a sense of inevitability. It emulates our own ageing, the very process of living. As it ticks by we move inexorably to the end of Hannah's life and the beginning of Mary's babies' lives. It is over time that we fulfil our purpose in life. Time marks our beginning and our end; time is what makes the difference between those two! It suggests a sense of movement, of going forward towards a realisation of our own future.

You may have noticed during one of your numerous readings of the extract, several references to nature. Look yet again at the passage and note these now before comparing your notes with the list below.

One muggy evening;
All that month there was a heatwave, wind blew from the east . . . sky was a hard and cloudless blue;
The pump ran dry. The mud cracked. Swarms of horseflies buzzed about the nettles; blood and nasturtiums;
the heat of the day;
beat to death an adder;
Wreath of yellow roses/lilies;
the weather broke;
scything the last of the oats;
All the birds were silent in the stillness that precedes a storm;
Thistledown floated upwards; and
The rainwater hissed on the rooftiles.

We have already considered the aspect of inevitability in that life and death are both part of existence. Note the elements of sympathetic background in the extract. (This is discussed in detail in Chapter 4 – 'Tools of analysis – features of text' on page 60.) Several references to nature can be compared to what is happening in the life of the human beings in the story. Look at these references again and see what connections you can make between natural conditions/events and those of the characters. *When you have done that* consider the following:

- 'One muggy evening'/oppression suggested by the arrival of Hannah;
- 'All that month there was a heatwave'/discomfort brought by Hannah;
- 'wind blew from the east'/a harsh presence (like Hannah);
- 'the sky was a hard and cloudless blue'/unforgiving, merciless, unequivocal (like Hannah);
- 'The pump ran dry. The mud cracked'/nothing to soothe or bring relief;
- 'Swarms of horseflies buzzed about the nettles'/Hannah hovering menacingly over Mary – the threat of a sting;
- 'blood and nasturtiums'/suffering, pain and flames – the heat;
- 'beat to death an adder'/Hannah's prediction, 'that means a death in the family';
- 'Wreath of yellow roses'/nature and death are linked;
- 'the weather broke'/Mary's waters break and labour is about to begin;
- 'scything the last of the oats'/image of the Grim Reaper;

- 'All the birds were still in the silence that precedes a storm' and 'Thistledown floated upwards'/the stillness of the foetus immediately prior to birth – a sense of expectation; and
- 'The rainwater hissed on the rooftiles'/Mary is under a sinister presence (Hannah).

The suggestions offered here are not definitive and there may be other ways of explaining some of the natural events and conditions, and the manner in which they mirror the world of humankind. What we can see is that there are links between the world of nature and that of human beings. Where does this take us? We have already established that there is a sense of inevitability about the extract. Think of that alongside the sympathetic background and you have the idea that the duality of existence that previously one might have thought was only to do with human beings can now be applied to the whole of creation.

Human life is frequently mirrored in the world of animals and natural phenomena suggesting that human beings and nature share much. What is emerging is a real sense of unity between:

- life and death; and
- humans and nature.

The message then would seem to be something to do with life and death both being part of human existence, and human existence being reflected in the world of nature, leading us to the idea that *all* existence is about endings and beginnings, that life is about running the race for the time that we are given and relinquishing the baton when the ticking tells us to stop. In this way, the race is forever being run, and all creation enters and exits the arena at its allotted time. The art is knowing when and how to hand over the baton to the next person.

## How does it end?

This question is not an easy one to answer in a sense, because the end of the extract is not necessarily the end of the whole text *but*, as was said before, you must only discuss the extract that is in front of you in the examination and not venture into a discussion of the rest of the novel. So we must still consider the end of the piece as a conclusion to a work in its own right.

Tension mounts as the pace of the writing increases. Amos is distraught amid the business of childbirth, and Chatwin brings us quickly to the end with the announcement of the arrival of twins, followed shortly by the death of Hannah.

There is a dramatic and momentous juxtapositioning of life and death which encapsulates the paradox of existence, and the reference to Hannah's relentless knitting of her socks reminds us of the preparation and accomplishment aspects of life.

The two women in this passage are characterised by what they represent, and in that sense they are more symbols than rounded characters. Mary stands for youth, life, new beginnings and the future; Hannah for age, death, endings and the past. There is an irony in the fact that the two women come together at The Vision. Life and death come face to face.

Both women have passed through periods of preparation; for Mary it was nine months, for Hannah fifty years, yet both women seem to have achieved something. Mary's accomplishment is obvious – two baby boys; Hannah's perhaps less so. She began planning for the moment of death fifty years before, and her timing has been impeccable. Are you familiar with the sound that is made by someone knitting? Perhaps the clicking needles act as a clock that is ticking away the moments of her life. We are aware that the socks are the last preparations to be made for her death, and she times it so that just three days after the second sock is finished and the new life arrives, she dies.

Some people believe that for every birth there is a death, that it is as if a new soul occupies a space that has been left by the departure of another. It is easy to believe that in this extract. There is a sort of dovetailing, a harmony, a balance in the final accomplishment that soothes the anxiety and the jitteriness of the passage. After the storm there is calm, and we have a sense of everything being just as it should be.

## Summarise your response

Let us return, as we always must, to the *start* of the piece. We see Hannah arrive and state gloomily, 'I belong by the bedside'. What sense can we *now* make of this? Perhaps it is that Hannah knew the end from the beginning. She knew that as the new life came, she would go. Life and death belong together because they are both part of the same plan; they both constitute essential elements of the cycle of life. She belonged 'by the bedside'. If, by 'bedside', we mean Mary's bedside and childbirth, then Hannah *did* belong there in a sense, because Hannah is the other half of the story, the other element of the pair, the other aspect of existence.

'Her skin . . . appeared to be transparent. Her breath came in cracked bursts and she had difficulty moving her tongue.' Dying is a painful business, but Chatwin paints with equal clarity a vivid picture of the pains of childbirth: 'Mary lay writhing, moaning, kicking off the sheets and biting the pillow.' Both processes involve hard work and suffering; both are inevitable parts of existence. 'It was obvious to everyone but Amos that she had come to The Vision to die.' *We* know that from her gloomy statement at the start of the extract. She 'belong[ed] by the bedside' because that was where life and death met, the beginning and the end, the alpha and the omega; both extremes of existence face-to-face with one another, each accomplishing what it must through the actions of its players.

So, once again, we ask *how* we arrived at this reading of the text:

- The first step was that of **close reading and thinking**.
- Then we **focused on the central conflicts**.
- The next step was to **track this theme throughout the passage**.
- We then looked at the **ways in which this was developed and explored elsewhere**.
- Finally, we **thought about the end and reflected on our whole response to the extract**.

## Sample essay – *On the Black Hill*

This extract is a tale of life and death embodied in the arrival of an old woman at the bedside of her pregnant daughter-in-law, Mary. It is a time of preparation for both, as they each negotiate different ends of the same journey.

Chatwin's use of language and references to the physical world of which his highly symbolic characters are a part, mean that the entire piece is imbued with a sense of life and death; their coexistence and the journey between the two. The most obvious manifestation of this is in his frequent bringing together of opposites, many of which are binary in nature and therefore dependent upon each other (much like life and death) for their definition and very existence. The black of Hannah's shawl contrasts with the white of the socks that she knits as she sits and shivers with cold 'in the heat of the day'. Hannah's grim prediction of 'a death in the family' conflicts with what we know are Mary's preparations for the birth, and reiterates Mary's own fear that 'the baby would be . . . born dead'. Indeed, in this phrase, Chatwin effectively draws together the essential conflicting elements in a striking and resonant way, which is all the more powerful because this is the written word and we can see the words 'born' and 'dead' actually next to each other on the page.

Soon, however, Chatwin employs the power of the reader's imagination to create a tableau, which becomes a powerful visual image. We see the young, pregnant mother – a symbol of life and fertility – reading to her ageing, 'gloomy' mother-in-law who has, with her black shawl and physical and social coldness, become a symbol of death. Unpack this moment more fully and the juxtapositions continue to reveal themselves. Mary is reading about floral tributes – beautiful representations of nature's bounty and fertility – to mark death at a funeral. This image gives way to another physical representation of the life/death conflict in the form of a 'rocking cradle from Watkins the coffin'. The resting place of the new-born life is thus linked to the final resting place of death in a way that is reminiscent of the words of the Christian funeral service – 'dust to dust'. Thus the interdependence of life and death and the notion that they are part of the same cycle – a journey that we must all travel – is also brought to the fore.

To reinforce this, Chatwin refers to Hannah's plans for her own funeral, which started on the day of her wedding over fifty years beforehand when 'she had kept, from her bridal trousseau, a single unlaundered white cotton night-dress to wear with the white socks when they laid her out as a corpse'. This alludes to the idea that from the day we are born, we begin to die. Hannah's wedding, conventionally representing new futures, new hope and potentially new life, thus becomes just another event in preparation for her death. This, in combination with the reader's realisation that the socks she is knitting are the finishing touches to her own funeral outfit (rather than babies' bootees, as one might expect) seems to confirm that the death she has predicted is, in fact, her own. From this point on, the clicking of the knitting needles, which must resound in the house, become indicative of the ticking of a clock, and the counted stitches become a countdown to Hannah's death.

Time also holds great significance in this extract as both women prepare for a single moment – birth or death. Here we see the final month or so of Mary's nine-month journey, and of the pilgrimage towards death that Hannah consciously began over fifty years before and has been making unconsciously all her life. Throughout the piece Chatwin punctuates his narrative with references to the passing of time. Indeed, it opens with a location of events in 'the first week of July', then 'a day or two later', 'all that month', '15th July' and so on, sometimes with subtle references to speed: 'very slowly' and 'cantered . . . helter skelter'. Indeed, just as the piece opens with two references to time in one sentence, so it ends with 'That night . . . and three days later'.

Another element of the first sentence that may be traced throughout the piece before figuring in the final sentence is the use of pairs. These function in a similar way to the opposites in that they emphasise the duality of life – the fact that life and death are partners that belong together, just as Hannah claimed to 'belong to the bedside' where life was to be created. So it is that pairs of things figure throughout the extract, from the 'pair of bundles' in the first paragraph to the 'second sock' of the final one. Days pass in pairs: 'a day or two later'; people come in pairs: 'Lloyd and Lloyd'; actions occur in pairs: 'ergot into one pocket, a bottle of chloroform into the other'; and, possibly most significantly, Mary's babies are a pair – 'two of them'. Indeed, to highlight the coexistence of life and death, not only do we follow the end of Hannah's life and the beginning of the twins' simultaneously, but the events of birth and death happen eventually within three days of each other: 'Two of them' and 'That night, Hannah rounded off the toe of the second sock and, three days later, died.'

Thus Chatwin creates a sense of inevitability as life must lead to death, the journey must be made and the 'goal' achieved, be it the knitting of a sock, the birth of a child, or the death of an old woman. This inevitability or natural combination of things is also suggested in Chatwin's use of natural detail. Once again, the author includes this important element right at the beginning of the extract and indeed uses it to set the whole scene: 'one muggy evening'. There is a whole paragraph (the fifth) placing the action in its natural setting. As we trace these references throughout the piece, however, it becomes increasingly clear that they function as more than a physical setting; they also act as a sympathetic background to the action. Thus they reflect the events and feelings of the human story.

The 'muggy evening' conjours a sense of oppression, which is also caused by Hannah's arrival in the same way that the 'heatwave' reflects the intensity and discomfort of the situation. The cracking mud and buzzing flies may reflect decay and ageing linked to Hannah, or the pain and the 'something [which Mary thought had] snapped inside'. Chatwin himself makes clear the link between nature and these lines when Hannah predicts 'a death in the family' as a result of seeing Amos 'beat to death an adder'. Thus, when 'the weather broke' there was a suggestion of Mary's waters breaking, and the natural 'silence that precedes a storm' could be seen as mirroring both the stillness of the foetus before

*x*
*conjures*

birth and the stillness before death, and certainly adds to the sense of expectation. Man and nature are thus brought together and, along with life and death themselves, are reflected as part of the same cycle. In this way, the whole of life is seen to be governed by the beginnings and endings referred to in this extract.

So it is that Chatwin creates a piece in which every aspect of the writing – its use of opposites, its pairs, its natural backdrop and even its disjointed, fractured paragraph structure – come together to create a complete picture. The reader is presented with a remarkably unified extract, reflecting the cyclical journey that characterises the whole of nature, from birth to death. He vividly suggests a sense of duality, inevitability, an acceptance of life's ordained patterns and its own achievement of these through the actions of its players.

# 9 Practical criticism of drama – Shakespeare

## Practical criticism of Shakespeare

Some examining boards require students to study a set Shakespeare play in advance of the practical criticism paper and the examination question contains an element of contextual analysis as well as practical criticism.

The set questions might be:

1. Discuss the presentation of Edmund – what he says and the language he uses.
2. What effect does the extract have on your thoughts and feelings as you read it/see it performed?
3. Explain its importance to the rest of the play.

**King Lear**, Act 1, Scene 2
*(Enter Edmund the bastard)*

<pre>
 1      Thou, nature, art my goddess; to thy law
        My services are bound. Wherefore should I
        Stand in the plague of custom, and permit
        The curiosity of nations to deprive me,
 5      For that I am twelve or fourteen moonshines
        Lag of a brother? Why bastard? wherefore base?
        When my dimensions are as well compact,
        My mind as generous, and my shape as true,
        As honest madam's issue? Why brand they us
10      With base? with baseness? bastardy? base, base?
        Who in the lusty stealth of nature take
        More composition and fierce quality
        Than doth, within a dull, stale, tired bed
        Go to the creating a whole tribe of fops
15      Got 'tween asleep and wake? Well then,
        Legitimate Edgar, I must have your land.
        Our father's love is to the bastard Edmund
        As to the legitimate; fine word, 'legitimate'!
        Well, my legitimate, if this letter speed
</pre>

20    And my invention thrive, Edmund the base
       Shall top the legitimate. I grow; I prosper.
       Now gods, stand up for bastards!

## Focus on and analyse the question

Look at the first question and do a focusing exercise on it.

> **Discuss** the **presentation** of Edmund – **what** he says and **the language** he uses.

Simply:

> **Talk about what Edmund is like in this extract. Look at what he says and the way he says it.**

For 'look at' you should read '*analyse*'.
 Next, look at the second question and do a focusing exercise on that.

> **What effect** does the extract have upon **your thoughts and feelings** as you read it/**see it performed**?

Simply:

> What do you think and how do you feel when you watch it?

You may be wondering why only half of the last part of the question has been addressed; 'read it' has been ignored. There is a very good reason for this. If you are studying drama it is essential to remember that the text you have in your hand is in fact a written script for a piece of live theatre, and as such drama is a unique genre. It has a dimension that neither poetry nor prose has to the same degree. Because certain pieces of drama are texts of such quality they are often studied in written form, but this was never the main intention of the writer. They were written to be performed on a stage, with all the visual and aural richness that drama offers us.

 If you choose to answer the 'read it' part of the question you run the risk of ignoring what are arguably some of the text's most distinctive and fertile elements.

 Now look at the third question and focus on that.

> **Explain** its **importance** to the **rest of** the **play.**

Simply:

> **Why is this extract important to the play?**

The focusing exercise has helped us to concentrate on the baseline instructions. It has cut straight to the heart of the question and told us *simply* what we must do. It is essential that you *keep* referring to the *highlighted* question *frequently as you work on the analysis and the writing of your essay.*

 We shall now:

- Work through the six stages of analysis;
- Look at some of the tools of analysis – the features of the text, that are relevant to the extract;

- Answer the question in note form; and
- Write an essay.

# The six stages of analysis

## Read closely and think

Read the passage *three* times. While *reading* every word carefully you are also *thinking* about the *issues* at work in a text. You want to know what it is 'about', so ask yourself six key questions.

### 1   *What* is happening?

- Edmund *addresses nature* and *swears allegiance* to her and not to human society.
- He then *challenges* society's values and judgements regarding illegitimacy and therefore his place in the world.
- Finally, he *determines to overthrow* his legitimate brother, Edgar.

### 2   To *whom* is it happening?

- It is happening to *Edmund* in that we see him alone on stage, therefore we know that what he says is true and it is here that he swears allegiance to the law of the jungle, that he dedicates himself to nature and refutes society's mores.
- It is also happening to *society*, because Edmund turns his back on it in this scene.
- It is happening to *Edgar*, because Edmund decides to dupe him and take his land. The letter to which Edmund refers is one that he himself has written, as if it were from Edgar, the legitimate son, to their father, Gloucester. In it are Edgar's supposed intentions to overthrow his father and seize his inheritance.
- It is happening to *Gloucester*, because he is about to be deceived.

### 3   *Why* is it happening?

- It is happening *because Edmund is angry* that he is considered to be sub-standard by (Elizabethan) society simply because he is illegitimate. He stands alone (physically on stage and metaphorically) *because he is challenging* Elizabethan concepts of order and position. As an illegitimate child he stands to inherit nothing under the law and he wants to redress the balance by taking the land, and therefore power and status, that rightfully belongs to his legitimate brother, Edgar. Quite simply, *he wants revenge.*

### 4   *When* is it happening?

- It is happening *in three periods simultaneously*, in a sense because the play is set in ancient Britain, but the audience for whom it was written was Elizabethan, and the audience reading/watching it now belongs to the twenty-first century. Therefore, being, like any other text, a product of its time, its appeal is to an audience of the seventeenth century, and indeed it reflects the laws and social attitudes of that time, but we must look at it with twenty-first-century eyes and interpret it with *all three eras in mind*; not an easy task! If we do not do this, we will have lost valuable insights into meaning and a great deal of depth and richness.

- He is *looking both back and forward* because he does not like the way that society has treated him in the past and is going to ensure that he secures more for himself in the future.
- It happens *early in the play*, straight after the end of Act 1, Scene 1, so the audience is informed early about the nature of Edmund and his intentions. It happens early because the rest of the play sees the development and fulfilment of his plans.

## 5    *Where* is it happening?

- It is happening in *ancient Britain*, which gives the play a primitive, primordial, dark feeling. This darkness blends well with the chaos that is created in the minds of an Elizabethan audience who were so preoccupied with notions of order. The abdication of a king who then goes mad, the duping of a good brother, the blinding of an innocent (if a little naïve) father, the banishment of the king's favourite daughter and best friend, and the ruling of Britain by two evil sisters would have instilled considerable fear into those watching these events being acted out on stage. Today's observers would be equally appalled. To an audience deeply concerned about order, the fact that evil would be seen to reign creates a sense of horror.
- It is happening *in the sub-plot* which runs parallel to the main plot. In this play, both plots mirror each other, and comparisons are constantly being drawn between the two. The fact that *both plots* present similar pictures gives the themes universality.

## 6    *How* is it happening?

- It is happening with *anger, bitterness, resentment* and a *desire for revenge*. It happens with a *cold determination* by Edmund to get even with the world, and with his *fervent plea* to a higher power to help him and all the other bastards for whom he stands.
- It happens with a *resolve* that is chilling, and a lack of fear that is frightening.

So, although we have not yet started to examine the language closely, we have gone a long way towards establishing 'the facts' about this extract, and once these are ascertained, we can start a more detailed analysis.

Now read the passage *again* and try to identify the feelings more accurately.

## Summarise the central conflict/s

Start to look for signs of conflict and note these carefully. Ask yourself:

- **What** is the conflict?
- **Who** is involved?

- **Why** is it there?
- **When** is it taking place?
- **Where** is it?
- **How** is it being acted out?

Remember that conflict can be signified by opposites or pairs of words. Now look at the sheet of conflict annotations.

---

*Box 9.1*   **CONFLICT ANNOTATIONS**

Act 1, Scene 2

*(Enter Edmund the bastard)*

*human laws/ natural laws*

*Edmund's inner conflict*

| | | |
|---|---|---|
| 1 | **Edmund** | Thou, nature, art my goddess; To thy law |
| 2 | *Conflict* | My services are bound. Wherefore should I |
| 3 | *between* | Stand in the plague of custom and permit |
| 4 | *what he* | The curiosity of nations to deprive me, |
| 5 | *wants and* | For that I am some twelve or fourteen moonshines |
| 6 | *what he* | Lag of a brother? Why bastard? Wherefore base? |
| 7 | *has* | When my dimensions are as well compact, |
| 8 | | My mind as generous, and my shape as true, |
| 9 | *Edmund/* | As honest madam's issue? Why brand they us |
| 10 | *society* | With base? with baseness? bastardy? base, base? |
| 11 | | Who in the lusty stealth of nature take |
| 12 | *Conflict* | More composition and fierce quality |
| 13 | *between* | Than doth, within a dull, stale, tired bed |
| 14 | *Edmund* | Go to the creating a whole tribe of fops |
| 15 | *and 'fops'* | Got 'tween asleep and wake? Well then, |
| 16 | | Legitimate Edgar, I must have your land. |
| 17 | *legitimate/* | Our father's love is to the bastard Edmund |
| 18 | *illegitimate* | As to the legitimate; fine word, 'legitimate'! |
| 19 | | Well, my legitimate, if this letter speed |
| 20 | | And my invention thrive, Edmund the base |
| 21 | *good/evil* | Shall top the legitimate. I grow; I prosper |
| 22 | *overcome* | Now, gods, stand up for bastards! |
| | *(conflict)* | *(Enter the Duke of Gloucester. Edmund reads a letter)* |

*Society/the individual – interdependence/ independence*

*status quo/desires for the future*

*Contrast – Edmund versus the legitimates*

*split : 'I'/ 'your'*

*Conflict between Edmund and his father*

*past + present/future*

*right/wrong (conflict)*

---

- **What** is the conflict?

The conflict is between:

- legitimacy and illegitimacy;
- Edmund's perception of the status quo/what he wants for the future;
- Edmund's previous acceptance of human society and its laws/his present dedication of himself to nature and her laws;

- good/evil;
- society/the individual; and
- independence/interdependence.

- **Who** is involved?

  - Edmund/society;
  - Edmund/his brother Edgar; and
  - Edmund/his father.

- **Why** is it there?

  - Because it is to do with one of the central themes of the play – families as well as legitimate positions. Cordelia is legitimate and entitled to rule with her sisters, but she is banished and disowned; and
  - Because it creates one of the central conflicts that provide the play with its action and its motivation. This is what moves it towards its resolution.

- **When** is it taking place?

  - It has its roots in the world beyond that of the play but his resolve is very much a here-and-now event. We in fact witness the moment when he commits himself to self-interest and self-gratification. We eavesdrop on this dedication and then follow his fortunes throughout the action of the rest of the play.

- **Where** is it?

  - It is within Edmund;
  - It is between Edmund and his brother;
  - It is between Edmund and his father;
  - It is between Edmund and society;
  - It is between right and wrong;
  - It is between justice and mercy;
  - It is between independence and interdependence;
  - It is between the past and the future;
  - It is between innocence and guile; and
  - It is between human laws and nature's laws.

- **How** is it being acted out?

  - It is being acted out with bitterness, anger, indignation and a spirit of revenge;
  - It being acted out coldly, resolutely; and
  - It is going to be acted out publicly but this preparation for it is very private – he is alone on stage and no one else knows his secret intent.

## Track the themes

If we agree that the central conflicts in this extract are those stated in the previous section, then our job now is to *track* those through the piece. They run like a thread that weaves its way through the fabric of the text. Our task now is to identify those threads. It is similar to detective work; we've found some clues and now we need to take our magnifying glass and follow the trail.

## Conflicts

*Within Edmund*

'Thou, nature, art my goddess; to thy law My services are bound. *Wherefore* should I ...'. Edmund tears himself away from society's rules to swear allegiance to the laws of nature. 'Why?' is *always* a challenging question. Inner turmoil drives him to detach himself from the judgements of human society.

*Between Edmund/Edgar*

The nature of this conflict is quite simply that Edmund is illegitimate and Edgar is legitimate. Notice Edmund's use of the word 'legitimate' throughout the speech.

*Between Edmund/Gloucester*

'Our father's love is to the bastard Edmund/As to the legitimate. Edmund refutes social custom on the grounds of Gloucester's equal love for both his sons, but his manipulation of his father suggests that he merely uses Gloucester to exact revenge.

*Between Edmund/society*

'the plague of custom' reflects Edmund's view of society at that time. Notice the language of sickness and death.

*Between justice/mercy*

'Wherefore should I/Stand in the plague of custom and permit/The curiosity of nations to deprive me,/For that I am twelve or fourteen moonshines/Lag of a brother? Why bastard? wherefore base?' This sees Edmund question the rightness of society's choosing justice over mercy.

*Between right/wrong*

'wherefore base?', 'Why brand they us?' depict a man who challenges society's perceptions of justice. Notice that 'brand' is a word used to refer to the naming or marking of animals or slaves to denote possession by another. It also marks thieves and criminals.

*Between past/future*

'Edmund the base shall top the legitimate' and 'Now, gods, stand up for bastards!' portray a man who is determined that the future will be different from the past.

| | |
|---|---|
| *Between independence/ interdependence* | 'I grow; I prosper' shows us someone focused entirely upon himself. Interdependence with society has got him nowhere; now it's every man for himself – the law of the jungle. |

## Develop the themes elsewhere

### Conflicts

| | |
|---|---|
| *Within Edmund* | Inner turmoil is near the surface as Edmund shares with the audience his refusal to accept his position in the world; '*Why* bastard? *wherefore* base?'. He tries to reason through this with, 'Our father's love is to the bastard Edmund/As to the legitimate.' |
| *Between Edmund/Edgar* | Edmund makes comparisons between himself and his legitimate brother and cannot accept society's discrimination against him. He believes that his mind is 'as generous' and '[his] shape as true,/As honest madam's issue' and he claims 'more composition and fierce quality' from his lusty conception than legitimate children are ever likely to enjoy. |

Looking more closely at Edmund's use of the word 'legitimate' we can see it used in some interesting and revealing ways:

- The word becomes an *adjective* for his brother. He calls him 'Legitimate Edgar'(line 16), not 'brother Edgar'.
- The word becomes a *noun* when he refers to his brother as 'the legitimate' (line 18). He fails to use either his name or his relationship to Edmund; Edgar is neither 'Edgar' nor 'brother'. All that Edmund can see about Edgar is his legitimacy.
- 'Well then,/Legitimate Edgar, I must have your land'. Edmund distances himself from Edgar again by use of *personal pronouns*; 'I'/'your' as he determines to rob Edgar of his birthright.

| | |
|---|---|
| *Between Edmund/society* | 'to thy law/My services are bound', Edmund tells nature. 'Thou', he says, 'art my goddess'. Use of the words, 'law', 'services', 'bound' and 'goddess' suggests a bond. No longer will he tie |

himself to man-made rules; natural law is now his choice.

*Between justice/mercy*

'Now, gods, stand up for bastards!' is an appeal to greater powers to defend the rights of the illegitimate against human society's disregard of them.

*Between past/future*

Now it is Edmund's turn to flourish and he claims the future: 'I grow; I prosper'. The tables are about to turn; things are going to be very different from now on.

*Between independence/ interdependence*

'And my invention thrive, Edmund the base/Shall top the legitimate.' Edmund now replaces the close family bonds that keep society together with self-interest. Rather than interdependence with his brother, Edmund's goal is now to overthrow him. He needs to go it alone to get on. Notice the way in which Edmund not only separates himself from societal values but he allies himself with all other bastards. See the 'Independence/Interdependence' annotations sheet.

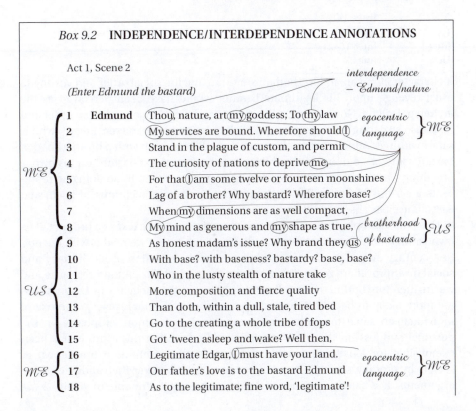

**Box 9.2  INDEPENDENCE/INTERDEPENDENCE ANNOTATIONS**

Act 1, Scene 2

*(Enter Edmund the bastard)*

|  |  |  |
|---|---|---|
| 1 | Edmund | Thou, nature, art my goddess; To thy law |
| 2 | | My services are bound. Wherefore should I |
| 3 | | Stand in the plague of custom, and permit |
| 4 | | The curiosity of nations to deprive me |
| 5 | | For that I am some twelve or fourteen moonshines |
| 6 | | Lag of a brother? Why bastard? Wherefore base? |
| 7 | | When my dimensions are as well compact, |
| 8 | | My mind as generous and my shape as true, |
| 9 | | As honest madam's issue? Why brand they us |
| 10 | | With base? with baseness? bastardy? base, base? |
| 11 | | Who in the lusty stealth of nature take |
| 12 | | More composition and fierce quality |
| 13 | | Than doth, within a dull, stale, tired bed |
| 14 | | Go to the creating a whole tribe of fops |
| 15 | | Got 'tween asleep and wake? Well then, |
| 16 | | Legitimate Edgar, I must have your land. |
| 17 | | Our father's love is to the bastard Edmund |
| 18 | | As to the legitimate; fine word, 'legitimate'! |

$\mathcal{ME} \left\{ \begin{array}{l} 19 \\ 20 \\ 21 \end{array} \right.$
$\mathcal{US} \{ \; 22$

19   Well, (my) legitimate, if this letter speed   *egocentric*   $\left.\right\} \mathcal{ME}$
20   And (my) invention thrive, Edmund the base   *language*
21   Shall top the legitimate. (I) grow; (I) prosper.   *brotherhood*   $\left.\right\} \mathcal{US}$
22   Now, gods, stand up for bastards!   *of bastards*

*(Enter the Duke of Gloucester. Edmund reads a letter)*

Look now at the 'independence/interdependence' annotations, as this theme needs to be developed more fully. We have already noted that Edmund is now driven by self-interest, and the fact that he is physically alone on stage reinforces his isolated position in Elizabethan society. But does he keep himself apart from *all* other people?

**Close reading** of the text will have highlighted Edmund's use of *personal pronouns*. To new students of practical criticism this might seem to be insignificant, but they are one of the most informative types of language used. They may be little but they are powerful indicators of attitude.

Look now at the annotations on independence/interdependence. Notice how Edmund breaks away from family and conventional society, and by so doing makes a bid for independence, but also at times allies himself with other bastards, showing interdependence not between himself and the social order but with those quite outside it. Let us examine the pattern. 'Me' indicates Edmund standing alone, distancing himself from 'acceptable' society and 'Us' suggests the points at which he joins society's other bastards.

| 'Me'/'I' | lines 1–8 |
| 'Us' | lines 8–15 |
| 'Me'/'I' | lines 15–21 |
| 'Us' | line 22 |

A character alone on an Elizabethan stage cursing the social order and vowing to exact revenge upon his legitimate brother would have been perceived as the archetypal villain. Not only is he illegitimate and therefore outside that order, but he is also swearing revenge upon a socially acceptable character (Edgar), who is safely within it. Added to that, this man then allies himself with a brotherhood of bastards and by so doing makes himself more powerful; a bastard on his own is one thing – but uniting with all the others is quite another. By so doing he represents a serious threat to Elizabethan society and its perceptions of itself, and casts himself as absolute villain.

This is an example of times when it is essential to see the text as a product of its own social and historical context, and to remember that we read it with twenty-first-century eyes. Generally, our responses to the question of illegitimacy and social disapproval are *quite different* from the typical Elizabethan response and we are therefore bound to see Edmund in quite a different light – our sympathies are more likely to be with Edmund than with conventional society. The rise of individualism since the Industrial Revolution lays far more emphasis on the personal and less on the social. Some would argue that this attitude has been responsible for loosening familial ties and for the continuing breakdown of society by eroding society's respect for the rules. Whatever the validity of these arguments, it is safe to suppose that Edmund assumes the role of villain *to the audience for whom the play was written, and therefore it was Shakespeare's inten-tion.* We can see two possible responses to Edmund's speech, but we must not allow the twenty-first-century 'layer' of meaning to cloud the writer's intent.

## How does it end?

Notice that the speech ends somewhat menacingly on the 'us' note. Edmund exhorts the gods to 'stand up for bastards' and the speech that has dominated the whole scene closes on the villain invoking supernatural powers to further the cause of the brotherhood of illegitimate children *everywhere*. The suggestion is that there is going to be an army of bastards, empowered by the gods. This sort of imagery would not have endeared Edmund to the Elizabethan audience.

The movement is upward at the end. Notice how, just after the reference to animals and slaves in the word 'brand', there are numerous repetitions of the word 'base' in various forms (line 10) emphasising the *low* status of bastards. From line 19 onwards there is talk of 'letter speed', 'invention thrive', 'top', 'grow', 'pros-per', 'gods' and 'stand up'. There is a distinct feeling of speed, energy and upward movement that whisk us along to the climax, by which time we are prepared for anything. Edmund is poised for action and we can only wait and watch to see exactly how he intends to exact revenge on his brother for his preferential treat-ment by a society that discriminates against bastards.

## Summarise your response

We have followed Edmund through his dedication to nature, his challenging of society's values, his derision of his legitimate brother, his intention to revenge him-self upon Edgar, and his exhortation to the gods to empower him and all other bas-tards in their attempts to correct what he sees as injustice. The issue of the Elizabethan and the twenty-first-century reactions to this character must be borne in mind as we try to formulate our responses to Edmund at this point in the play. The layers of interpretation mentioned before are important considerations in this passage. How are we supposed to feel about him?

What is interesting to note is that this extract takes us along an undulating emotional path with Edmund, and he succeeds in engaging us thoroughly as we are given an insight into his thoughts and feelings. He is alone on stage and there is nothing to distract us as he shares with us, the audience, his awful secret. We must remember that he *is* the villain and as such we should not be too sympath-etic towards him. Some members of a twenty-first-century audience are likely to be more tolerant than Shakespeare ever intended, and it is important to be aware of this in your response.

In Chapter 4, 'Tools of analysis – features of text' deals with numerous features of literary texts which act as vehicles for a writer's meaning. We shall now address our-selves to some of those that have been employed by Shakespeare in this extract. Look at the sheet of language annotations.

Act 1, Scene 2

*direct address to a powerful force* — *tied/united* — *Connotations of dedication, worship and sacrifice*

*(Enter Edmund the bastard)*

*as opposed to human law – defiant*

| | |
|---|---|
| 1  Edmund | Thou, nature, art my goddess; To thy law |
| 2 | My services are bound. Wherefore should I |
| 3 | Stand in the plague of custom, and permit |
| 4 | The curiosity of nations to deprive me, |
| 5 | For that I am some twelve or fourteen moonshines |
| 6 | Lag of a brother? Why bastard? Wherefore base? |
| 7 | When my dimensions are as well compact, |
| 8 | My mind as generous and my shape as true, |
| 9 | As honest madam's issue? Why brand they us |
| 10 | With base? with baseness? bastardy? base, base? |
| 11 | Who in the lusty stealth of nature take |
| 12 | More composition and fierce quality |
| 13 | Than doth, within a dull, stale, tired bed |
| 14 | Go to the creating a whole tribe of fops |
| 15 | Got 'tween asleep and wake? Well then, |
| 16 | Legitimate Edgar, I must have your land. |
| 17 | Our father's love is to the bastard Edmund |
| 18 | As to the legitimate; fine word, 'legitimate'! |
| 19 | Well, my legitimate, if this letter speed |
| 20 | And my invention thrive, Edmund the base |
| 21 | Shall top the legitimate. I grow; I prosper. |
| 22 | Now gods, stand up for bastards! |
| | *(Enter the Duke of Gloucester. Edmund reads a letter)* |

*the deadly nature of convention*

*language of comparison low*

*Comparison*

16 *not 'brother'*
17 *'Edgar'*

22 *not 'my brother' (legitimacy replaces family bond)*

*pun on 'tup' meaning animals mating*

*Challenging language*

*plosive 'b' repetition accumulation*

*Questions-challenge questions – challenge*

*harsh, monosyllabic, determined*

*his illegitimacy is as much a part of him as his name*

*Sarcastic tone*

*Upward movement of the language – tumescent*

## Form and structure

The form is a soliloquy of twenty-two lines without a break, which constitutes the whole scene and represents a significant length of uninterrupted speech with which Edmund can hold the stage. Unrhymed iambic pentameters give the speech a conversational feel. Convention has it that we can believe the soliloquist as he/she is sharing with the audience, and indeed with us, his/her inner thoughts and feelings. Here, then, we have a lengthy, rather natural speech delivered without pausing. This suggests genuineness and a considerable force behind the words. He has much to say to us (ostensibly to himself) and nothing is going to stem his flow. This is from the heart.

## Tone

The tone is aggressive and challenging but at times there is a sense of genuine puzzlement at society's attitude to illegitimacy; 'wherefore' and 'why' reflect both of these attitudes. Towards the end of the speech the tone becomes downright threatening, with Edmund's promise (or threat) to, 'grow' and 'prosper', and by his exhortation to the gods to empower all bastards. By the last line the audience is left wondering just what this villain will do to execute his plan for revenge.

## Imagery

You might have to look hard to find imagery worthy of comment in this speech, but it is there. Let us focus on the words 'base' and 'bastard'. The first means low and it is interesting to note that the second comes from an Old French word 'bast' meaning a pack saddle. If someone was described in Old French as a 'fils de bast' (son of a pack saddle) that meant conceived on horseback as opposed to a bed. The connections between lowness and animals need no explanation and the suggestion is that conception took place 'on the road' and not within a settled relationship.

Beds are also used in the imagery to highlight that the issue of illegitimacy is quite simply a matter of where a child was conceived.

Line 21 contains the word 'top', and we assume from this language that Edmund is keen to redress the balance and allow himself not only to rise from his low place in the world, but also to overthrow his brother. It is most likely that the word 'top' was pronounced 'tup' in the Elizabethan theatre and this word has another meaning. It is the word used to describe a ram mating with a ewe. This imagery throws some light on an interesting theme that runs throughout the play and this speech – that of nature. It also refers to base behaviour, and again to the idea of conception. Add to this the notion of 'being on top' in the sexual act and you have a pool of vivid and animalistic images which all contrive to paint Edmund as a creature concerned with his own power and survival.

It has already been said that Edmund no longer wants to adhere to the laws of human society, and in the first line of this speech he dedicates himself to nature. Once he turns his back on the human-imposed order he is left with the law of the jungle – the survival of the fittest. When he predicts that he will 'top' his legitimate brother he is implicitly referring to 'natural' behaviour, in other words behaviour that has no sanctions. In Freudian terms it is the 'id'; a human being behaving in his/her natural state, without a conscience from within, or social control from outside. It is interesting to note that the word 'natural' was the name given to an illegitimate child in Elizabethan England. This being so, it is almost as if Edmund is playing with the word and deciding to act according to his name.

## Repetition and accumulation

In purely numerical terms, the most frequently repeated words are:

why/wherefore × 4;
legitimate × 4; and
base/bastard × 10.

It is interesting to note that if we string together these key words (and they *are* key because they are there in such numbers) we have the basis of the speech; why legitimate/bastard? Is this not exactly what Edmund is asking? Surely he is saying, 'Why are you discriminating between legitimacy and illegitimacy?' He wants an explanation for the discrimination that he has experienced, just as in the twenty-first century people question discrimination on the grounds of gender, race, religion or any number of issues.

The repetition of the key words quite simply betrays Edmund's preoccupation with the matter. Remember that repeated or accumulated words, either identical or similar, are proof of the *significance* of that subject to the speaker. Is it not just the same in everyday human speech?

## Word order

Although not exclusively in this position, it is interesting to see that at times the key words appear at the end of lines:

Line 6   – base;
Line 10 – base;
Line 18 – legitimate;
Line 20 – base; and
Line 22 – bastards.

You will remember from 'Tools of analysis – features of text' that this is one of the most significant positions in a text and therefore such a location emphasises the meaning.

## Unusual juxtapositions and binary opposites

The very fact that the speech contains so many references to 'legitimate' and 'bastard' is central to its meaning, and the frequent use of these two opposite terms serves to highlight the nature of the conflict.

## First person soliloquy

Although ostensibly Edmund is talking to nature, then to himself and finally to the gods, there seems to be a desire on Shakespeare's part to establish this character quite firmly in the audience's mind as a villain and therefore it bears the signs of a public soliloquy; in other words, he is speaking to us, the audience.

Edmund is using the device to share quite openly with us the thoughts and feelings that are to motivate his actions throughout the rest of the play, but because it is the villain who is doing this, it creates an uncomfortable feeling among the audience to have him share them with us. We would rather not know his wicked intentions; his confiding in an Elizabethan audience might have made them wonder if perhaps they could be thought of as colluding with the villain. We don't really want to hear it.

Edmund discloses all to the audience in this speech and in so doing sets up much of the dramatic irony for the rest of the play. The first example of this is at the end of this speech, when Gloucester enters and Edmund reads the false letter that is the illegitimate son's first step along the path to revenge.

vengance?
not ve?

## Punctuation

Lack of an end stop at many line ends in this speech suggests a full and free sharing with the audience. What is interesting to note is that in some versions of the text there are quotation marks around the terms to do with the central issue that Edmund uses, such as 'bastard', 'base', 'baseness', 'bastardy' and 'legitimate'. What effect do you think they could have on the speech? Think about normal human speech. What happens when we quote or use a word as if we are actually quoting? We *slow down* our speech *just before the word*. Why? To *emphasise* its use and to highlight the fact that *it is not our word but someone else's*. Try this yourself or listen carefully next time someone else quotes another source.

Edmund very much *needs* to emphasise these words; they are the basis of his speech. He also wants to explain to the audience that these are *not his terms but society's because they are not his values but society's*. It is as if he is borrowing the words but they are not part of *his* language because he makes no such distinctions.

Notice in line 10 how fractured and broken the verse feels. The punctuation creates several breaks in the line, either by a question mark or a comma, and it is appropriate that the word 'base' in all its forms should be at the heart of a line that conveys Edmund's strong emotions and the reasons for them.

## Caesura

There is a telling pause in the middle of line 18 that enables 'legitimate' to appear *twice* in one line, once in the middle and once at the end. The semi-colon mid-line allows Edmund to end both the sentence and the line with that same key word. Ends of sentences and ends of lines are both significant places, so the concept of illegitimacy is given *two* prime sites in *one* line of verse.

# Answering the question in note form

We need to look again at the questions we explored at the beginning of the chapter:

1. Discuss the presentation of Edmund – what he says and the language he uses.
2. What effect does the extract have on your thoughts and feelings as you read it/see it performed?
3. Explain its importance to the rest of the play.

Look back at that section now to remind yourself of the way the questions were focused on and simplified.

## Answer to Question I in note form

### What he says

Edmund swears allegiance to nature and turns his back on the laws of human society ('*Thou*, nature, art my goddess; to *thy* law/My services are bound').

Questions society's discrimination against him on grounds of his illegitimacy ('*Why* bastard? wherefore base?'). Compares himself favourably with many legitimate children who lack his fire ('. . . Who in the lusty stealth of nature take/More composition and fierce quality/Than doth, within a dull, stale, tired bed/Go to the creating a whole tribe of fops'), and swears revenge on his legitimate brother ('Legitimate Edgar, I must have your land') invoking the power of the gods to help him further the cause of all bastards everywhere ('Now, gods, stand up for bastards!').

## How he says it

- He says it with **conviction**; he is unequivocal ('Thou, nature, art my goddess; to thy law/My services are bound'). There is little doubt as to where his allegiance lies.
- He says it **legalistically**, with an awareness of an agreement or a contract: 'law', 'services' and 'bound'.
- He says it **challengingly** ('Wherefore should I stand in the plague of custom'). The question why is *always* one of challenge.
- He says it **cynically**; 'the plague of custom' shows that he sees the rules of society in terms of disease and death to bastards like himself.
- He is **fierce**; he refers to the 'fierce quality' that illegitimate children possess.
- He is **bitter**; 'Well then,/Legitimate Edgar' highlights the legitimacy issue and replaces the term 'brother'.
- He is **sarcastic**; 'fine word, 'legitimate' shows his disdain at the high status enjoyed by Edgar simply because of his birth.
- He is **coldly determined**; 'I must have your land'.
- He is **hell-bent on revenge**; 'I grow; I prosper'.
- He is **bold** enough to invoke the power of the supernatural to help him to further his cause; 'Now, gods, stand up for bastards!'.
- He **addresses nature directly**: 'Thou, nature . . .'.
- He **declares his devotion** to nature his 'goddess'.
- He uses **egocentric language**: 'My', 'I' and 'me' (independence).
- He **allies himself to all other bastards**; the 'I'/'us' distinction (interdependence, not with conventional human society but with others like himself.
- He uses **sexual imagery**; 'thrive', 'grow', 'prosper' and 'stand up' could all be read as tumescent language, referring to swelling in response to sexual stimulation, and links to the idea of 'tup' and 'base', and to conception generally.
- He speaks **emphatically** by using repetition and accumulation: 'base', with 'baseness, bastardy, – base, base'.
- He speaks **explosively and in a sinister way**. Notice the plosive 'b' and the hissing 's' in the word 'base' in its various forms.
- He speaks **threateningly**. The 'I grow; I prosper' is an overt threat to society and to the audience.

Let us now look at Question 2, focused:

> **What** is the **effect** of the extract on **your thoughts and feelings** as you read it/ see it performed?

## Answer to Question 2 in note form

- We cannot fail to be **impressed** by the sheer power of Edmund in this speech. That is not to say that we necessarily think he is admirable; 'impressed' is used in its more literal sense here, meaning that he makes his mark. His direct address to nature shows us that he is a man who is not afraid to petition face to face, as it were, what Elizabethans saw as the ultimate power. This tells us that Edmund is going to be a force to be reckoned with. He is not going to be fobbed off and he is not afraid to fight for what he thinks should rightfully be his.

- A twenty-first-century audience might feel **sympathy** for him here when he questions why he should 'stand in the plague of custom and permit/The curiosity [meaning conventions] of nations to deprive' him of what he feels he is owed. Remember the discussion about 'layers' of interpretation, and distinguish between a contemporary response and an Elizabethan one.

- An Elizabethan audience would have been **horrified** by Edmund's attitude, and he would have been seen quite unequivocally as a villain.

- For this reason we might feel **ambivalent** towards him. The twenty-first-century response may well provoke sympathy for his situation, but can we truly condone such ruthless intentions on an innocent brother? The Elizabethan response condemns him more readily and completely.

- We must be **concerned** about his declaration in this scene. Edmund is on the way up and his cold determination is **frightening**.

- Our **sense of right and wrong is affronted** *if* we are not too sympathetic towards him. He is planning to destroy an innocent brother whose only crime is to be the legitimate son of Gloucester. This cannot be right and we now have to **prepare ourselves for the moral battle between the forces of good and evil** that will work themselves out on the stage before our eyes. We see conflict ahead and we must now wait to see it resolved.

- The speech creates a **feeling of expectation and tension**. We ask ourselves, 'Who will win?' and 'What will be the costs?'

- We are **in awe** of him at the end of the speech. He stands alone on stage and in the world, facing the multitude, invoking the powers of the gods and allying himself to the brotherhood of bastards. We *know* this is a **dangerous and deadly man**, and that this is just the beginning.

- We also **know that this course of action cannot be right**, whatever the reason and we cannot help but **anticipate his downfall**.

- We are also **anxious** for Edgar's safety. Edmund is a **ruthless** man, **determined to have his way**.

Let us look now at Question 3: **Explain** its **importance** to the **rest** of the **play**.

The examiners are looking for evidence of your having seen the **patterns** that emerge in the extract. They want to see that you can analyse it in detail as a piece of literature in its own right, yet view it as an integral part of a greater whole and be able to say which marks it bears of that totality.

This question can be answered by using the following list of points:

## Plot

What does it do for the plot? How does it develop it? It is never enough merely to say that any extract develops the plot; you must say precisely *how* this is achieved. How does this extract handle any possible interplay between a main and a sub-plot?

## Character

Does the key character develop or change in any way in this extract, or does the text at this point merely serve to reinforce what we already know about him? How?

## Framing/flanking

Look at the extract in context. What is on either side of it? What does it help to frame? Is there evidence of symmetry? In other words, are there two similar extracts which sit on either side of one that is quite different?

## Mirroring/echoing

Does this extract mirror or echo any previous parts of the text in terms of events/ language/behaviour and so on?

## Foreshadowing/presaging

Does this passage foreshadow any future events/language/behaviour and so on?

## Contrast

Does the extract contrast significantly with any others? What contrasts are there within the passage?

## Fulcrum/turning point

Is this extract a turning point in the text as a whole?

## Themes

Which themes dealt with in the text are also referred to in this passage?

Once again, do not use this list in such a way that you approach the passage coldly and *too* methodically. It is intended to be merely a prompt for you to keep in the back of your mind.

## Answer to Question 3 in note form

### Plot

- Very important as this scene discloses precisely where Edmund stands in relation to society, and what are his aims.
- Establishes the plot. We now know what his objectives are and how he hopes to meet them.

- Establishes some of the essential conflict that will be resolved through development of the plot.
- Interplay of plot/sub-plot. The sub-plot in this extract echoes the main plot with Lear and his three daughters in that the innocent child is badly treated and the treacherous ones seem to thrive. Both plots have fathers who are foolish and easily duped and do not know their own children, or indeed themselves. As the play develops, the closeness of the two plots becomes ever more apparent.

## Character

- Sudden and dramatic character development. Until now Edmund was just Gloucester's son and the butt of his father's insensitive jokes about his being a bastard.
- How? By being in soliloquy. His innermost thoughts and feelings are revealed.

## Framing/flanking

- The extract follows a scene in which the king abdicates and banishes a daughter who truly loves him because he is stupid enough to fall for the lies of two daughters who do not. In this extract we see Edmund about to seriously mistreat an innocent brother.
- The extract is followed by the entrance of Edmund's father, who is about to be caught up in his bastard son's foul plan for his legitimate brother. Dramatic irony when Gloucester enters after Edmund finishes speaking in Act 1, Scene 2.

## Mirroring/echoing

- The speech by Edmund is mirrored later in Act 2, Scene 3, when Edgar occupies the stage alone for one whole scene and shares with the audience both his plight and his intentions.

## Foreshadowing/presaging

- Contrary to Edmund's intentions it does *not* foreshadow future events as Edmund would like to see them develop, and for this reason his words in Act 2, Scene 1 create dramatic irony instead, because quite the reverse occurs and Edgar 'tops' Edmund by killing him.

## Contrast

- The speech opens with Edmund's references to himself (singular) and his plight as an illegitimate son. He speaks of 'my', 'I' and 'me'. This contrasts sharply with the move to 'us' (plural) in line 9, referring to all bastards, and then back again to 'I' in line 16.
- He explains his own position in society, allies himself with the forces of all illegitimate children and finally states unequivocally what he himself intends to do to address the injustice he perceives. Can you see the way in which the theme of independence/interdependence is handled here?
- Note also the contrast between 'base'/'legitimate', 'base'/'thrive' and 'base'/ 'grow' and 'prosper'.

## Fulcrum/turning point

- Although the extract does not represent a turning point it *is* central to the play because it establishes vital developments in the sub-plot which are reflected in the main plot.

## Themes

- The themes of family ties, disloyalty, self-interest, nature, independence/interdependence and order all appear in the passage.

We now have more than enough for an essay, a sample version of which follows.

# Sample essay – *King Lear*

This essay is longer and more detailed than anything that you would be expected to produce in one hour in an examination. However, it is an example of a well-developed and clearly expressed discussion that demonstrates the ability to focus closely on the smallest textual detail while also identifying major twists and developments in the movement of the text. It also deals fully with the points raised in the criticism section you have just read, and for all these reasons it has been included in its present form.

Bear in mind as you read it that you can only deal realistically with a handful of points in an examination essay. It might be a useful exercise for you to identify from this sample essay five or so issues that *you* think are the most significant.

## *King Lear,* Act 1, Scene 2

In this soliloquy Edmund has the stage to himself and the opportunity to express honestly to the audience his thoughts, feelings and plans. In this way we are given an insight into the workings of a devious and fascinating mind in a speech which sets up many of the play's themes, triggers much of the action and is later mirrored by Edgar's soliloquy in Act 2, Scene 3.

Edmund's opening sentence is curt and striking, thereby immediately attracting the audience's attention and highlighting one of the key issues in the soliloquy. Here is a man who is switching allegiances, challenging human laws and setting himself apart from others. Standing alone on stage, 'the bastard Edmund' makes a direct address to nature, evoking a powerful force and at the same time allying himself with that power. 'Thou, nature, art my goddess', he declares with conviction. The image before the audience is one of solitude, as Edmund turns his back on the laws of human society. The repetition in this first line of 'thou' and 'thy', sandwiching the reference to himself with 'my', acts to separate him from the rest of society, and he reinforces this with the language of a binding legal contract: 'To thy law my services are bound'.

The explanation for this decision to break with society comes in the form of a challenge, which is enhanced throughout the soliloquy in the repeated use of the words 'why' and 'wherefore': 'Why bastard?' 'wherefore base', 'Why brand they us'. Edmund asks, 'Wherefore should I/Stand in the plague of custom', and the rules of society are thereby given the qualities of a killer disease – undesirable and something that must be fought in order to survive. This essential conflict between Edmund and society is further developed as he challenges 'The curiosity of nations' which sets him apart from the majority and 'deprive[s]' him of what he sees as his rightful inheritance. He attacks the reasoning behind such judgement, since he believes himself to be as much a human being as 'honest madam's issue'.

It is at this point (line 9) that he ceases to be a solitary, independent figure and connects himself to a whole brotherhood of dispossessed, illegitimate children with the challenge, 'Why brand they us...'. Indeed, the sentence structure is such that 'us' receives emphasis from its position at the end of the line as well as from the fact that it appears next to 'they', once again highlighting the 'them and us' conflict. Similarly, the full stop in the middle of the line adds emphasis to the two sides of the balance, where it acts as a pivot between 'honest madam's issue' and 'brand[ed] us'. At the same time the 'why' draws attention to the nature of Edmund's challenge.

The focus of the soliloquy thus shifts from Edmund's personal situation to the broader issue of illegitimacy and society's perception of it. Once he identifies with a group, he draws strength from numbers and turns around the general movement of the speech. From his concentration on the low social position of the 'bastard' who is 'base' and 'Stand[s] in the plague of custom', Edmund argues that they are not only equal to 'honest madam's issue' but in fact in someway superior to it, because in their conception there was a great deal more 'lusty stealth' and a certain 'fierce quality'. This would seem to apply to both the original lovemaking and its illegitimate issue, in comparison with the 'dull, stale, tired' process involved in 'creating a whole tribe of [legitimate] fops'.

It is significant that even in his description of his very conception, Edmund refers to 'nature', alluding to his recent devotion to her laws and also to the Elizabethan description of illegitimate children as 'natural', in other words not in accordance with human laws.

The realisation that he need not remain alone and down at heel results in a determination to take control of his destiny and wreak revenge on 'Legitimate Edgar'. Indeed, this very term reveals that Edmund's position as illegitimate and his alliance with others in his situation has created a certain interdependence with the brotherhood of bastards that was formerly a characteristic of his relationships with his family. So 'brother' Edgar becomes 'Legitimate Edgar'. Once again, Edmund employs egocentric language while explaining just how he is going to have his way. 'I must have your land' is a clear, stark statement that highlights the gap between the brothers – 'I' and 'your' – and reveals Edmund's cold determination to serve his own ends. This self-centred commitment to revenge is similarly reflected in his triumphant call, 'Edmund the base/Shall top the legitimate'. Here we see all relations collapse into outright conflict between 'legitimate' and 'illegitimate', and the 'base', with its connotations of lowliness, turns the world of the play on its head as he rises to the 'top' and declares his passionate and chilling prophecy, 'I grow; I prosper'.

As if he has not risen enough in terms of imagery and aspiration, Edmund closes his soliloquy with an appeal to the 'gods', [to] 'stand up for bastards!' This takes us back to the opening line, as his first direct address to the supernatural sees him dedicating himself in 'service' to a greater power. Twenty-two lines later Edmund really has grown and prospered, as he demands of the gods that they defend him and all those like him. He is no longer weak and alone.

This change in position driven by his own determination can be traced in Edmund's changing use of the terms 'base' and 'bastard'. The fact that these words appear in ten lines out of twenty-two shows how essential they are to the piece. The movement is from 'bastard' and 'base' as 'plague[s] of custom' which serve only to deprive, to 'baseness, bastardy, base, base' as a drive to anger itself expressed through the tightly packed repetition of the key words with their plosive 'b' sound and fragmenting punctuation in line 10, and finally to Edmund's acceptance of 'bastards' as a call to arms and a source of strength.

It is the sheer power of this speech that impresses the audience as they behold a man standing alone, unafraid to renounce a whole society and appeal to other, marginalised individuals as well as to the gods themselves for support. It is important to consider that audiences of Shakespeare's contemporaries may have responded differently from the way in which a modern audience would.

Nature, for the Elizabethans, was the ultimate power, and social solidarity an unchallenged inevitability. The whole was far more important than the individual and it was guarded by strict moral codes and expectations. Edmund's renouncing of the glue that held society together, his appeal to the ultimate power, and his alliance with other bastards would have fixed him firmly in the role of villain and horrified an Elizabethan audience. A twenty-first-century audience may be less ready with complete condemnation. The ambivalence of our emotional response shows changes in the position of the illegitimate child and an increased awareness of social injustice, human rights and the rights of the individual. For this reason we may feel sympathy and perhaps an element of support for someone fighting for equal rights for themselves and for other members of a minority of which they are a part. Despite these differences in stance, however, neither audience can condone Edmund's vicious intent to destroy his innocent brother, whose sole crime is his legitimacy. As has already been seen, the speech gains momentum, power, direction and determination, until lines 20–22 culminate in a declaration that instils fear and tension in the audience. Edmund sounds a warning that 'the base/Shall top the legitimate'.

At the same time as reflecting Edmund's ruthlessness, these lines state clearly his intention, bringing observers into collusion with a person we have already classed as a villain. This is unnerving to the audience and we begin to feel uncomfortable with being 'part' of the plan. Thus we are drawn into the moral battle between good and evil as we watch it unfold, and the sense of expectation and tension is thereby increased. Being taken into Edmund's confidence through soliloquy means that we suddenly know more about him and his thought processes and plans than we do about others on stage. We also know more about him than do the characters around him. He moves from being the butt of insensitive jokes to being a prime mover in the play.

So, just as it establishes an essential conflict to be resolved through development of the plot, so irony is also set up in this soliloquy. The first instance of this is immediately after Edmund's speech, when his father enters the scene bemoaning the chaos of the court and is clearly about to be duped. This, of course, only worsens the sense of disorder.

Just as Edmund's speech is preceded by a revelation of Lear's stupidity as he falls for the lies of his evil daughters and banishes the one who 'legitimately' deserves not only his land, but his love, so it is followed by a scene of similar naïvety as Gloucester falls into his evil son's trap and banishes the one who truly loves him. In this way we see sub-plot and main plot reflect one another, and this soliloquy functions clearly to raise common themes of family ties, disloyalty, self-interest, nature, independence/interdependence and order. A vital extract therefore in the development of plot, character and themes, this soliloquy serves as an intense concentration of much of what Shakespeare is discussing in *King Lear*, as well as functioning structurally to help to craft what is, arguably, Shakespeare's greatest work.

# ◧ ⊠ 10  Practical criticism of modern drama

## Practical criticism of modern drama – *Waiting for Godot*

What do you find interesting about this extract from *Waiting for Godot* by Samuel Beckett?

| | |
|---|---|
| *He spits.* | *Estragon moves to centre, halts with his back to auditorium.* |
| Estragon | Charming spot. (*He turns, advances to front, halts facing the auditorium.*) Inspiring prospects. (*He turns to Vladimir.*) Let's go. |
| Vladimir | We can't. |
| Estragon | Why not? |
| Vladimir | We're waiting for Godot. |
| Estragon | (*despairingly*). Ah! (*Pause.*) You're sure it was here? |
| Vladimir | What? |
| Estragon | That we were to wait. |
| Vladimir | He said by the tree. (*They look at the tree.*) Do you see any others? |
| Estragon | What is it? |
| Vladimir | I don't know. A willow. |
| Estragon | Where are the leaves? |
| Vladimir | It must be dead. |
| Estragon | No more weeping. |
| Vladimir | Or perhaps it's not the season. |
| Estragon | Looks to me more like a bush. |
| Vladimir | A shrub. |
| Estragon | A bush. |
| Vladimir | A –. What are you insinuating? That we've come to the wrong place? |
| Estragon | He should be here. |
| Vladimir | He didn't say for sure he'd come. |
| Estragon | And if he doesn't come? |
| Vladimir | We'll come back tomorrow. |
| Estragon | And then the day after tomorrow. |
| Vladimir | Possibly. |
| Estragon | And so on. |
| Vladimir | The point is – |
| Estragon | Until he comes. |

| | |
|---|---|
| *Vladimir* | You're merciless. |
| *Estragon* | We came here yesterday. |
| *Vladimir* | Ah no, there you're mistaken. |
| *Estragon* | What did we do yesterday? |
| *Vladimir* | What did we do yesterday? |
| *Estragon* | Yes. |
| *Vladimir* | Why... (*Angrily*). Nothing is certain when you're about. |
| *Estragon* | In my opinion we were here. |
| *Vladimir* | (*looking round*). You recognise the place? |
| *Estragon* | I didn't say that. |
| *Vladimir* | Well? |
| *Estragon* | That makes no difference. |
| *Vladimir* | All the same...that tree... (*turning towards the auditorium*) ...that bog. |

The first thing to do is to focus on the key words of the question: 'What do **you find interesting** about this extract from *Waiting for Godot* by Samuel Beckett?'

This type of task is highly personal and it allows you to focus on whatever features of the passage *you* find interesting. This question is, in many senses, a gift, but its lack of structure can be a pitfall for some students. You need to think clearly *before* you start to write, about the features upon which you intend to focus and make a definite, if brief, essay plan, otherwise you may find yourself rambling and drifting. If the question lacks structure, as this one does, you need to make some of your own so that your response shows a clear sense of purpose and direction.

## Read closely and think

As usual, the first step is to read the extract carefully and to think about its meaning. This is not an easy task with drama of this kind; we have to work hard to help to create meaning, and working with only a short extract from a play makes it harder. Do not be discouraged if you find this excerpt difficult to understand; this is all part of the process and you will not be alone. Try to *summarise* its most obvious and straightforward meaning in a brief overview of the passage – no more than one short paragraph.

As usual, it may help you to ask yourself the basic comprehension-type questions:

- **What** is happening? Two male characters are unable to go anywhere; they are waiting for Godot.
- To **whom** is it happening? It is happening to Vladimir and Estragon.
- **Why** is it happening? They are waiting because they hope that Godot will come, and this is important to them.
- **When** is it happening? As it is live drama, it is happening *now*.
- **Where** is it happening? It is happening on a stage that is bare except for a what is possibly a dead tree.
- **How** is it happening? It is happening with feelings of uncertainty and tension.

These are very basic answers at this stage, but from these you should be able to write something that will act as a foundation from which to work.

Perhaps you have something along the lines of, 'The extract deals with two characters who are "waiting for Godot". They are stuck where they are and *cannot* leave because their purpose is to wait. A strong sense of uncertainty pervades the passage – the state and nature of the tree that is on stage, the location for the proposed meeting with Godot, and even what they did yesterday – doubt abounds. They are locked into a situation and seem to make no progress. Everything is questionable.'

This is *not* a definitive summary and you may have expressed these ideas quite differently, but all that matters is that you have identified the key issues at work in the extract right at the start of your discussion. This is helpful because:

- It gives you *and* the examiner a sense of direction for the essay that is to follow;
- It provides you with a solid framework on which to build the rest of your argument; and
- It keeps you focused on the meaning so that you are less likely to stray from this as your discussion develops.

## Summarise the central conflict/s

Because of the nature of modern literature, many of the features of traditional drama, with which we are so familiar, are missing. We tend to look for plot and progress on the stage; we expect action – we feel that something is going to *happen*. This is not necessarily the case with some modern dramas, and it is certainly not a feature of this play. There is much more emphasis on 'the moment', the situation, and the movement in the piece can feel more circular than linear. Sometimes it seems that the characters do not in fact get anywhere, and that nothing really 'happens'. Look carefully at this issue of action versus inaction, for it is here that the most significant conflict lies. With this extract it might also be fruitful to examine the use of *questions* in an effort to identify the central conflict/s. Think about the way in which they are used by both characters. Remember that questions can signify doubt or challenge.

Ask yourself the basic questions as in the section entitled 'read closely and think'.

### What?

Look at the passage again and try to identify the key areas of conflict by focusing on simple opposites. Do this now and *then* compare your list with this one:

- action/inaction;
- right place/wrong place;
- don't know/do know;
- tree/bush/shrub;
- Godot will come/Godot will not come;
- should keep coming back/should not keep coming back;

- came here yesterday/did not come here yesterday;
- recognise the place/do not recognise the place; and
- Vladimir/Estragon.

Now look at the Conflict Annotations sheet to see where these areas of conflict lie.

---

### Box 10.1   CONFLICT ANNOTATIONS

*He spits.* *Estragon moves to centre, halts with his back to auditorium.*

Estragon: Charming spot. (*He turns, advances to front, halts facing the auditorium.*)

Inspiring prospects. (*He turns to Vladimir.*) Let's go. — *action/inaction*

Vladimir: We can't.

Estragon: Why not?

*challenge*
Vladimir: We're waiting for Godot.

Estragon: (*despairingly*). Ah! (*Pause.*) You're sure it was here?

Vladimir: What?

Estragon: That we were to wait.

Vladimir: He said by the tree. (*They look at the tree.*) Do you see any others? — *right place/wrong place*

Estragon: What is it?

*don't know/do know*
Vladimir: I don't know. A willow.

Estragon: Where are the leaves?

Vladimir: It must be dead.

*tree/*
Estragon: No more weeping.

*bush/*
Vladimir: Or perhaps it's not the season.

Estragon: Looks to me more like a bush.

*shrub*
Vladimir: A shrub.

Estragon: A bush.

Vladimir: A – What are you insinuating? That we've come to the wrong place?

*Godot will come/*
Estragon: He should be here.

Vladimir: He didn't say for sure he'd come.

*Godot will not come*
Estragon: And if he doesn't come?

Vladimir: We'll come back tomorrow.

Estragon: And then the day after tomorrow.

Vladimir: Possibly.

Estragon: And so on.

*should keep coming back/*
Vladimir: The point is –

Estragon: Until he comes.

*should not keep coming back*
Vladimir: You're merciless.

Estragon: We came here yesterday. — *came here yesterday/did not came here yesterday*

Vladimir: Ah no, there you're mistaken.

Estragon: What did we do yesterday?

| | Vladimir: | What did we do yesterday? |
| | Estragon: | Yes. |
| | Vladimir: | Why ... (*Angrily*). Nothing is certain when you're about. |
| | Estragon: | In my opinion we were here. |
| *recognise* | Vladimir: | (*looking round*). You recognise the place? |
| *the place/* | Estragon: | I didn't say that. |
| *do not* | Vladimir: | Well? |
| *recognise* | Estragon: | That makes no difference. |
| *the place* | Vladimir: | All the same ... that tree ... (*turning towards the auditorium*) ... that bog. |

*(marginal annotation: Vladimir/Estragon)*

Now try to answer the rest of the questions on this subject of conflict/s: **Who? Why? When? Where? How?**

You should by now have thought carefully enough about the content of the passage and the nature of the conflict/s to be able to move to the next stage of the process. It is important *not* to skimp on this exercise. Unless you have done this *thoroughly*, your foundation will *not* be firm enough for you to move on in your analysis. However, once you have progressed carefully through **read closely and think** and **summarise the central conflict/s** you are ready to explore the ways in which these concepts are developed.

## Track the themes

- **action/inaction**

Estragon says, 'Let's go'; he wants action. Vladimir replies, 'We can't'; action is denied. Estragon challenges this inaction with the question, 'Why not?' and is told that they must wait. Can you feel the tension between these two stances?

- **right place/wrong place**

Estragon questions the location for the meeting with Godot – 'You're sure it was here?' Vladimir states confidently, 'He said by the tree. Do you see any others?' and later, 'What are you insinuating? That we've come to the wrong place?' Conflict and doubt exist over the issue of whether this is the right place to meet Godot.

- **don't know/do know**

Notice that Vladimir says that he does not know what type of tree it is, and then immediately states that it is a willow. He is uncertain whether he knows or not.

- **tree/bush/shrub**

The question of whether or not it is a tree at all is then raised and they argue as to whether it is in fact not a tree at all but a bush or a shrub. Their immediate environment (and the only other thing on stage apart from themselves) is clouded with doubt.

- **Godot will come/Godot will not come**

Estragon asserts, 'He should be here' but Vladimir counters this with, 'He didn't say for sure he'd come'. They are waiting for someone or something but are not sure whether he or it will turn up; the future is uncertain.

- **should keep coming back/should not keep coming back**

The interchange about their returning to the spot to meet Godot increases in pace, until Vladimir suddenly turns on Estragon and accuses him of being 'merciless'. This sting adds to the conflict.

- **came here yesterday/did not come here yesterday**

Estragon says positively, 'We came here yesterday' but Vladimir counters this with, 'Ah no, there you're mistaken'. Even their past is uncertain.

- **recognise the place/do not recognise the place**

Estragon declares to Vladimir that '[they] were here'. When Vladimir then assumes that he 'recognise[s] the place', Estragon points out sharply, 'I didn't say that'. It seems that nothing can be taken for granted.

- **Vladimir/Estragon**

There is a constant tension between the couple that seems to coexist with the familiarity. Alongside the intimacy of the interlaced dialogue is a conflict that reminds us of that between a married couple. Vladimir tells Estragon that he is 'merciless' and then says '*angrily*', 'Nothing is certain when you're about'. Estragon replies irritably to Vladimir's 'You recognise the place?' with a pedantic, 'I didn't say that'.

I hope you will have noticed that very little has actually *happened* in this extract. What has been established clearly, however, is the uncertainty that exists in the world of this play. We can be sure of nothing and neither can the two characters on stage. *We must not be tempted into speculating about what happens or does not happen in the rest of the play.* All we can deal with is what is before us, and that is uncertainty.

## Develop the themes elsewhere

Let us remind ourselves of the situation so far. The two men are unable to go anywhere because they are waiting for Godot. They do not know if they are in the right place. They are not sure about the type of tree they are near, nor if it is a tree at all, or a bush or a shrub. Godot's arrival is debatable, as is the wisdom of their continually returning to the spot to meet him. They are not sure if they came here yesterday, or whether they even recognise the place.

We have searched for the conflict and what we have found is that we, the audience, and Vladimir and Estragon can be sure of nothing. What can we make of this? All we know is that we know very little. Our analysis of the conflict in the extract has brought us to an overwhelming sense of uncertainty and this is central to the meaning of the play. We have very little to work on and this is part of the challenge with which this type of pared-down drama presents us.

It is stark; all we have is the interaction between two people, and it is their interaction and their situation that strikes the audience so forcefully. It is stripped down; there is no scenery except for one dead tree. It is bleak and smacks of T. S. Eliot's *The Waste Land*; even the tree, frequently a symbol of life in literature, in this play is dead at this point. The place is nowhere that we recognise; it has no name, therefore it is *anywhere* and, by extension, *everywhere*. The people are not defined in any way other than by their names. They are not princes, noblemen or bastards, but merely ordinary people like you and me, therefore they are *anybody* and, by extension, *everybody*. There is a twentieth-century universality about these lines, and therefore a suggestion that we are in fact looking at ourselves when we watch Estragon and Vladimir. We know that *they* are looking at *us*, because Estragon '*halts facing auditorium*', addressing us with, 'Inspiring prospects' and, at the end of the extract, Vladimir '*turning towards the auditorium*' says, ' . . . that bog'. So, *they* are looking at *us*, *we* are looking at *them*, but *we* are also looking at *ourselves*. Note the circular quality referred to above in summarising the central conflict.

The extract is taken from early in the play and perhaps by now you are beginning to feel that this drama operates on more than one level. Maybe you have seen that it could be a metaphor for the nature of human life. What is disconcerting is that we don't really know what's going on. What does it all mean? It is clearly not a revenge play, nor a murder mystery, so what *is* it? *We*, along with Vladimir and Estragon, are waiting for Godot – but who or what is Godot? The similarity to 'God' is unlikely to be coincidental, so we assume that it is God or something that will take the place of God – a mythical person whose coming is expected to affect the world? Whatever or whoever Godot is, his exact nature is less important than the waiting, for this is the subject of the play, indeed it is its title. Waiting is, after all, a significant part of the human condition; we all wait for something in life – for a person, an event, death.

The passage is about action versus inaction. Estragon begins the extract with his words of action, 'Let's go', but he is prevented from going by Vladimir, who advises him, 'We can't . . . We're waiting for Godot.' The waiting thus becomes their purpose; their action is *in*action. It is in waiting that we experience most keenly the movement of time. Activity makes time pass (us by); waiting allows us to feel it as it goes. To experience time is to experience change, and yet this sets up a curious paradox in this passage because nothing actually happens, therefore nothing changes.

Further uncertainty is raised, this time about where to find Godot. Estragon asks, 'You're sure it was here? . . . That we were to wait'. Their search is utterly futile if they are waiting for him in the wrong place. When Vladimir cites the tree as the place, Estragon does not even recognise it as a tree. The appointed meeting place is now in doubt. After further debate, which reveals their anxiety to meet Godot, Vladimir then declares that, 'He didn't say for sure he'd come'. If meeting Godot is the object of Vladimir and Estragon's desire, then this seems sadly to be beyond their grasp; they are waiting in what is possibly the wrong place, for someone who may not even turn up. Their hope of meeting Godot is continually deferred, and this persistent advance and repudiation – this cycle of hope and despair – locks them into a wheel of suffering.

At this point, when the more faint-hearted among us might have given up, Vladimir determines that, 'We'll come back tomorrow'. Both men decide to persevere, until Vladimir tells Estragon that he is 'merciless'. However, surely this is the logic of waiting; it *is* remorseless. Both men live in hope; the coming of Godot will signify the end of their waiting.

We have two men waiting for God/ot. Could this be a religious play, or a play that is laden with religious significance – two people, a tree and God/ot? However, while it is possible to see here an allusion to the Garden of Eden, we must also remember that this tree looks dead, and there is a certain sterility and lack of meaning conveyed by this fact because trees are supposed to represent life. If Godot does represent a God-like being, the outlook is bleak. Repeated emphasis on the uncertainty of their appointment with him, his unreliability and the possible futility of the hopes that rest upon him all suggest an essential absurdity.

## How does it end?

It is important to remember that when you answer this question in relation to an extract of either prose or drama, the end of the passage is not necessarily the end of the text. All you can do is to consider the end of the extract *in relation to the rest of it*.

Looking at this passage, we could say that in some ways the end mirrors the beginning. Estragon starts the piece by turning to the audience and saying, 'Inspiring prospects'; Vladimir ends it by facing us with, ' . . . that bog'. If we hope to understand these two characters' perceptions of us by looking at the ways in which they address us, we shall be as confused as we are by just about everything else in the play; look at the contradiction in the opening and closing lines of this extract. Are we 'inspiring prospects' or 'a bog'?

The feelings we are left with at the end are those of doubt. Nothing seems certain and all we know is that Vladimir and Estragon are going to wait. Action in its conventional sense has been arrested, and our layers of certainties in and expectations of traditional drama have been peeled away. The linear movement that usually characterises conventional drama is absent. Both characters address us; we know that they are aware of our presence and we engage with the circular interaction between Estragon, Vladimir and ourselves. We are left with a bleak minimalism and a strong feeling that this play is going to challenge and engage us intellectually as we struggle to find meaning.

## Summarise your response

Your response to this extract will inevitably be coloured by your previous experience of modern literature. If your experience is scant, you will find some elements of this extract more puzzling than will people who have dealt with modern drama before.

When you are studying modern literature it is important to put aside the expectations acquired through your study of more conventional material. Modern literature breaks free from what its creators saw as 'stale' practices. It plays with the concept of time and the notion of action in an intense analysis of the moment. It aims to create a sense of freshness in its examination of human experience, and to give its readers and audiences something new in their encounters with time and with human action within it.

Initial responses from new readers of modern drama might include feelings of frustration and bewilderment. What is going on? Why doesn't something happen? What is this about? If you hang on to conventional expectations such as plot, you will make little progress in your appreciation of such material. You may respond with confusion and uncertainty, not only because of the doubt that exists in the minds and situation of the two characters, but also because of the play's apparent lack of meaning and movement. However, you will fail to appreciate fully the writer's intention if you continue to expect the linear qualities associated with conventional literature.

## Language

It is a tragi-comedy because some of its elements are comic and some tragic. Look at this rapid interchange:

| | |
|---|---|
| *Estragon* | And then the day after tomorrow. |
| *Vladimir* | Possibly. |
| *Estragon* | And so on. |
| *Vladimir* | The point is – |
| *Estragon* | Until he comes. |
| *Vladimir* | You're merciless. |

It is as if each character is continuing his own conversation, which, while interlacing itself tightly with the other's, is also separate. It seems possible that these two characters are, in fact, two parts of a single personality – the conscious and unconscious minds – such is the extent of their intimacy. Yet, if we remove Vladimir's lines and look at the sequence of Estragon's, it appears that Vladimir's words are woven around those of Estragon in such a way that the latter's could make sense *without* Vladimir:

| | |
|---|---|
| *Estragon* | And then the day after tomorrow. |
| *Vladimir* | ........................... |
| *Estragon* | And so on. |
| *Vladimir* | ........................... |
| *Estragon* | Until he comes. |

However, this independence in no way lessens the intimacy that exists between these two; if anything it enhances it. The pace and closeness of this interaction produce comic effects at times, as do the characters' references to the audience as both 'inspiring prospects' and '...that bog'. The cross-talk is undoubtedly comic, as in these lines:

| | |
|---|---|
| *Vladimir* | I don't know. A willow. |
| *Estragon* | Where are the leaves? |
| *Vladimir* | It must be dead. |
| *Estragon* | No more weeping. |

It is almost like a double-act in places. Notice the way in which Estragon has 'picked up the ball from Vladimir'; the former mentions 'willow', and three lines later Estragon talks of 'weeping'. However, the tragic elements are also very real; interwoven with the comedy is the tragedy of human uncertainty and doubt. Vladimir tells Estragon that, 'Nothing is certain when [he] is about' and the bleakness of their situation is made real by the disturbing image of the tree – so often a symbol of life – which in *this* play, is probably dead.

This interlacing of their dialogue engages the audience, not so much in the emotional way that is so often a feature of conventional drama, but on an intellectual level. This bouncing off each other locks them into one another but also intrigues us. We observe but we are emotionally detached. In watching them, however, we are watching ourselves. What we see is the human condition played out in front of us, and we look on more with our minds and less with our hearts. This is a play for intelligent people. It is reminiscent of Stravinsky's attitude to music. He believed that people should listen to music actively, clearly and intelligently, that they should not allow themselves to be borne away on a sea of cloudy emotion.

The minimalism in this extract encourages us to respond intellectually. All we have are two men, a dead tree and a great deal of uncertainty. This starkness is enhanced by naturalistic dialogue; the language is disjointed, fractured. There are interruptions and single word lines, such as:

| | |
|---|---|
| *Vladimir* | Possibly. |
| *Estragon* | And so on. |
| *Vladimir* | The point is – |
| *Estragon* | Until he comes. |

You only have to look at the page to see that the lines are short and the interchange rapid. The diction is straightforward, pared down, the longest word in this extract being 'insinuating'. The language is not in any way rich, superfluous or elaborate (compare Shakespeare); its starkness mirrors the atmosphere and setting created by the doubt and the dead tree respectively.

Stage directions are more precise than in Shakespeare; for example, '*Estragon moves to centre, halts with his back to auditorium*' and '*He turns, advances to front, halts facing auditorium*'. They are also thematic – (*despairingly*) and (*Angrily*).

Now look at the Language Annotations sheet.

Box 10.2  LANGUAGE ANNOTATIONS

*He spits. Estragon moves to centre, halts with his back to auditorium.*

audience involved

Estragon: Charming spot. (*He turns, advances to front, halts facing the auditorium.*)

Inspiring prospects. (*He turns to Vladimir.*) Let's go.

comic effect

Vladimir: We can't.

rapid interchange/ straight forward diction

Estragon: Why not?

Vladimir: We're waiting for Godot.

Estragon: (*despairingly*). Ah! (*Pause.*) You're sure it was here?

Vladimir: What?

Estragon: That we were to wait.

Vladimir: He said by the tree. (*They look at the tree.*) Do you see any others?

minimalism

Estragon: What is it?

cross-talk (double act)

Vladimir: I don't know. A willow.

Estragon: Where are the leaves?

Vladimir: It must be dead.

tragic

Estragon: No more weeping.

Vladimir: Or perhaps it's not the season.

Estragon: Looks to me more like a bush.

Vladimir: A shrub.

fractured language (interruption)

Estragon: A bush.

naturalistic dialogue – stark

Vladimir: A – What are you insinuating? That we've come to the wrong place?

Estragon: He should be here.

Vladimir: He didn't say for sure he'd come.

Estragon: And if he doesn't come?

Vladimir: We'll come back tomorrow.

rapid inter-change tragi-comedy

Estragon: And then the day after tomorrow.

Vladimir: Possibly.

Estragon: And so on.

Vladimir: The point is –

Estragon: Until he comes.

Vladimir: You're merciless.

Estragon's own conversation interlaced with Vladimir's – 2 parts of a single personality

fractured language (interrup-tion)

Estragon: We came here yesterday.

Vladimir: Ah no, there you're mistaken.

Estragon: What did we do yesterday?

Vladimir: What did we do yesterday?

2 parts of a single personality – mirrored speech

Estragon: Yes.

Vladimir: Why . . . (*Angrily*). Nothing is certain when you're about.

Estragon: In my opinion we were here.

tragic

Vladimir: (*looking round*). You recognise the place?

Estragon: I didn't say that.

Vladimir: Well?

*Box 10.2   (Contd)*

Estragon:   That makes no difference. ─────────── *audience involved*
Vladimir:   All the same . . . that tree . . . (*turning towards the*
            *auditorium*) . . . that bog. ─── *comic effect*

## Positioning of characters/on stage and auditorium

Stage directions suggest some interesting positioning on stage. We can see the comic effect when Estragon '*halts with his back to the auditorium*' and declares his view to be a 'Charming spot' – in other words not the audience. He then '*turns, advances to front, halts facing auditorium*' and states that we are 'Inspiring prospects'. '*Turn[ing] to Vladimir*' he suggests, 'Let's go.' Notice how Estragon has thus addressed, and thereby acknowledged the existence of, three distinct areas – the back of the stage; us, the audience; and his counterpart, Vladimir. The visual impact of his physically turning to face each component means that Estragon shares with us his awareness of the stage, of the only other person on it with him, and of us. By doing this, he draws us into the drama's circular movement that was discussed earlier when summarising the central conflict.

The stage in this play has four sides – but they are left, right, stage and auditorium, rather than the conventional left, right, stage and offstage, and the audience's inclusion in the field of action is part of what makes it so definingly twentieth century. This interaction with the audience causes a certain anxiety in us; will he come off stage and enter our territory? We are used to clearly-defined boundaries in much (but not all) conventional drama; the proscenium arch and the stage curtain help to mark the limits of the actors' territory and ours. However, in this extract, both characters address us, assess us and we do not feel quite so safe. This intimacy and interaction with us is somewhat unexpected (depending on your familiarity with modern drama) and uncomfortable, but we should be getting used to both those responses by now.

## Centre of power or dominance/grouping

There would appear to be no clearly dominant character in this pairing. The fact that there are only two characters in this extract means that we cannot examine the grouping in the way that we would were there more actors on stage. However, it does suggest that these two are equals, a view supported by the notion that both characters are the two halves of the same personality. It could be argued that there is never true equality between two individuals, and it seems that Vladimir is perhaps marginally the driver in this pairing, but the real power would appear to lie in the interaction between the two. This extract is not grand, public drama, nor is it even social drama. We are not looking at a family or a society, and the absence of the group dynamic helps to define their isolation.

It could be said that the power in this extract lies more in the hands of the actors than the audience. What do they think of us? What's going to happen next? Will they join us in the auditorium? This suspense is a traditional component of drama and yet it is interesting to see the way in which it is created here – not by the conventional method of a linear plot but by utter uncertainty about almost everything. The old certainties fall away; we are sure of nothing, as indeed are the characters, and in this way we are drawn powerfully into a shared experience of doubt with those on stage. In *Waiting for Godot* Samuel Beckett is redefining not only the concepts of positioning of characters, the centre of power and onstage/offstage but also our *expectations* of these things on the stage.

## Sample essay – *Waiting for Godot*

The extract focuses on two characters who are 'waiting for Godot'. They are locked into a situation in which they seem unable to move; they cannot leave because their purpose is to wait, and yet they are not sure that they are waiting in the right place, or that the person for whom they are waiting will even turn up. A strong sense of uncertainty pervades the passage – the state and nature of the tree that is on stage, the location for the proposed meeting with Godot, and even what they did yesterday – neither they nor we can be sure of anything. They seem to go nowhere, to make no progress. Both the situation and the language are bleak and stark. Everything is questionable.

The passage is full of conflict. First there is the question of action versus inaction. Estragon says, 'Let's go'; he wants action, movement, progress. Vladimir replies, 'We can't', and the action is denied. Estragon challenges this inaction with the question, 'Why not?' and is told that they must wait. There is considerable tension between these two stances, established within the first four lines of the extract.

There is conflict over whether or not this is the right place. Estragon questions the location for the meeting with Godot – 'You're sure it was here?' Vladimir states confidently, 'He said by the tree. Do you see any others?' and later, 'What are you insinuating? That we've come to the wrong place?' While there is an obvious tension created by this conflict, there is also a strong sense of uncertainty and potential futility. Waiting for Godot has become their purpose; their action will be pointless if they are waiting in the wrong place.

Even Vladimir's powers of discernment create conflict. First, he says that he does not know what type of tree it is, and then immediately states that it is a willow. Similarly, the question of whether or not it is a tree at all is then raised and they argue as to whether it is in fact not a tree, but a bush or a shrub. Their immediate environment (and the only other thing on stage apart from themselves) creates tension between them and is clouded with doubt.

We *know* that the act of waiting for Godot is central to this play, and of enormous significance to Estragon and Vladimir. The sense of uncertainty in the audience and the characters is thus enhanced greatly when Estragon asserts, 'He should be here' and Vladimir counters this with, 'He didn't say for sure he'd come'. They are waiting – an act, which in itself creates suspense – for someone or something whose arrival is uncertain.

They do not know whether or not they should keep coming back to the spot to meet Godot. The interchange about this increases in pace:

| | |
|---|---|
| *Vladimir* | Possibly. |
| *Estragon* | And so on. |
| *Vladimir* | The point is – |
| *Estragon* | Until he comes. |

until Vladimir suddenly turns on Estragon and accuses him of being 'merciless'. This sting in the tail hurts all the more for the intimacy and interlacing of dialogue that precedes it, and thus the effect of the conflict is enhanced.

It seems that there can be no agreement between this couple – not even on whether or not they came here yesterday. Estragon says positively, 'We came here yesterday', but Vladimir counters this with, 'Ah no, there you're mistaken'. We already know that their future is uncertain; now it seems that their past is also in doubt.

It seems that nothing can be taken for granted in this play. Estragon declares to Vladimir that '[they] were here'. However, when Vladimir then assumes that he 'recognise[s] the place', Estragon points out sharply, 'I didn't say that'. This leads us to the final and perhaps most tangible area of conflict: that between Vladimir and Estragon themselves. There is a constant tension between the couple that seems to coexist with the familiarity. Alongside the intimacy of the interlaced dialogue is a conflict that reminds us of that between a married couple. Vladimir tells Estragon that he is 'merciless' and then says '*angrily*', 'Nothing is certain when you're about'. Estragon replies irritably to Vladimir's 'You recognise the place?' with a pedantic, 'I didn't say that'.

It is clear that there is an all-pervasive feeling of conflict in this extract, but it is interesting to see the way in which it leads us toward a powerful sense of doubt and uncertainty. Vladimir and Estragon argue over what has been and what has not, what is and what is not, what is to be and what is not; there is no certainty in the past, the present or the future.

An interesting feature of this passage, alongside the conflict and doubt, is the element of universality invested in it by this same uncertainty. Our lack of knowledge about the identity of the characters (apart from their names), the location, or anything else, come to that, gives the drama a universal application. It is possible that this characteristic owes much to the accompanying starkness, which itself robs the extract of any readily identifiable features. It is a barren wasteland that they inhabit; the only possible marker is the tree, which is probably dead and which no one can clearly identify.

We are locked into this wasteland with Vladimir and Estragon in a powerful and bewildering circular movement between the two men; their past, present and future; and us, the audience. They cannot move; 'Let's go', says Estragon. 'We can't' replies Vladimir. They wait and we wait with them. It seems as if no one is going anywhere, and while we wait, we wonder what it all means. We ask why there is no action, no progress; the feelings of uncertainty that blight Vladimir and Estragon are ones that we soon begin to experience ourselves.

While the hope of meeting Godot drives Vladimir and Estragon and gives their lives purpose, we cannot help but see both the tragic and comic elements of their search for him. If Godot represents God and the extract is about waiting for him, then it is possible to see the drama in terms of a metaphor for the nature of human existence, which itself is a mixture of comedy and tragedy. Perhaps many of us are looking for God in some form or another and we are concerned about where we might find him. Religion offers us few certainties in human terms and maybe it is more about the waiting than the event – the journey than the destination.

Woven into this, at times frustrating, wait are strands of the tragic and comic. Vladimir tells Estragon that he is 'merciless', and that 'nothing is certain when [he] is about' but then we are treated to Estragon's description of us as, 'inspiring prospects' and later to Vladimir's opinion – 'that bog'.

Equally closely woven is the language of the intimate repartee between these two characters which almost 'ping-pongs' to and fro across the stage, sometimes at tremendous speed. The language, like the set, is minimalist, shorn of richness and all superfluity, pared down to basics. It is fractured and blunt:

> *Estragon*   Looks to me more like a bush.
> *Vladimir*   A shrub.
> *Estragon*   A bush.
> *Vladimir*   A – .

The starkness is powerful, as is the actors' use of the stage *and* the audience. From the start of this extract we witness their awareness of us when Estragon looks our way and says, 'Inspiring prospects'. This sense of our presence is mirrored at the end with Vladimir's quite different, but equally comic, 'that bog'. The stage in this play has four sides – but they are left, right, stage and auditorium, rather than the conventional left, right, stage and offstage, and the audience's inclusion in the field of action is part of what makes it so definingly twentieth century. In this way we are drawn into the action, or lack of it.

While we are part of the drama, this involvement clearly does not invest us with any real power, because in this play it lies firmly in the hands of the characters. They have acknowledged our presence and commented upon our potential, or lack of it; we wonder what they will do next. Are they going to leave the stage and join us? Things become uncertain for us too. The power between the two characters lies marginally with Vladimir, inasmuch as there is unlikely ever to be true equality between any two people, but much of the time the conflict between them clouds any such distinction.

What is interesting in this passage is that action in its conventional sense has been arrested, and our layers of certainties in and expectations of traditional drama have been peeled away. The linear movement that usually characterises conventional drama is absent; progress has given way to a circular movement and the passage engages us and challenges us intellectually, as we struggle to find meaning.

The old certainties fall away; we, like Vladimir and Estragon, can be sure of nothing, and in this way we are drawn powerfully into a shared experience of doubt with those on stage. However, the involvement is not primarily an emotional one, although it does provoke feelings of uncertainty and even fear. We are detached onlookers. If we accept *Waiting for Godot* as a metaphor for the nature of human existence, we can say that Samuel Beckett is redefining not only the concepts of action in drama, positioning of characters, the centre of power and notions of onstage and offstage, but also our *expectations* of these things on the stage and in real life.

Practical criticism of prose
(eighteenth-century)

## Practical criticism of prose (piece from 1792)

### Focus on and analyse the question

A focusing exercise will bring to our attention the key instructions. (AQA (AEB) June 1998)

Read the following passage carefully then write about your response to it. You should consider the following in your essay:

- **What** the writer is saying about **the position of women in society**;
- **How** she says it; and
- **How effective** she is in **attracting and holding your attention**.

*A Vindication of the Rights of Woman* by Mary Wollstonecraft (1792)

My own sex, I hope, will excuse me, if I treat them like rational creatures, instead of flattering their *fascinating* graces, and viewing them as if they were in a state of perpetual childhood, unable to stand alone. I earnestly wish to point out in what true dignity and human happiness consists – I wish to persuade women to endeavour to acquire strength, both of mind and body, and to convince them that the soft phrases, susceptibility of heart, delicacy of sentiment, and refinement of taste, are almost synonymous with epithets of weakness, and that those beings who are only the objects of pity and that kind of love, which has been termed its sister, will soon become objects of contempt.

Dismissing then, those pretty feminine phrases, which the men condescendingly use to soften our slavish dependence, and despising that weak elegancy of mind, exquisite sensibility, and sweet docility of manners, supposed to be the sexual characteristics of the weaker vessel, I wish to show that elegance is inferior to virtue, that the first object of laudable ambition is to obtain a character as a human being, regardless of the distinction of sex; and that secondary views should be brought to this simple touchstone.

This is a rough sketch of my plan; and should I express my conviction with the energetic emotions that I feel whenever I think of the subject, the dictates of experience and reflection will be felt by some of my readers. Animated by this important object, I shall disdain to cull my phrases or polish my style; – I aim at being useful, and sincerity will render me unaffected; for, wishing rather to persuade by the force of my arguments, than dazzle by the elegance of my language, I shall not waste my time in rounding periods, or in fabricating the turgid bombast of artificial feelings, which, coming from the head, never reach the heart. I shall be employed about things, not words! – and, anxious to render my sex more respectable members of society, I shall try to avoid that flowery diction which has slided from essays into novels, and from novels into familiar letters and conversations.

These pretty superlatives, dropping glibly from the tongue, vitiate the taste, and create a kind of sickly delicacy that turns away from simple unadorned truth; and a deluge of false sentiments and overstretched feelings, stifling the natural emotions of the heart, render the domestic pleasures insipid, that ought to sweeten the exercise of those severe duties, which educate a rational and immortal being for a nobler field of action.

The education of women has, of late, been more attended to than formerly; yet they are still reckoned a frivolous sex, and ridiculed or pitied by the writers who endeavour by satire or instruction to improve them. It is acknowledged that they spend many of the first years of their lives in acquiring a smattering of accomplishments; meanwhile strength of body and mind are sacrificed to libertine notions of beauty, to the desire of establishing themselves, – the only way women can rise in the world, – by marriage. And this desire making mere animals of them, when they marry they act as such children may be expected to act: – they dress; they paint, and nickname God's creatures: – Surely these weak beings are only fit for a seraglio*! – Can they be expected to govern a family with judgement, or take care of the poor babes whom they bring into the world?

## Read closely and think

*Always consider the title of any work*; it has been attributed to the text for a good reason and can be extremely helpful to us in our efforts to establish precisely what a piece 'is about'. The title points to the writer's wish to establish the merits or justice of women's rights, so it is no surprise that even after only one reading of this passage, we can see that it is to do with the social situation of women at the time of writing.

Now is the time to answer the basic comprehension-type questions. Remember the key points to consider?

- **What** is happening? It is an appeal to other women of her time to become strong and to shake off society's view of them as weak and worthy of pity.
- To **whom** is it happening? The focus is upon all the women of her time.

* Seraglio: harem

- **Why** is it happening? Wollstonecraft is writing this because she senses the inequality surrounding society's perception of women.
- **When is it happening?** It is happening in 1792, with all the social and historical implications that accompany that period.
- **Where** is it happening? It could safely be assumed that the writer is English, and that the piece refers to English women. There are no striking cultural differences apparent in the text.
- **How is it happening?** It is written with energy, strength and passion.

## Summarise the central conflict/s

Again, the key questions to ask are: **what? who? why? when? where?** and **how?**

### What?

- 'I' (line 1)/'the men' (line 11). There is conflict between the way *she* sees her fellow women and the way in which 'the *men*' perceive them;
- 'rational creatures' (line 1)/'state of perpetual childhood, unable to stand alone' (line 3). There is conflict between what she sees women as being and what she thinks men see them as;
- 'strength' (line 5)/'weakness' (line 8). She wants to persuade women to become strong; the traditionally feminine qualities, she argues, are 'synonymous with epithets of weakness';
- 'pity' (line 8)/'contempt' (line 10). The 'pity' that women receive because of this weakness will change to 'contempt';
- 'sickly delicacy' (line 31)/'simple unadorned truth' (line 31). She complains that the 'flowery diction' associated with women of the time has little to do with truth;
- 'false sentiments' (line 32)/'natural emotions' (line 33). She believes that true feelings are suppressed by a stream of 'false sentiments', which it has become socially desirable to express; and
- 'only fit for a seraglio' (line 45)/'govern a family with judgement' (line 45). There is an implied conflict here between the likely focus and ability of a woman in a harem and that of one who manages a family wisely.

### Who?

The conflict exists in the mind of the writer but she sees it taking place in the lives of the women around her.

### Why?

The conflict exists because the writer believes that men are keeping women in 'a state of perpetual childhood, unable to stand alone' and she believes that women should be treated like 'rational creatures', suggesting a sense of adult independence.

# When?

This conflict occurs in 1792 and this is partly what makes the writing quite exceptional for its time. When the date of the piece has been concealed from successive generations of students it is interesting to note that their assumption is that it was written towards the middle of the twentieth century.

# Where?

Social and cultural context can be assumed to be British or similar, as there are no overt indications to the contrary.

# How?

The conflict is expressed:

- personally – 'I hope', 'my plan' (line 18);
- vehemently – 'energetic emotions that I feel' (line 19);
- cogently – the lists (lines 3–15) suggest organisation and thought;
- assertively – 'Surely...' (line 44); and
- challengingly – 'Can they be expected ... the world?' (line 45).

Look now at the sheet entitled 'Conflict Annotations, Question 1'.

---

*Box 11.1*  **CONFLICT ANNOTATIONS, QUESTION 1**

Read this passage carefully, then write about your response to it.

You should consider:

- what Mary Wollstonecraft is saying about the position of women in society;

  *how she would like to treat them versus how men treat them*

- how she says it;

  *I/them*

- how effectively she engages your attention.

*2 conflicting ways of treating women*

My own sex, I hope, will excuse me, if I treat them like rational creatures, instead of flattering their *fascinating* graces, and viewing them as if they were in a state of perpetual childhood, unable to stand alone. I earnestly wish to point out in what true dignity and human happiness consists – I wish to persuade women to endeav-  5
our to acquire strength, both of mind and body, and to convince them that the soft phrases, susceptibility of heart, delicacy of senti-  *suggestion of conflict – changes need to be made*
ment, and refinement of taste, are almost synonymous with epi-

*opposites*

thets of weakness, and that those beings who are only the objects of pity and that kind of love, which has been termed its sister, will  10
soon become objects of contempt.  *male/female*

Dismissing then, those pretty feminine phrases, which the men condescendingly use to soften our slavish dependence, and despising

---

that weak elegancy of mind, exquisite sensibility, and sweet docility of manners, supposed to be the sexual characteristics of the     15
weaker vessel, I wish to show that elegance is inferior to virtue     *Conflict*
that the first object of laudable ambition is to obtain a character
as a human being, regardless of the distinction of sex; and that
*conflict –* secondary views should be brought to this simple touchstone.
*she refuses*
*to behave* This is a rough sketch of my plan; and should I express my con-     20
*in a stereo-* viction with the energetic emotions that I feel whenever I think of
*typically* the subject, the dictates of experience and reflection will be felt by
*feminine* some of my readers. Animated by this important object, I shall
*way* disdain to cull my phrases or polish my style; – I aim at being
useful, and sincerity will render me unaffected; for, wishing rather     25
*opposites* to persuade by the force of my arguments, than dazzle by the     *Conflicting*
elegance of my language, I shall not waste my time in rounding     *methods of*
periods, or in fabricating the turgid bombast of artificial feelings,     *persuasion*
*tangible* which, coming from the head, never reach the heart – I shall be
*versus* employed about things, not words! – and, anxious to render my     30
*intangible* sex more respectable members of society, I shall try to avoid that     *contrast*
*Suggesting* flowery diction which has slided from essays into novels, and
*that they* from novels into familiar letters and conversations.
*are not*
*respectable* These pretty superlatives, dropping glibly from the tongue, vitiate     *opposites*
*now* the taste, and create a kind of sickly delicacy that turns away from     35
simple unadorned truth; and a deluge of false sentiments and     *conflict –*
*opposites* overstretched feelings, stifling the natural emotions of the heart,     *overstretched*
render the domestic pleasures insipid, that ought to sweeten the     *feelings/*
*some* exercise of those severe duties, which educate a rational and     *natural*
*change in* immortal being for a nobler field of action.     *emotions*
*attitudes*     40
*over time* The education of women has, of late, been more attended to than     *'but' means*
formerly; yet they are still reckoned a frivolous sex, and ridiculed     *conflict*
*opposites* or pitied by the writers who endeavour by satire or instruction to
improve them. It is acknowledged that they spend many of the
*What* first years of their lives in acquiring a smattering of accomplish-     45  *Conflict*
*women* ments; meanwhile strength of body and mind are sacrificed to
*aspire to/* libertine notions of beauty, to the desire of establishing them-
*what they* selves, – the only way women can rise in the world, – by mar-
*become in* riage. And this desire making mere animals of them, when they
*marriage* marry they act as such children may be expected to act: – they     50
dress; they paint, and nickname God's creatures: – Surely these
*how they* weak beings are only fit for a seraglio*! – Can they be expected to
*act in* govern a family with judgement, or take care of the poor babes     *Conflict*
*marriage/* whom they bring into the world?
*what is*
*expected* Source: MARY WOLLSTONECRAFT, *A Vindication of the Rights of Woman*, 1792
*of them*
\* Seraglio: harem

# Track the themes and develop the themes elsewhere

Sometimes it is possible, and indeed expedient, to handle stage 3 – tracking the theme, and stage 4 – developing the theme, together and this is what we shall do here.

The theme of conflict is subtly sustained and developed in the language. For example, in line 5 Wollstonecraft says that she wishes to 'persuade women' and to 'convince them'. This suggests that she is trying to change their attitudes and behaviour, which in turn, belies a conflict.

This conflict is evident again in the language in line 13, when she no longer speaks with a solitary voice but unites with all other women in her attempts to improve their status by discussing '*our* slavish dependence'. Note the dramatic and emotive language denoting the submissive behaviour she is trying to change.

Developing the theme of 'false sentiments' (line 36) / 'natural emotions' (line 37), she talks of 'fascinating graces' (line 2), 'soft phrases, susceptibility of heart, delicacy of sentiment and refinement of taste' (line 7), which all suggest a certain falseness. This idea is further cultivated with 'pretty feminine phrases' (line 12), 'weak elegancy of mind' (line 14), 'exquisite sensibility and sweet docility of manners' (line 14).

These delicate descriptions contrast strongly with her own 'energetic emotions'. She is 'animated by this important object' and she will 'disdain to cull [her] phrases or polish [her] style'. Her honesty and refusal to submit to typically feminine affectation are evident in her clear statement in line 24, where she points out that she aims 'at being useful' and says that 'sincerity will render me unaffected'.

Her honesty will motivate her to 'persuade by the force of [her] argument' rather than 'dazzle by the elegance of [her] language'. Note this continued conflict in the language in which she juxtaposes her own directness and integrity with the insincere affectation with which women of her time were forced to behave.

She goes on to declare boldly that 'these pretty superlatives, dropping glibly from the tongue, vitiate the taste'. See the contrast in the language as 'vitiate' cuts sharply across the 'pretty superlatives' and 'glibly'. Such 'niceties', she explains, spoil, degrade and devalue, and she goes on to contrast again very clearly the two approaches in lines 35–6 by talking about 'sickly delicacy' and 'simple unadorned truth'.

There are more examples but there is sufficient evidence here to substantiate the point in any essay.

Notice the way in which the language becomes more powerful and serious in the fourth paragraph. She explains how the 'false sentiments and overstretched feelings . . . render the domestic pleasures insipid, that ought to sweeten the exercise of those *severe duties*, which *educate* a *rational* and *immortal being* for a *nobler field of action*'. Here she explains how the 'false sentiments' in fact spoil women's experience of 'domestic pleasures', which ought to prepare 'rational and immortal beings', such as women are, for higher and nobler things.

The final conflict she deals with is that of marriage. It is ironic, she observes, that marriage is 'the only way women can rise in the world', but this desire to 'establish themselves' merely makes 'animals of them' because 'when they marry they act as such children may be expected to act' (line 50).

She goes on to point out that women who behave in such a way as to 'dress...paint and nickname God's creatures' are surely fit only for a 'seraglio'. Why, then, are they expected to 'govern a family with judgement or take care of the poor babes whom they bring into the world?' This rhetorical question on which she ends focuses sharply on the conflict between society's *treatment* of women and its *expectations* of them.

Look now at the sheet 'Language Annotations, Questions 2 and 3'.

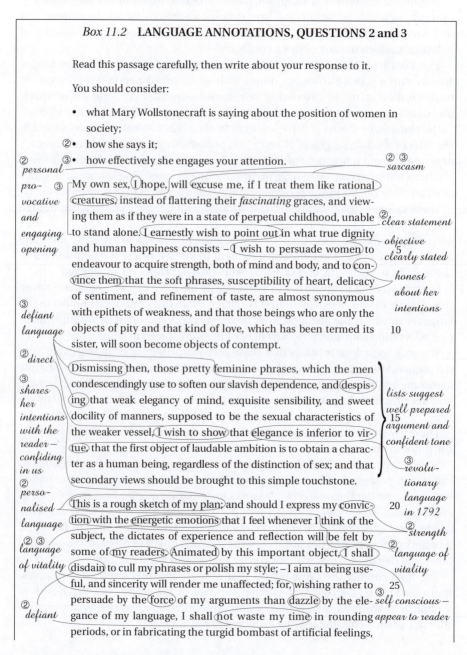

Box 11.2  **LANGUAGE ANNOTATIONS, QUESTIONS 2 and 3**

Read this passage carefully, then write about your response to it.

You should consider:

- what Mary Wollstonecraft is saying about the position of women in society;
- ② how she says it;
- ② ③ how effectively she engages your attention.

② *personal*

*pro-* ③
*vocative*
*and*
*engaging*
*opening*

③
*defiant*
*language*

② *direct*

③
*shares*
*her*
*intentions*
*with the*
*reader –*
*confiding*
*in us*

② *perso-*
*nalised*
*language*

② ③
*language*
*of vitality*

② *defiant*

② ③ — *sarcasm*

My own sex, I hope, will excuse me, if I treat them like rational creatures, instead of flattering their *fascinating* graces, and viewing them as if they were in a state of perpetual childhood, unable to stand alone. I earnestly wish to point out in what true dignity and human happiness consists – I wish to persuade women to endeavour to acquire strength, both of mind and body, and to convince them that the soft phrases, susceptibility of heart, delicacy of sentiment, and refinement of taste, are almost synonymous with epithets of weakness, and that those beings who are only the objects of pity and that kind of love, which has been termed its sister, will soon become objects of contempt.

Dismissing then, those pretty feminine phrases, which the men condescendingly use to soften our slavish dependence, and despising that weak elegancy of mind, exquisite sensibility, and sweet docility of manners, supposed to be the sexual characteristics of the weaker vessel, I wish to show that elegance is inferior to virtue, that the first object of laudable ambition is to obtain a character as a human being, regardless of the distinction of sex; and that secondary views should be brought to this simple touchstone.

This is a rough sketch of my plan; and should I express my conviction with the energetic emotions that I feel whenever I think of the subject, the dictates of experience and reflection will be felt by some of my readers. Animated by this important object, I shall disdain to cull my phrases or polish my style; – I aim at being useful, and sincerity will render me unaffected; for, wishing rather to persuade by the force of my arguments than dazzle by the elegance of my language, I shall not waste my time in rounding periods, or in fabricating the turgid bombast of artificial feelings,

② *clear statement*
*objective*
5 *clearly stated*
*honest*
*about her*
*intentions*

10

*lists suggest*
*well prepared*
15 *argument and*
*confident tone*

③ *revolu-*
*tionary*
*language*
20 *in 1792*

② *strength*

② *language of*
*vitality*

25

③ *self conscious –*
*appear to reader*

**194** Mastering Practical Criticism

Box 11.2   (Contd)

which, coming from the head, never reach the heart. – I shall be employed about things, not words! – and, anxious to render my ② sex more respectable members of society, I shall try to avoid that ~ *personal* flowery diction which has slided from essays into novels, and from novels into familiar letters and conversations.

30

② ③
*gustorial*
*imagery*
*– vivid*

These pretty superlatives, dropping glibly from the tongue, vitiate } 35 the taste, and create a kind of sickly delicacy that turns away from simple unadorned truth; and a deluge of false sentiments and overstretched feelings, stifling the natural emotions of the heart, render the domestic pleasures insipid, that ought to sweeten the exercise of those severe duties, which educate a rational and immortal being for a nobler field of action.

② ③
*confident;*
*assertive*
*tone*

40

② ③
*balanced – she*
*acknowledges*
*some*
*progress …*

The education of women has, of late, been more attended to than formerly; yet they are still reckoned a frivolous sex, and ridiculed or pitied by the writers who endeavour by satire or instruction to improve them. It is acknowledged that they spend many of the first years of their lives in acquiring a smattering of accomplishments;

*but still*
*sees the*
*need for*
*more*

45

② ③
*emotive*
*language*

meanwhile strength of body and mind are sacrificed to libertine notions of beauty, to the desire of establishing themselves, – the only way women can rise in the world, – by marriage. And this desire making mere animals of them, when they marry they act as such children may be expected to act: – they dress; they paint, and nick-name God's creatures: – Surely these weak beings are only fit for a seraglio*! – Can they be expected to govern a family with judgement, ⌐ or take care of the poor babes whom they bring into the world? ⌐

② ③
*dramatic*

50

② ③
*emotive*

② ③
*rhetorical*
*and sarcastic*

*Source*: MARY WOLLSTONECRAFT, *A Vindication of the Rights of Woman*, 1792

* Seraglio: harem

③ *question engages the reader*

# How does it end?

In the discussion below, emboldened words represent the key features of her conclusion.

Where has the essay taken us? Through what territories of the writer's mind have we travelled? It is *her* viewpoint. Where does she stand at the end? Summarise concisely the ground that we have covered in the essay. What are we left with at the end? Response is about feelings, so focus on these too.

The conclusion dealt with in the previous section suggests that the piece has moved steadily towards a **strong** and **challenging climax**. Wollstonecraft **starts** on a note of biting sarcasm, asking the forgiveness of her sex for treating them 'like rational creatures, instead of flattering their fascinating graces', and she is **direct** and **forceful** throughout the piece, perhaps to illustrate the fact that the women of her time are not allowed to be.

Looking at the last paragraph, she **concludes** her argument by putting the issue of the position of women in society into its social and historical **context**, which makes it seem more **reasoned**, **conceding** that 'the education of women has of late been more attended to than formerly'. However, she then goes on to point out that 'they are still reckoned a frivolous sex, and ridiculed or pitied by the writers who endeavour by satire or instruction to improve them'. Her 'It is acknowledged' exemplifies her ability to present her material in what appears to be a **balanced** and reasonable way; it is **hard to argue** with any claim that something 'is acknowledged'. She then goes on to **document** the way in which women grow into their social roles and develop according to what society deems they should be.

Her argument is powerful yet rational and **cogent**. Her purpose is laid bare in the third paragraph, when she explains that 'this is a rough sketch of [her] plan' and she moves methodically through the essay towards a **vehement** and challenging conclusion that asks **provocative** questions: why do women pursue marriage when this desire makes mere 'animals' of them? And why does society treat them as if they are fit only to be in a harem when it these same women into whose hands it places the government of a family and the rearing of children these women have brought into the world?

The questions are **rhetorical**; neither Wollstonecraft nor we need the answers because we know there are none. Such questions succeed in highlighting the stupidity and unfairness of society's attitudes towards women at the time.

The **crescendo** reached towards the end of the last paragraph is **emotional** and she concludes, as has been discussed already, on a **stirring** note of **challenge** to all those who shared society's views of women in 1792. Whatever one's views on the rights of women, it is difficult to suggest that 'making mere animals' of them or consigning them to a harem is either right or desirable. We cannot fail to be **moved** in *some* way by her argument. Whether this is in her favour or not depends, to some extent, upon the reader.


## Summarise your response

As above, emboldened words are used; in this case to represent the key features of the reader's response.

It is important for students of practical criticism to see texts in their social, cultural and historical contexts, and it is *essential* with a piece such as this. Wollstonecraft's discussion must be seen *in the light of eighteenth-century life* and when we do this, the **shock value** of the essay becomes apparent. It really is a remarkably outspoken and direct piece of prose, propounding **progressive** and **challenging** ideas **for its time** and it is important to try to look at it through eighteenth-century *as well as* twenty-first century eyes. If we fail to do this, we miss entirely the *intended* impact on the reader. This is not always easy, and does not come naturally perhaps, but it is a prerequisite for *all* study of literature. You will already have encountered this need in your study of Shakespeare.

The student's own **gender** will, to some extent, influence his/her response to the piece. Female readers are perhaps more likely to sympathise with

Wollstonecraft's argument and approach, and males maybe less so, but these gender differences are gradually disappearing. There will inevitably, however, be a substantial difference between male/female responses now and those of **the period**. One can only wonder about the way in which men of the time received this text and this *must* be considered in your essay. The modern reader (gender differences notwithstanding) might respond with admiration for Wollstonecraft and for her directness, but also with some sense of shock at the suggestions made, particularly at the end of the piece, to do with harems and animals.

Twenty-first-century readers may appreciate the piece for the **background** it offers to the whole issue of feminism. We can look at the question now and compare the twenty-first-century situation with that of 1792. If we do that, it is possible that our sympathies will be moved in Wollstonecraft's direction. Alternatively, our response might be suddenly to gain a new sympathy with all those who still resist feminism, on the grounds that angry women like Wollstonecraft do their gender no good at all by behaving in such an **unconventional** way. Another response might be to realise that, although vehement in her approach, Wollstonecraft is actually quite intelligent and her **argument** is a **cogent** one. Notice her clear statement of intent in 'I earnestly wish to point out' (line 4); her self-awareness in 'I wish to persuade' (line 5); and her reasonable 'I wish to show' (line 6). All these sound rational and balanced. This is not an hysterical woman speaking, and the suggestion of intelligence and rationality that she creates counters the contemporary stereotype of women she is trying to change. This might serve to heighten our **sympathy** for her cause because we are more likely to concede to her demands on the grounds of her common sense. Simply put, things must have been bad if a sensible woman like this becomes so angry about it.

This is the time for **personal response** and, as discussed earlier, our responses to literature depend so much on our own past experiences, prejudices and sympathies. Response suggests feelings. What emotions are we left with at the end? Are we stirred by her language, ready to join the battle? If we *are* ready to join the battle, on whose side will we be? Are we angry at what she says, or the way in which she says it? Has she won us or alienated us?

Returning to the question, it would seem that we have still to consider the last part of it. How effectively does she engage your attention? To answer this question we need to look at the devices she has used and evaluate their success in engaging the reader.

The 'vindication' of the **title** is an **emotive** word. It is to do with defending, justifying and supporting, and when we combine it with 'the Rights of Woman' we have what promises, from the outset, to be a controversial and provocative piece of writing. It would, undoubtedly, have been all those things to the average reader in 1792, and it could be argued that little has changed. Feminism is, in some ways, even more of an issue today, as it is very much in evidence in the climate of political correctness and equality that characterises much of life in the twenty-first century. So, the title engages the reader.

Wollstonecraft's use of the **first person narrator** is an engaging device. The piece promises to be personal and subjective, and by very definition suggests a subjectivity that invariably draws the reader in to its intimate view of the world.

Her first sentence is **direct** and **sarcastic**, and both qualities will undoubtedly engage the attention of most readers. Her language is **challenging** – she is 'anxious to render [her] sex more respectable members of society', and it could be argued that she is **presenting opinion as fact** when she refuses to 'view [women] as if they were in a state of perpetual childhood'. This technique will attract the reader's attention, if only to criticise her lack of objectivity. She states early on that she 'earnestly wish[es] to point out' (line 4) and 'to persuade women' (line 5), denoting a certain **self-consciousness**. She is aware of her own writing as a vehicle to express her ideas and persuade others, and this is in itself engaging.

She is **states openly** that she is 'dismissing' (line 12) the devices used by men to manipulate women into a certain position in society and that she 'wish[es] to show' (line 16) or prove her argument. We are aware of a woman **with a mission**, we are struck by her **candour** and we inevitably *respond* to this *in some way*.

She **shares** with us her **intentions**: 'This is a rough sketch of my plan' (line 20); 'I shall disdain to cull my phrases' (line 23); 'I shall not waste my time' (line 27); and we feel as if we are her **confidantes** – we know how she is going to approach the problem of vindicating the rights of women.

Throughout the piece her **language** is **provocative** – she talks of '*fascinating graces*', 'pretty superlatives', 'sickly delicacy' – and **extreme** with references to 'animals' and 'a seraglio' in an effort to **evoke a response** in the reader.

The **tone** is **bold** and **unequivocal** throughout, and within the first sentence we are made aware of Wollstonecraft's stance on the subject of women's rights.

Now let us review how we approached our analysis:

- The first step was that of **close reading** and **thinking**.
- Then we **focused** on the **conflict** throughout the essay.
- The next step was to **track** this **conflict** and **trace** its **development**.
- We then **thought** about the **end** of the essay and the ground that we had covered.
- Finally we considered our **responses** to the piece.

We now have enough material for an essay on the text, a sample version of which follows.

## Sample essay – *A Vindication of the Rights of Woman*

In this passage Mary Wollstonecraft presents an outline of her intentions for the work to follow. Her style is such that the reader is awakened and engaged by sarcasm in the opening line then given a clear synopsis of the writer's ideas and desire to influence in the first paragraph before she becomes more passionately critical. As the piece develops, the language becomes stronger, more confrontational and even more persuasive, thereby reflecting the very process she urges women to undergo.

This is a courageous piece – written not in the twenty-first century as one might assume from its outspokenness and its essential message, but in the eighteenth century. Bearing this in mind as we read makes the argumentative style and content even more outstanding. This is an appeal to both women and men to open their eyes and see the injustice of patriarchal perceptions of women and femininity. Men need to stop limiting and silencing women with their expectations, and women need to stop complying. This is an incitement to rebellion and as such its underlying conflicts are plain to see and openly reflected in the language and structures Wollstonecraft uses.

The opening words place her clearly in the conflict; this is her 'own sex' that is under attack and she is going to fight 'the men' who are attacking. The language of conflict and determination peppers the first paragraph (and indeed the whole piece): 'I earnestly wish to point out . . . to persuade . . . to convince', she states as she calls women to fight 'the soft phrases, susceptibility of heart, delicacy of sentiment and refinement [which] are almost synonymous with epithets of weakness' by 'acquir[ing] strength of both mind and body'. She sees 'rational creatures' where men see women 'in a state of perpetual childhood, unable to stand alone'.

Her first action, therefore, is that of 'dismissing those pretty feminine phrases' she sees as a weapon of control 'which the men condescendingly use to soften our slavish dependence'. She employs the language of rational argument traditionally connected with men: 'wishing rather to persuade by the force of my arguments than dazzle by the elegance of my language'.

Thus her 'simple unadorned truth' is juxtaposed with the 'sickly delicacy' usually expected to be 'dropping glibly from the tongue' of her fellow women. This is therefore an internal conflict for Wollstonecraft, as she fights against society's expectations as well as an external conflict between men and women.

As has already been suggested, her language becomes stronger and more serious as the piece develops. From the unity suggested by 'our slavish dependence' and the emotive and dramatic imagery of slavery employed here, Wollstonecraft moves on to a clear attack on the nature of women's expression and the fact that it has a direct effect on their lives, their enjoyment and their usefulness or ability to fulfil their 'natural' role. Rather than simply being reflections of women's status, their 'pretty feminine phrases' reinforce women's 'meekness' and are described in more vicious terms as 'sickly', 'false', and 'overstretched'. As a result, they are actively 'stifling', so that 'weak elegancy of mind, exquisite sensibility, and sweet docility of manners' (lines 14–15) in fact 'render the domestic pleasures insipid, that ought to sweeten the exercise of those severe duties, which educate a rational and immortal being for a nobler field of action'.

Herein lies the crux of Wollstonecraft's argument, which is articulated numerous times in different ways throughout this piece, but arguably never more clearly than when she states in paragraph two that she wishes to 'show that elegance is inferior to virtue, that the first object of laudable ambition is to obtain a character as a human being regardless of the distinction of sex'.

This aim is clearly contrasted with the 'current' conception of women as 'the weaker vessel' – a lower grade inanimate and empty object – 'animals' and 'children' – who, by definition, are not capable of adult thought or responsibility.

Marriage, she acknowledges, is women's usual route to social advancement. She points out, however, that this is just another social trap that makes 'mere animals of them when they marry' because they 'act as such children may be expected to act' and therefore these 'weak beings are only fit for a seraglio!'

As such, marriage prevents women from fulfilling their potential as human beings. After all, Wollstonecraft concludes, in this weakened, devalued and dehumanised state, how 'can they be expected to govern a family with judgement, or take care of the poor babes whom they bring into the world?' This final note is a serious one, as women's unique role is referred to and their need to be in control – the use of 'govern', 'judgement' and 'take care' highlight this – despite their treatment at the hands of society, which expects them simultaneously to be mother, whore, child and pet.

Wollstonecraft's direct and forceful style thus comes to a strong and challenging climax as she appeals to women to fulfil their potential as mothers and homemakers. As has been shown, the language employed is provocative and stirring, in clear juxtaposition with that expected of women. It is, however, more than this. Wollstonecraft presents in this piece a cogent, reasoned argument employing much of the rhetoric of logical – one might even say, traditionally masculine – debate.

Having made her apologies to some of her audience in line 1, she moves on to outline her argument in the rest of the first paragraph, explaining what she wishes to achieve and why it is important. The second paragraph is a further development of her methods and aims, and here she employs the 'list' that clarifies the feminine characteristics which need to be overcome: 'weak elegancy of mind', 'exquisite sensibility and sweet docility of manners' and the 'stronger' attributes that should replace them: 'virtue' and 'obtain[ing] a character'.

The third paragraph seems to 'express [her] conviction' and to justify her direct style as a means to an important end: 'I shall be employed about things not words! and, anxious to render my sex more respectable members of society'.

As has been already discussed, the fourth paragraph then launches an all-out attack on the falseness of women's language and expected behaviour, and their stifling effects. Then the final paragraph places Wollstonecraft in context, providing some sociohistorical background to the situation of women. She acknowledges that, 'The education of women has of late been more attended to than formerly' but ensures that this concession is followed by 'yet', thereby indicating that this is not enough. Similarly, she adds weight to her observation by her phraseology: 'It is acknowledged', which serves to summon other minds who agree.

It is clear that Wollstonecraft uses two important persuasive techniques to hold and influence her readers. It is the intermingling of the coldly rational language of debate and the emotive diction of the personal appeal of a member of the oppressed group concerned, speaking directly to '[her] readers', together with what one might describe as the 'shock factor' of the author's candour that make this an engaging, inspiring and persuasive piece. It has the potential to appeal in differing ways to both men (possibly through the rhetoric of debate) and women (through emotive appeal) of the eighteenth and twenty-first centuries alike.

# ◼ ☑ 12 Practical criticism of poetry – comparison

## The comparative question

Sometimes you will be asked to compare two pieces of literature, and we should now look at that task and at ways of approaching it. The choice of these two texts for comparative study does not always mean poetry; sometimes examining boards set a poem to be compared to a short piece of prose, or even drama. Students often shy away from this exercise, as they believe that they cannot hope fully to understand and appreciate two texts in the time usually given to analysing one, and the mixture of genres is sometimes off-putting. However, you are strongly advised to consider this option as a viable alternative. It is *not* impossible and in some ways it is easier than focusing solely on one.

You may be wondering how it could possibly be easier to deal with two texts rather than one in the same available time. The answer is simple; you will not be expected to analyse either to the same depth when handling two as you would when dealing with one. You can rely on the fact that both texts will have content in common: that is, the subject matter will be the same. It could be that one was written in *an earlier century* and the other is contemporary, or that one has a certain *viewpoint* and the other quite a different one. It is possible that the *forms* are different; one might be a poem and the other a letter or a diary entry. Be prepared for any combination, but rest assured that they will both be about the same 'thing' and do not panic when you see this option. It is set as a viable alternative to handling one text, and many students opt for this question every year, most successfully.

Students have often related to me that they found this option easier because the same subject matter was presented in two different ways, and if they found it hard to grasp in one form, they often understood it more clearly when seeing it in another. In terms of time in an examination, you would naturally only be expected to spend about half the time analysing each text that you would if you were dealing with a single text.

Another advantage to this option is that there will inevitably be a great deal more to say, and therefore you are unlikely ever to be stuck for material. So, you see, there are several good reasons to consider a question like this, and you should not discount it automatically before reading the texts involved.

A typical examination (AQA (AEB) Summer 1997) question might be:

Thomas Wyatt wrote his poem 'They Flee From Me That Sometime Did Me Seek' in the sixteenth century; Gavin Ewart wrote his poem with the same title in the second half of the twentieth century. Explore the similarities and the differences in the ways Wyatt and Ewart present their feelings about the breakdown of the relationships in the two poems.

### 'They Flee From Me That Sometime Did Me Seek'

They flee from me that sometime did me seek,
With naked foot stalking in my chamber:
I have seen them gentle, tame and meek,
That now are wild, and do not once remember
That sometime they have put themselves in danger
To take bread at my hand; and now they range,
Busily seeking with a continual change.

Thanked be fortune, it hath been otherwise
Twenty times better; but once, in special,
In thin array, after a pleasant guise,
When her loose gown from her shoulders did fall,
And she me caught in her arms long and small,
Therewith all sweetly did me kiss,
And softly said, *'Dear heart, how like you this?'*

It was no dream; I lay broad waking:
But all is turned, thorough my gentleness,
Into a strange fashion of forsaking;
And I have leave to go, of her goodness;
And she also to use new-fangleness.
But since that I unkindly so am served,
*'How like you this?'* – what hath she now deserved?

Sir Thomas Wyatt (1503–42)

### 'They Flee From Me That Sometime Did Me Seek'

At this moment in time
the chicks that went for me
in a big way
are opting out;
as of now, it's an all-change situation.

The scenario was once,
for me, 100% better.
Kissing her was viable
in a nude or semi-nude situation.
It was *How's about it baby?*,
her embraces were relevant
and life-enhancing.

I was not hallucinating.
But with regard to that one
my permissiveness
has landed me in a forsaking situation.
The affair is no longer on-going.

She can, as of now, explore new parameters –
*How's about it?* indeed!
I feel emotionally underprivileged
What a bitch!
(and that's meaningful!)

Gavin Ewart (1916–)

## Focus on and analyse the question

As you well know by now, the first task when approaching any question is a focusing exercise, so take a moment to practise that now, then compare your response to the one below.

> **Explore** the **similarities** and the **differences** in the ways Wyatt and Ewart present their **feelings** about the **breakdown** of the **relationships** in the two poems.

It is important to note exactly what is implied by this focusing. You are asked to 'explore the similarities and the differences' – in other words, to state what is similar and what is different. You must look at **how** each poet presents his feelings about the breakdown of the relationship; you are *not* asked to concentrate on **what** he feels, although this is, to some extent, inexorably linked with the '**how**'. The 'what' is a matter for basic comprehension, and that is not what critical appreciation is all about. It is assumed that you have managed to figure out *what* each feels; focus now on *how* each poet expresses it.

## Read closely and think

The first, and most useful, question that we can ask when dealing with any text is, 'What is happening?' It might be rather basic, but it forms the foundation of our building and it needs to be established from the outset, before we build any more of our structure on top of it. Although practical criticism seeks to go a great deal further than 'mere' comprehension, this *has* to be the first stage. Close reading and careful thought will reveal that these poems deal with the thoughts and feelings of the narrator, who has observed a change in the behaviour of women towards him.

Let us look more closely at what is happening and pose the questions that we have asked before:

| Questions to ask | The answers to give |
|---|---|
| • **What** is happening? | The action |
| • To **whom** is it happening? | Main protagonists |

- **Why** is it happening?  Explanations
- **When** is it happening?  Past/present/future historical setting
- **Where** is it happening?  Context
- **How** is it happening?  Feelings in the work

## Thomas Wyatt's version (1503–42)

- **What** is happening? The narrator is bemoaning the changing behaviour of women and the rejection he is experiencing because of it.
- To **whom** is it happening? The main protagonists are the narrator and the potential female partners of his time.
- **Why** is it happening? It is happening because the behaviour of women is changing.
- **When** is it happening? It is happening now, but he is also reflecting on how it was in the past. Historically, the original version is set in the sixteenth century.
- **Where** is it happening? It is happening close to him, in his own life.
- **How** is it happening? He feels confused and badly treated.

## Gavin Ewart's version (1916–)

- **What** is happening? The narrator is complaining about the rejection he has experienced at the hands of modern women.
- To **whom** is it happening? The main protagonists are the narrator and the potential female partners of his time.
- **Why** is it happening? It is happening because the behaviour of women is changing.
- **When** is it happening? It is happening now, but he is reflecting on how it was in the past. Historically, this version is set in the twentieth century.
- **Where** is it happening? It is happening close to him, in his own life.
- **How** is it happening? He feels angry and yet sounds cool-headed.

Notice how the *feelings* differ in the two poems. Although there is common ground between the two, the emotions expressed are not quite the same. Ewart's verse has a much sharper edge than its sixteenth-century counterpart, and remember that the question asks you to focus on the respective narrators' 'feelings about the breakdown of the relationships'.

## Summarise the central conflict/s

Searching out the central conflict/s is easily achieved by identifying opposites in the language – pairs of words. See if you can spot any conflict that is reflected in the language of the poems, then compare your annotations with those on the 'Conflict Annotations' sheet that follows. As the content of both poems is so similar – Ewart's an updated version of Wyatt's – the conflict and time/change annotations will be on the original and the annotations on the language will focus on the modern version.

It is helpful to pinpoint the conflict precisely by answering questions about each version.

## Thomas Wyatt's version

- **What** is this conflict?
  The conflicts are:  time (past and present);
  behaviour (tame and wild);
  temperament (passive and active); and
  gender (feminine and masculine).
- **Who** is involved? The narrator and his potential female partners.
- **Why** is it there? It is there because women's behaviour has changed and the narrator is disturbed by this.
- **When** is it taking place? The conflict is taking place *now*, at the time of writing.
- **Where** is it? The conflict is within the narrator as well as between him and women.
- **How** is it being acted out? It is being acted out in the changing behaviour of the women and in his attitude to this. The women are becoming more independent and he is disturbed by this turn of events.

You will notice that the principal areas of conflict are all present in the *first* stanza. Remember that the beginning is always an important part of any text, and this poem is no exception. Notice: 'flee'/'seek', 'tame'/'wild', 'put themselves in danger to take bread at my hand'/'now they range, Busily seeking' and 'sometime'/'now'. *Simple pairs of opposites* encapsulate the nature and the extent of the conflict in the whole poem and *it this all in the first stanza.*

To be entirely clear about this conflict, we need to identify it accurately:

'flee'/'seek' – **attraction/disenchantment**;
'take bread'/'range'– **dependent/independent**;
'tame'/'wild' – **under control/out of control**; and
'sometime'/'now' – **past/present**.

These points of conflict act as early markers, and you should try to keep focused on these.

### Gavin Ewart's version

There is little point in replicating the points that are identical for both poems, and the answers to the questions: what? who? why? when? where? and how? are all similar. What is different, of course, is the language of conflict in the first stanza that establishes its nature in such a significant way:

'went for me'/'opting out'– **attraction/disenchantment**;
'went for me'/'opting out' – **dependent/independent**;
'went for me'/'opting out' – **under control/out of control**; and
'went'/'now' – **past/present**.

You will notice that the language in Ewart's verse offers much less variety than Wyatt's, and we draw *several* conclusions about the existence of conflict from just *two* phrases.

## Track the themes and develop the themes

Read through the poem with the areas of conflict outlined above firmly in your mind and look for further evidence of them. How does the writer *continue* to weave this thread of conflict throughout his work?

### Wyatt's version

Remember to use the approach discussed in Chapter 5. You should have these headings in the margin:

**attraction/disenchantment;**
**dependent/independent;**
**under control/out of control;**
**past/present;**

and to these headings should be 'tied' by a line, *all textual references that relate to each point*. **Remember always to do this** for the purposes of time management and organisation of your essay.

Now we need to consider what happens to these themes. Where do they go? How are they developed?

The elements of **attraction/disenchantment, dependent/independent, under control/out of control** and **past/present** that were identified in the first stanza can be seen recurring and being developed in subsequent stanzas. Go through the poem now and highlight all references to these elements. There should be no 'floating quotations' or 'loose comments' in the margin.

In the second stanza we see the recurrence of **past/present**: 'it hath been otherwise' and 'but once', together with continuous use of the past tense, contrasting with the present tense, that characterises the opening line of the poem.

This past tense continues in the third stanza, but soon changes to an appraisal of the way things are now with 'all *is* turned'. This is the last we hear of the past tense because the 'hath . . . deserved' at the end is interrupted by 'now', signifying the present.

The **attraction/disenchantment** idea is developed in the second stanza, with the narrator's romantic detail about a moment of seduction:

> When her loose gown from her shoulders did fall
> And she me caught in her arms long and small,

This picture of attraction is shattered in the third stanza, with 'But all is turned'.

The **dependent/independent** theme is also developed. In the first stanza the women were 'gentle, tame and meek' but 'now are wild'. They have forgotten that once they 'put themselves in danger/To take bread at my hand'; now he has 'leave to go', a victim of their 'strange fashion of forsaking'. She has 'leave' to 'use new-fangleness'. She has become independent, with the right to choose a new type of behaviour.

This is close to the idea of being **under control/out of control**. Notice the *nature* of the imagery used in the first stanza. The narrator is the man with the bread; the women are the animals, perhaps birds that risk danger to take the food from his hand. He is in a position of power – the traditional figure of a human being holding authority over the animals. Now they are wild, not tame. They 'range', out of his control; they are 'busily seeking' – actively searching for what they want, not merely risking danger to take whatever it is that he has to give them. He is now in a situation of 'continual change' and therefore he is no longer in control.

Look now at the sheet entitled 'Annotations on Time/Change'.

---

*Box 12.2* **ANNOTATIONS ON TIME/CHANGE**

**'They Flee From Me That Sometime Did Me Seek'**

*present tense*     They flee from me that sometime did me seek,    *change*
            With naked foot stalking in my chamber:

---

| | |
|---|---|
| *past tense* | I have seen them gentle, tame and meek, |
| | That now are wild, and do not once remember |
| *present tense* | That sometime they have put themselves in danger |
| | To take bread at my hand; and now they range |
| *past* | Busily seeking with a continual change.    *change* |
| *past/present* | Thanked be fortune, it hath been otherwise |
| | Twenty times better; but once, in special, |
| | In thin array, after a pleasant guise,    *past tense* |
| | When her loose gown from her shoulders did fall, |
| | And she me caught in her arms long and small, |
| | Therewith all sweetly did me kiss, |
| | And softly said, '*Dear heart, how like you this?*' |
| *past* | It was no dream; I lay broad waking:    *change* |
| | But all is turned, thorough my gentleness, |
| *present* | Into a strange fashion of forsaking;    *change* |
| | And I have leave to go, of her goodness; |
| | And she also to use new-fangleness.    *change* |
| | But since that I unkindely so am served, |
| | '*How like you this?*' – what hath she now deserved? |

Sir Thomas Wyatt, 1503–42

## Ewart's version

Follow a similar process for this version of the poem, going through it looking for the development of the principal themes:

**attraction/disenchantment;**
**dependent/independent;**
**under control/out of control;**
**past/present.**

Now compare your findings with what follows.

The **past/present** conflict is developed in the second stanza, with continuous use of the past tense – 'was'/'were', leading into the third stanza, which ends with 'The affair *is* no longer on-going' and the 'now' of the last stanza.

The **attraction/disenchantment** idea develops in the second and third stanzas, albeit in very different terms from those used by Wyatt. We have to look hard for it in 'Kissing her was viable/in a nude or semi-nude situation' and in 'her embraces were relevant/and life-enhancing'.

The idea of **dependent/independent** evolves in the last stanza with her new ability to 'explore new parameters' after his 'permissiveness has landed [him] in a forsaking situation'. She is exercising her right to end their relationship and to look elsewhere, and this leads us to the **under control/out of control** idea. Notice the *active* tone of the word 'explore' and the way in which she has *chosen* to leave him after his self-confessed 'permissiveness'. She has done what she needed to do; he is left feeling 'emotionally underprivileged', and resenting her for it.

# How does it end?

## Wyatt's version

I hope that you noticed the sting in the tail at the end. We are led through this tale of woe by a narrator who bemoans the changing behaviour of women in his time. He even blames his own 'gentleness' for the loss of one particular temptress and her dreamlike powers of seduction. However, as the poem ends we sense that a burning retaliation is imminent. He quotes the words that she used in a moment of passion to reveal his desire to exact his revenge upon her and this twisting and 'misquoting' adds an almost sadistic tone to the end of the verse. We are left wondering what exactly he intends to do. The poem ends with a question; he is deciding what she deserves and we have the distinct feeling that he intends to mete out her punishment according to the pain that her changed behaviour has caused him.

## Ewart's version

Interestingly, there would appear to be less of a sting in the tail in the later version than the earlier. Ewart's narrator states how he feels – 'emotionally underprivileged' – and calls her 'a bitch', but his recycling of her 'How's about it?' lacks the venom in Wyatt's verse because it is followed by 'indeed!' This means that we do not get a sense of his asking her if she likes what he is about to do to her in revenge.

Ewart's ending, much like the rest of the verse, is a bland version of the original. So, what has the end achieved? It has:

- Returned the reader to the beginning of the poem, inviting him/her to compare the two situations; and
- Revealed the writer's thoughts and feelings about the event or experience that 'gave birth' to the poem.

## Wyatt's version

Compare the end with the beginning. The tone of the first line is forlorn, almost melancholy; that of the last, angry and vengeful. His reflections have brought him to the point where he seeks revenge upon womankind for his pain.

It is interesting, in the twenty-first-century climate of feminism, to see the issues of women, men and power being addressed in the poetry of the sixteenth century. It is also interesting to note this particular narrator's response to the changing behaviour of women. Perhaps this poem asks a modern audience to consider its *real* reactions to the same issue. I am not suggesting that this was Wyatt's intention in writing this verse, merely that as an audience, we should consider our reaction to the changing position of women in society and its effect on men in our personal response to this particular text.

### Ewart's version

Compare the end with the beginning. The tone of the first line is bland – an unemotional statement about the status quo. That of the last *tries* to be controlled and passionless, but the feeling breaks out in 'What a bitch!'. His reflections have brought him to the point where he finds it difficult to remain entirely free from emotion.

## Summarise your response

We need to summarise concisely the ground we have covered, and establish what we are left with at the end. Response suggests *feelings*, so we must focus on these too, remembering always that poetry is about *emotion*. If we have failed to identify and respond to *that*, then we have neither understood nor appreciated it.

### Wyatt's version

The poem moves towards anger and revenge for the hurt sustained by the narrator, with a heavy emphasis on conflict, opposition and contrast, and yet there is also a depiction of mutual attraction and passion in the past. The narrator confides in us, the readers, sharing his feelings about the change in women's behaviour and the way this has affected him. We hear *his* thoughts, but interestingly, *her words*, suggesting her dominance and his subordination, and we enter the world of this man's relationship to women through *his* perceptions of it.

### Ewart's version

This poem moves towards anger at women, but there is less of a sign of a desire for revenge than in the original. Much of our response to the Wyatt version is applicable to Ewart's, except that the modern version is a much blander and more watery affair than the original. There is less variety in the language, which we shall look at now, and the very nature of the diction robs it of the passion and colour that was so evident in Wyatt's version.

## Language

### Gavin Ewart's version (twentieth century)

We have seen that there are numerous points of comparison between the two poems, and some would argue that they are almost identical. However, it is clear that the language that both poets use is very different. Surely, as we have already established, the 'how' is an intrinsic part of the 'what' in any piece of literature, it is not possible to say that the content is *precisely* the same if the language that is used is different.

Read the poem again and annotate it with your responses to Ewart's choice of language. Remember to look for *patterns*. When you have done this, refer to the Annotations on Language sheet and compare your responses. It is important that you do this exercise *before* looking at the sheet in the book. The poem requires close reading and careful thought about the *attitude* that is expressed by Ewart's choice of language, which is radically different from the original version. It might help you to think about life in the twentieth/twenty-first centuries and about the types of language people use today.

You should consider:

- What type/s of language are used; and
- The effect this has upon the text as a whole.

Now do the exercise.

---

*Box 12.3* **ANNOTATIONS ON LANGUAGE**

**'They Flee From Me That Sometime Did Me Seek'**

| | |
|---|---|
| pseudo educated/ serious | At this moment in time the chicks that went for me in a big way — 20th century |
| business-speak | are opting out; as of now, it's an all-change situation. 5 business-speak |
| | The scenario was once, for me, 100% better. business/economics |
| matter-of-fact/ business | Kissing her was viable business/logical in a nude or semi-nude situation. |
| | It was How's about it, baby?, 10 direct/unromantic her embraces were relevant |
| pop psychology | and life-enhancing. business-speak/pop psychology |
| business-speak | I was not hallucinating. But with regard to that one 20th century culture my permissiveness (drugs) 15 |
| business-speak | has landed me in a forsaking situation. direct/unromantic The affair is no longer on-going. |
| 20th century | She can, as of now, explore new parameters business-speak How's about it? indeed! |
| 20th century | I feel emotionally underprivileged 20 What a bitch! psychobabble (and that's meaningful!) psychobabble |

Gavin Ewart, (1916–)

---

I hope you will have noticed that Ewart's language is deeply rooted in the twentieth/twenty-first centuries. It is full of clichés and terms with which we are all familiar, but which, because of over-use, have become meaningless and lifeless. The annotations largely speak for themselves and need little explanation. I have used the following 'shorthand' to describe the diction:

## pseudo educated/serious

By this I mean the way people sometimes speak in order to sound educated, precise and official; for example, 'At this moment in time'. This is typical perhaps of a spokesperson who is trying to sound impressive and professional when being interviewed on television. 'At this moment' is all that is needed; 'in time' is obvious and the addition of this rather 'overdoes' the formality.

## business-speak

This refers to words and phrases that are common in the world of business. For example: 'no longer on-going'. This is the sort of long-winded language that adds a note of formality and seriousness to what could quite simply have been expressed as 'stopped' or 'ended'. The language of business/economics is usually formal and contains numerous expressions that come into fashion and go out again just as quickly.

## psychobabble/pop psychology

Colloquial terms for the type of language that was originally used by therapists and psychologists but which is now finding its way into our social discourse, hence the term 'pop'; for example, 'I feel emotionally underprivileged'. This is the type of language with which people declare their emotions in an unemotional and objective way. It is a clear statement of the way he feels, but it has none of the force of powerful feeling attached to it.

## direct/unromantic

This refers to language that lacks the subtlety and romance of Wyatt's diction. For example: 'in a nude or semi-nude situation'. This is direct, unemotional and unromantic. It is blunt yet accurate – a clear statement of the 'situation', with no suggestion of amorous extravagance.

## twentieth century

This applies to words that are part of twentieth/twenty-first-century culture; for example, 'chicks', 'hallucinating' and 'in a big way'. The first two exemplify the language of the 1970s drug culture, while the third typifies contemporary collo-quial language.

So we have established that there are various *patterns* of language at work in Ewart's verse that are quite different from Wyatt's. The next important question we must ask is, 'What *effect* do these have on the text?'

## pseudo educated/serious

This adds a certain sense of control and distance to the piece. He maintains control by sounding official, and the distance comes because he gives the matter considerable *thought* while there is little evidence of *feeling*, until the penultimate line.

## business-speak

This technique sets the verse firmly in the twentieth/twenty-first centuries. The language of business pervades most areas of human life and the influences of commerce are to be felt in fields of work that were once untouched by such forces. This narrator's use of business-speak makes him appear cool-headed, objective and powerful. It also suggests opportunism; this man sees the male/female relationship in terms of business opportunities – notice how 'she can, as of now, explore new parameters'.

## psychobabble/pop psychology

This type of language points to a man who is aware of the existence of emotions but who is, ironically, expressing his in unemotional terms. He *knows* that women's changing behaviour has affected him adversely but he does not show that he *feels* it. The only sign of real, uncensored emotion is in the penultimate line, and the poem ends on an explosive note. Much of his feeling is covered up with his use of pseudo psychological/therapeutic terms and there is a sense of his playing some sort of game. It is too wordy, too deliberate and too professional to be honest or spontaneous.

## direct/unromantic

This characteristic adds bluntness to the poem. It suggests a man who sees his relationships with women in terms of facts, not feelings. If you are acquainted with Charles Dickens' Mr Gradgrind from *Hard Times*, this will sound familiar. This man is unlikely to be carried away on a wave of emotion, and his unromantic, factual account lacks the sensuousness and sensuality that is so evident in Wyatt's original.

## twentieth century

This type of language roots the verse firmly in the twentieth or twenty-first centuries, giving it a very contemporary feel. Because the diction is so obviously and deliberately modern, it works in part by relying on *our* bringing to the text the whole range of connotations that go with it. That is why I suggested to you before you analysed the poem that you thought carefully about life in the twentieth/twenty-first centuries and the type of language in use today.

We have already said that Ewart's language lacks the colour, variety and life that is evident in Wyatt's poem; in short, it is unpoetic and banal, partly because of the clichés which are, by definition, overworked and stale forms of language. Ewart's language is stereotypical of a contemporary businessman who has been on the usual management courses and emerges from them with the customary hoard of jargon with which to impress and exclude those who have not. Language is an effective carrier of power, and Ewart's verse presents a man whose language of business suggests that he is successful and whose language of therapy suggests that he is enlightened.

Ask yourself what Ewart might be trying to say about contemporary life by choosing to use this type of diction in his modern version of Wyatt's original. He is saying a great deal about life and priorities in the modern world, about image and attitudes. You could say that the language is, to some extent, a bland, prosaic cover-up for honest feeling. It lacks both the colour and the vibrancy of Wyatt's vivid honesty and it is diluted by contemporary influences that rob the male/female experience of its richness, spontaneity and 'poetry'. Surely this is part of Ewart's message. As a satirist, his role is to expose human folly and vice to ridicule and we should not allow his lightness and humour to detract from the force of his comment on the tendency of contemporary life to deaden and make bland our richest human experiences.

In putting the matter of the changing behaviour of women into a contemporary context, it suggests that the problem Wyatt's narrator had several hundred years ago is one that still exists. It also explores the ways in which some men in the present century handle that problem. If we compare the two, Wyatt's original seems a great deal more alive and real; Ewart's is more censored and conditioned. Perhaps this tells us as much about the changing behaviour of men as it does about the new face of women.

So, how did we get here? Again, we seem to have come a long way and yet the process has really been a simple one, following the methodology as before:

- The first step was that of **close reading** and **thinking**;
- Then we **focused** in the first stanza on the central **conflict**;
- The next step was to **track** this theme in the rest of the poem;
- We then looked at the ways in which this was **developed** elsewhere; and
- Finally, we thought about the **end** and reflected upon our whole **response** to the poem.

You now have all you need for a sound and analytical essay, an example of which follows.

## Sample essay – 'They Flee From Me That Sometime Did Me Seek'

The same title, the same form and much the same content, but such different pieces – this is the reader's immediate response to a comparison of Wyatt and Ewart's poems of the same title. The similarities jump out, from the title onwards. Both are male writers addressing the changing behaviour of women and its effect on them. While they share both theme and title, each is very much rooted in the linguistic traditions of its day. Thus our attention is drawn to the language they use and therefore to the way they express their different responses to the same situation.

Both pieces start in the present tense: 'At this moment in time' and 'They flee from me' but move quickly into an exploration of the past and the changes leading to the present 'situation', which is then returned to in the final stanza. Ewart's version exemplifies this particularly well, with the opening lines of each stanza setting it firmly in past or present: 'At this moment', 'The scenario was once', 'I was not hallucinating' and finally 'She can of now, explore new parameters', which hints at the future. This sets up a conflict between what has been and what is now, thereby highlighting the central theme of 'continual change' that is encapsulated in the title of both poems and the first line Wyatt's sixteenth-century version:

They flee from me [in the present] that sometime did me seek [in the past],

The first stanza of each poem also employs the animal, or more specifically, bird imagery in reference to women. Wyatt develops this overtly throughout the first stanza. His previous conquests are referred to as 'stalking . . . tame and meek', willing to 'put themselves in danger to take bread from my hand'. That is to say, they were dependent on the man, under his control and relatively passive. This is brought into stark contrast with 'new women', even in the sixteenth century. 'Now' they are 'wild' and 'range/Busily seeking with a continual change'; in other words, they are gaining their independence and making moves for themselves, looking for and taking what they want, rather than accepting what they are given. This notion is repeated in the final stanza, where Wyatt's lament that 'all is turned' links with the 'continual change' of line 7, and he refers to the behaviour he has outlined in stanza one as 'a strange fashion of forsaking . . . and . . . also to use new-fangleness'.

This is a story of disenchantment, both of women with men – 'They flee from me that sometime did me seek' and also of the narrator with 'new-fangleness'. Ewart expresses this very succinctly while drawing on the bird imagery and all its connotations, both in twentieth-century discourse and with reference to Wyatt's work as he complains that 'the chicks that went for me/in a big way/are opting out'. Now, he points out, 'it's an all change situation'.

Indeed, it could be argued that Ewart's version is almost an exact paraphrase, stanza by stanza, of the original, with Wyatt's final verse becoming Ewart's last two. It is certainly clear that both poets reflect on a better time in their second stanza. It is in a comparison of these two approaches that the coldness of Ewart's writing is brought into most stark contrast with the passion of Wyatt's. Wyatt paints a picture of seduction with references to 'her loose gown', 'her shoulders', 'her kiss' and, in contrast to the 'wild' women of the first stanza, the adverbs he uses are similarly feminine; she conducts herself 'sweetly' and 'softly'. This is sensual, sensuous and emotive language, and we can almost hear her devotion and submission as she asks, *'Dear heart, how like you this?'*

In his rendition of this 'scenario', Ewart strips away the passion, sensitivity and feminine beauty of the scene and plunges it into the icy language of the boardroom. This is no longer 'fortune' but a 'scenario', not 'special' but 'viable'.

The sensual image of a 'loose gown' falling to the floor is replaced by the blunt acknowledgements of the facts of 'a nude or semi-nude situation', and finally the 'sweet' kiss is rendered 'relevant' and, at best, 'life enhancing'. It is possible to see, in the contrast between the events described which are by definition loving, and the cold, unemotional mode of expression, the change that is essential to both works – the wildness of the formerly tame creature, the breaking away from expectation and the norm.

It cannot be said, however, that Ewart's poem lacks emotion and sentiment where Wyatt's is loving if a little bewildered. The final verse of each work reveals a different side of the poets from that previously shown. Wyatt expresses his shock at the change he sees in women's behaviour when he explains that, 'It was no dream; I lay broad waking', and this is mirrored in the penultimate stanza of Ewart's version. These lines bring us face to face with twentieth-century drug culture with his assertion that he 'was not hallucinating'. Nevertheless, whether it be 'new-fangleness' or 'new parameters' that women are now free to explore, the male recipients of their behaviour feel resentment. Wyatt considers himself 'unkindely... served' and responds to this with a real sting as he plots his revenge, ironically expressed through a corruption of the woman's own words in a previous and better time – '"*How like you this?*" – what hath she now deserved?'

The words of devotion, endearment and passivity of the second stanza have thus become weapons of the gender war by the end of the poem. This perhaps suggests that changing female behaviour necessarily results in changing male behaviour, and that women are not the only ones who can get tough!

Ewart also repeats his lover's words, but his tone is indignant – '*How's about it?* indeed!' This exclamation mark, however, reveals emotion behind the stilted psychobabble and pseudo-serious jargon of the verse. So it is that we believe his admission, 'I feel emotionally underprivileged', and glimpse true feeling behind language designed to hide it. In case we are unsure, or have missed the subtleties of this revelation, the narrator explodes with, 'What a bitch!' Our attention is drawn by parentheses to '(and that's meaningful!)' and we are prompted to ask, 'What is meaningful?' Is it the emotion, the expression of it, the relationship, or the poem or form itself? The inevitable emphasis on the word 'that's' suggests that something else is *not* as meaningful. This could almost be a literary pulling of the rug from beneath our feet. Is the poet suggesting that the psychobabble and pseudo-serious language of his own verse is in fact meaningless, and that it is only the spontaneous and free expression of emotion that means anything?

By the end of each very different work there is a twist, a sense of unease which itself reflects the discomfort caused by the changing nature of women's behaviour. Each poet approaches the same issue in a remarkably similar way, but from four hundred years apart, and as a result the reader is made aware not only of changing times but also of the constancy of human nature. In this way the poems function well together, but they are equally forceful when they stand alone. However, the exploration of their language reveals two very different types of impact, each a symptom of its time.

## Antony and Cleopatra and 'Funeral'

Read closely and carefully the following extract from Shakespeare's *Antony and Cleopatra*, and the poem 'Funeral' by W. H. Auden.

In the extract from Shakespeare's play, Cleopatra, the heroine, the Queen of Egypt, expresses her grief at the death of her lover, Antony, a famous soldier and joint ruler of the Roman Empire.

What do the extract and the poem have in common? How do they differ?
Your answer should consider:
– feelings and attitudes
– language and style.

(AQA (AEB) June 1996)

### *Antony and Cleopatra*, Act IV. Sc xv

| Cleopatra | O, See my women. | [*Antony dies*] | 1 |
| | The crown o' th' earth doth melt. My lord! | | |
| | O, withered is the garland of war, | | |
| | The soldier's pole is fall'n: young boys and girls | | |
| | Are level now with men. The odds is gone, | | 5 |
| | And there is nothing left remarkable | | |
| | Beneath the visiting moon. | [*Faints*] | |
| Charmian | O, quietness, lady! | | |
| Iras | She's dead too, our sovereign. | | |
| Charmian | Lady! | | 10 |
| Iras | Madam! | | |
| Charmian | O, madam, madam, madam! | | |
| Iras | Royal Egypt! Empress! | | |
| Charmian | Peace, peace, Iras! | | |
| Cleopatra | No more but e'en a woman, and commanded | | 15 |
| | By such poor passion as the maid that milks | | |
| | And does the meanest chares. It were for me | | |
| | To throw my scepter at the injurious gods, | | |

To tell them that this world did equal theirs
Till they had stol'n our jewel. All's but naught.                    20
                                        William Shakespeare

### 'Funeral'

Stop all the clocks, cut off the telephone,                          1
Prevent the dog from barking with a juicy bone,
Silence the pianos and with muffled drum
Bring out the coffin, let the mourners come.

Let the aeroplanes circle moaning overhead                          5
Scribbling on the sky the message He is Dead,
Put crepe bows round the white necks of the public doves,
Let the traffic policeman wear black cotton gloves.

He was my North, my South, my East, and West,
My working week and my Sunday rest,                                  10
My noon, my midnight, my talk, and song;
I thought that love would last forever; I was wrong.

The stars are not wanted now: put out every one;
Pack up the moon and dismantle the sun;
Pour away the ocean and sweep up the wood.                          15
Nothing now can ever come to any good.
                                        W. H. Auden


## Focus on and analyse the question

Let us begin by doing a focusing exercise on the question: What do the extract
and the poem **have in common** and how do they **differ**? In your answer you
should consider the **feelings** and **attitudes** as well as the **language** and the **style**.

If we extract the bare essentials in terms of focus, we are left with: **same/differ-
ent**, **feelings**, **attitudes**, **language** and **style**.

As usual, we start with the first step of the six-stage method.


## Read closely and think: *Antony and Cleopatra*

Now is the time to answer the basic comprehension-type questions. Remember
the key points to consider; and the reasons why we ask them.

| Questions to ask | What the answers give us |
|---|---|
| • **What** is happening? | Basic action |
| • To **whom** is it happening? | Main protagonists |
| • **Why** is it happening? | Explanations |
| • **When** is it happening? | Past/present/future historical setting |

- **Where** is it happening?          Context
- **How** is it happening?          Feelings in the work

We shall consider the Shakespeare extract from *Antony and Cleopatra* first.

- **What** is happening? Cleopatra is expressing to her maids, Charmian and Iras, her intense grief at the death of her lover, Antony. Her maids try to comfort her but she will not be consoled.
- To **whom** is it happening? It is happening to Cleopatra, and her maids are involved because it is in them that she confides.
- **Why** is it happening? It is happening because Cleopatra is grief-stricken and can see no point in living now that her lover is dead.
- **When** is it happening? As the text is drama, it is 'happening' now, because the actors are in front of us if we are watching it in a theatre, and in front of us in terms of visual imagination if we are reading the play. In the sense of historical time, it is set at the height of the Roman Empire and the language bears witness to that.
- **Where** is it happening? We are told that it is happening at a monument in Alexandria, in Egypt. We need to bear in mind the exotic connotations of Egypt and the Pyramids, and the sympathetic background that is suggested by the monument in the context of the death of this great man.
- **How** is it happening? It is happening with much grief and sorrow. Cleopatra's expression of grief is passionate and her sense of despair overwhelming. Charmian and Iras are similarly distraught at their mistress's suffering.

## Summarise the central conflict/s

The conflict in this extract is subtle, and the reader has to look for it and help to construct it, as indeed happens in any text. If we consider pairs of words or phrases we can begin to see some sort of opposition emerging: 'crown'/'melt', 'withered'/'garland', 'pole'/'fall'n', 'boys and girls/Are level now with men', 'the odds is gone', 'nothing left remarkable beneath the visiting moon', 'no more but e'en a woman', 'as the maid that milks/And does the meanest chares', 'stol'n our jewel', 'throw my scepter at the injurious gods', 'tell them that this world did equal theirs/Till they had stol'n our jewel' and 'All's but naught'.

At first glance, you might not find it easy to spot the conflict or tension in these quotations, and you should spend some time thinking about this now. Unless you are able to do this, you will not grasp the central opposition that acts as the text's driving force. Until you can do this, you have little upon which to work in your analysis.

Let us look at each quotation in turn.

### 'crown'/'melt'

The word 'crown' signifies power and force. To say that this concept is the opposite of 'melt' is to consider both ideas on a *connotative* as opposed to a *denotative* level. The word 'crown' does not literally mean the opposite of 'melt' but it *connotes* something that creates a tension between the two ideas. The word 'melt' suggests a disappearance, a blending, an evaporating into nothing, whereas 'crown' is a word that distinguishes from the ordinary he or she who wears it. It is a mark of distinction, of separateness.

### 'withered'/'garland'

The word 'withered' suggests dying, similar in a way to 'melt', and this is perhaps more obviously opposed to 'garland', which connotes life. A garland is a form of 'crown', a symbol of respect.

### 'pole'/'fall'n'

The word 'pole' connotes something tall and straight and upright, whereas 'fall'n' suggests quite the opposite.

### 'boys and girls/Are level now with men'

We know perfectly well that children are not 'level . . . with men'; they are different. Cleopatra is linking two things that are not the same. The conflict here is child/adult.

### 'the odds is gone'

This suggests that the difference has disappeared and it reminds us of 'crown'/'melt'.

### 'nothing left remarkable beneath the visiting moon'

The tension here is subtle and it is similar to 'the odds is gone'. Cleopatra is saying that now there is nothing exceptional in the world, which is, in a sense, a contradiction in terms, because the world is composed of a plethora of different and extraordinary phenomena.

### 'No more but e'en a woman'

The conflict here lies in the fact that Cleopatra is a great deal more than 'just' a woman; she is the Queen of Egypt. The tension comes from her public/private roles, emphasised by reference to 'Lady' (an ordinary position), then 'Madam', followed by 'Royal Egypt'(queen) and finally Empress (identifying her political power).

### 'as the maid that milks/And does the meanest chares'

Comparing herself to an ordinary woman merely serves to highlight her status as Queen of Egypt and lover of the joint ruler of the Roman Empire. Here is also the idea that in love and loss we are all equal.

### 'throw my scepter at the injurious gods'

The conflict here lies in two areas. The gods are abstract, yet if we interpret Cleopatra's words literally, she talks of throwing her scepter at them. There is a mismatch here between the solid scepter and the intangible gods. If we respond to her on a figurative level, we see that she is talking about 'throwing' her 'weight' as a mortal ruler of Egypt at the gods – to face them with the fact that her world with Antony in it was as extraordinary as theirs, 'Till they had stol'n our jewel'. There has been a fall from demigod to milkmaid.

## 'tell them that this world did equal theirs/Till they had stol'n our jewel'

Notice the conflict in 'did'/'Till', which signifies past/present and 'this world'/ 'they', which suggests a conflict between her world and the gods.

## 'stol'n our jewel'

Look again at 'crown'/'melt' and you should be able to see a similarity between the two quotations. Once more, we have this sense of something extraordinary disappearing. Something precious, which should be cherished and guarded, has been taken away.

## 'All's but naught'

Simply put, Cleopatra is saying that everything is nothing. This conflict is self-explanatory.

Again, the key questions to ask, this time about the conflict in the extract, are:

- **What is the conflict?** The conflict would seem to be between what the world *was* like for Cleopatra *with* Antony and what it *is* now like *without* him. It is to do with the *special* and the *ordinary*. So, we can summarise this as:

  - past/present;
  - with him/without him; and
  - special/ordinary.

- **Whom is the conflict between?** The conflict is between:

  - Cleopatra and the gods;
  - Cleopatra and her maids; and
  - Cleopatra and the world.

- **Why does the conflict exist?**

  - Cleopatra and the gods: she is angry with them at the death of her lover;
  - Cleopatra and her maids: she is distraught and they are trying to soothe her; and
  - Cleopatra and the world: she does not see the point of living in a world without Antony.

- **When is the conflict taking place?** Because the genre is drama, the time is now, although we are aware of the play's historical context. We are involved in Cleopatra's suffering as it happens and we follow her to her suicide.

- **Where is the conflict taking place?** The conflict occurs:

  - In the geographical context of Egypt, towards the end of Cleopatra's life (69 BC–30 BC);
  - Between the world of the gods and the mortal world;
  - Between the royal status of the queen and the servant status of Charmian and Iras; and
  - Between Cleopatra and the world.

- **How is it manifesting itself?** It is painful:

  - Cleopatra suffers because of the loss of her lover; and
  - Her maids suffer because their mistress is distraught and they are unable to comfort her.

Look now at the sheet entitled 'Conflict Annotations'.

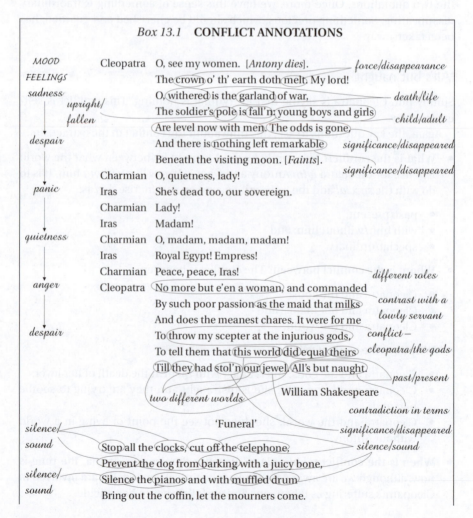

Box 13.1   **CONFLICT ANNOTATIONS**

| | | | |
|---|---|---|---|
| MOOD | Cleopatra | O, see my women. [*Antony dies*]. | force/disappearance |
| FEELINGS | | The crown o' th' earth doth melt. My lord! | |
| sadness | | O, withered is the garland of war, | death/life |
| *upright/ fallen* | | The soldier's pole is fall'n; young boys and girls | |
| | | Are level now with men. The odds is gone, | child/adult |
| despair | | And there is nothing left remarkable | significance/disappeared |
| | | Beneath the visiting moon. [*Faints*]. | significance/disappeared |
| panic | Charmian | O, quietness, lady! | |
| | Iras | She's dead too, our sovereign. | |
| | Charmian | Lady! | |
| | Iras | Madam! | |
| quietness | Charmian | O, madam, madam, madam! | |
| | Iras | Royal Egypt! Empress! | |
| anger | Charmian | Peace, peace, Iras! | different roles |
| | Cleopatra | No more but e'en a woman, and commanded | contrast with a |
| | | By such poor passion as the maid that milks | lowly servant |
| | | And does the meanest chares. It were for me | |
| despair | | To throw my scepter at the injurious gods, | conflict – |
| | | To tell them that this world did equal theirs | cleopatra/the gods |
| | | Till they had stol'n our jewel. All's but naught. | |
| | | | past/present |
| | *two different worlds* | William Shakespeare | |
| | | | contradiction in terms |
| silence/ | | 'Funeral' | significance/disappeared |
| sound | | Stop all the clocks, cut off the telephone, | silence/sound |
| | | Prevent the dog from barking with a juicy bone, | |
| silence/ | | Silence the pianos and with muffled drum | |
| sound | | Bring out the coffin, let the mourners come. | |

Box 13.1   (Contd)

Let the aeroplanes circle moaning overhead         *direction/circling*
Scribbling on the sky the message He is Dead,
Put crepe bows round the white necks of the public doves,         *black/white*
*public/*  Let the traffic policeman wear black cotton gloves.
                                                                 *directions*
*private*   He was my North, my South, my East, and West,
*work/rest*  My working week and my Sunday rest,         *week/weekend*
                                                         *work/rest*
*time of day*  My noon, my midnight, my talk, my song;         *way of*
I thought that love would last forever; I was wrong.         *communicating*

                                                         *thinking/reality*
The stars are not wanted now: put out every one;         *light/dark*
*night/day*  Pack up the moon and dismantle the sun;
Pour away the ocean and sweep up the wood.         *human acts/*
For nothing now can ever come to any good.         *natural life*

*life/no hope*                     W. H. Auden

## Track the themes and develop the themes elsewhere

At this stage, read through the text with the areas of conflict outlined above firmly in your mind and look for further evidence of them. How does Shakespeare *continue* to weave this thread of conflict throughout his work?

Once the nature of the central conflict/s has been established clearly, you need to consider how these ideas have been developed. The commentary in note form that follows tracks this growth:

- **Dramatic language**, suggesting intense emotion:
  Line 1: 'O, see my women'; and
  Line 3: 'O, withered is the garland of war'.
- **Fractured language**, suggesting drama and emotion:
  Lines 8–14.
- **Reflective language**:
  Lines 2–7; and
  Lines 15–20.
- **Symmetrical language**:
  Lines 2–7, reflective, longer lines;
  Lines 8–14, dramatic, shorter lines; and
  Longer, more contemplative lines frame shorter, 'breathy' lines of the maids in the middle of the extract.
- **Language of nothingness**:
  Line 2: 'melt';
  Line 3: 'withered';

Line 4: 'fall'n';
Line 5: 'level'; and
Line 6: 'nothing'.

- **Change in mood/feeling**:
  Lines 1–7, sadness;
  Lines 9–13, despair/panic;
  Line 14, quietness; and
  Lines 15–20 despair.
- **Public nature of Antony's status and Cleopatra's grief**:
  Line 2: 'crown of the earth';
  Line 3: 'garland of war';
  Line 4: 'soldier';
  Line 9: 'sovereign';
  Line 13: 'Royal Egypt'/'Empress'; and
  Line 18: 'scepter'.
- **Large scale**:
  Line 2: 'crown of the earth';
  Line 9: 'sovereign';
  Line 18: 'gods'; and
  Line 19: 'this world'.
- **Apocalyptic imagery**:
  Line 20: 'All's but naught';
  Lines 6–7: 'there is nothing left remarkable/Beneath the visiting moon'; and
  Line 9: 'She is dead too, our sovereign.'

Look now at the sheet entitled 'Language Annotations'.

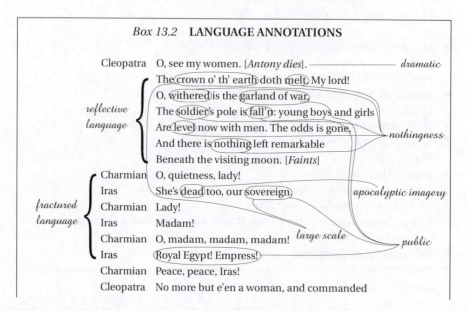

Box 13.2   **LANGUAGE ANNOTATIONS**

Cleopatra   O, see my women. [*Antony dies*]. ──────── *dramatic*

*reflective language*
{
The crown o' th' earth doth melt. My lord!
O, withered is the garland of war,
The soldier's pole is fall'n: young boys and girls
Are level now with men. The odds is gone,
And there is nothing left remarkable
Beneath the visiting moon. [*Faints*]
}
*nothingness*

*fractured language*
{
Charmian   O, quietness, lady!
Iras   She's dead too, our sovereign.
Charmian   Lady!
Iras   Madam!
Charmian   O, madam, madam, madam!   *large scale*
Iras   Royal Egypt! Empress!
Charmian   Peace, peace, Iras!
Cleopatra   No more but e'en a woman, and commanded
}
*apocalyptic imagery*

*public*

Box 13.2 (Contd)

*reflective*
*language* {

By such poor passion as the maid that milks   *public*
And does the meanest chares. It were for me
To throw my scepter at the injurious gods,  *apocalyptic imagery*
To tell them that this world did equal theirs
Till they had stol'n our jewel. All's but naught.

*large scale*

William Shakespeare

## How does it end?

It is important to remember that this extract does not represent the end of the play. All we can do is to consider it in context and comment on the *end of this extract* in relation to the rest of it.

The last point under the previous section provides us with the answer to the question of how this extract ends. It finishes on an apocalyptic note, with the imagery of nihilism. There is nothing left for Cleopatra and it is this realisation that leads her to suicide. The intensity of the emotion, the dramatic expression of grief and the utter despair of the maids are all encapsulated in Iras's 'She's dead too, our sovereign'. We are left with nothing at the end of the extract. Cleopatra's power, status and sovereignty have no meaning for her without Antony. She has no future for which to live.

From the dramatic 'O, see my women', we are taken through a range of emotions outlined in the previous section, to arrive at the end of this extract with 'naught'. There is at once a climax, and an anti-climax, and we cannot help but feel the heroine's utter despair. Her language is expansive – she lived and loved on a grand scale – but at the end, 'All's but naught'.

## Summarise your response

Cleopatra's grief is expressed in such a way that we cannot help but empathise with her sense of hopelessness. In confiding in her maidservants, she informs the audience of her utter despair in a world that no longer has her Antony in it. Now it is a place where 'the odds is gone' and we are left with the feeling that Cleopatra would be happier out of it.

She is inconsolable and Iras's comment when her mistress faints that, 'She's dead too, our sovereign', refers as much to the collapse of Cleopatra's spirit as it does to that of her body. Her fainting body and will to live foreshadow her later physical suicide, and by the end of this extract we cannot help but feel that, without Antony, this world holds nothing to keep her alive.

We follow Cleopatra through several changes in emotion, from the animated 'O, see my women' to the lifeless 'All's but naught' in the final line. There seems to be a note of resignation in this line, and the heavy, monosyllabic statement is a fitting final note to this extract.

We are left with the sense that the Queen of Egypt has shared with us her most intimate thoughts and feelings. We have heard her deepest sorrow expressed in terms of thoughtful observation about the world without Antony, but with an intensity of pain that makes her final declaration understandable. We are as helpless as her maids; she cannot be consoled.

Now let us look at W. H. Auden's 'Funeral'.

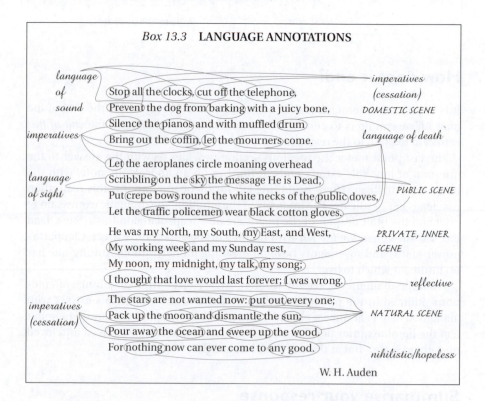

Box 13.3   **LANGUAGE ANNOTATIONS**

*language of sound*

*imperatives*

*language of sight*

*imperatives (cessation)*

Stop all the clocks, cut off the telephone,
Prevent the dog from barking with a juicy bone,
Silence the pianos and with muffled drum
Bring out the coffin, let the mourners come.

Let the aeroplanes circle moaning overhead
Scribbling on the sky the message He is Dead,
Put crepe bows round the white necks of the public doves,
Let the traffic policemen wear black cotton gloves.

He was my North, my South, my East, and West,
My working week and my Sunday rest,
My noon, my midnight, my talk, my song;
I thought that love would last forever; I was wrong.

The stars are not wanted now: put out every one;
Pack up the moon and dismantle the sun;
Pour away the ocean and sweep up the wood.
For nothing now can ever come to any good.

*imperatives (cessation)*
DOMESTIC SCENE

*language of death*

PUBLIC SCENE

PRIVATE, INNER SCENE

*reflective*

NATURAL SCENE

*nihilistic/hopeless*

W. H. Auden

# Read closely and think: 'Funeral'

Again, we must answer the basic questions:

- **What** is happening? Auden's narrator is grieving at the loss of a loved one. He issues instructions to the world about what to do, now that the object of his love has gone.
- To **whom** is it happening? It is happening to the narrator, whose grief is expressed in the first person.
- **Why** is it happening? It is happening because the narrator is stricken with grief with which he is trying to deal. It is his response to loss.
- **When** is it happening? His grief is present, with 'let' suggesting the future. We sense that the death is recent.

- **Where** is it happening? The setting is a domestic and urban one, although nature is mentioned at the end. Icons of modern life abound and there are references to traffic.
- **How** is it happening? It is happening sombrely and deliberately. This expression of grief takes the form of a list of instructions, which communicate his sense of loss.

## Summarise the central conflict/s

As with the extract from *Antony and Cleopatra*, we shall consider the pairs that suggest tension:

- **Stanza one**: 'Stop'/'clocks', 'cut off'/'telephone', 'Prevent the dog from barking', 'Silence the pianos', 'muffled drum'.
- **Stanza two**: 'Let the aeroplanes circle', 'crepe bows'/'white necks', 'public'/'my' (stanza 3).
- **Stanza three**: 'North'/'South', 'East'/'West', 'working week'/'Sunday rest', 'noon'/'midnight', 'talk'/'song', 'thought'/'was wrong'.
- **Stanza four**: 'stars'/'put out', 'Pack up the moon'/'dismantle the sun', 'Pour away the ocean', 'sweep up the wood', 'nothing'/'any good'.

As with the Shakespeare extract, we cannot say that each of these 'pairs' is a precise example of a binary opposite. The opposite of 'stop' is not 'clocks' but, as has been discussed before, when we look for tension or conflict, we need to explore the connotative levels of meaning as well as the denotative interpretations. To clarify that point, the opposite of 'stop' on a purely *denotative* level would be 'start' or 'begin'. The word 'clocks' can be the opposite of 'stop' *in this context*, on a *connotative* level because of the *associations* that come with the word. With 'clocks' we connect time and its seemingly endless passage, continuity and the sound of ticking. With these connotations in mind, it is then quite easy to sense the opposition and tension in the word 'stop'.

Using this approach to the interpretation of tension, we shall consider the other pairs:

- **Stanza one**
  - 'cut off'/'telephone'.
    The conflict here is similar to that discussed in 'stop'/'clocks'. The element of sound suggested by 'telephone' is abruptly contrasted by 'cut off'.
  - 'Prevent the dog from barking'.
    Again, this has the same feeling as the previous two pairs. Barking is a natural function of dogs; indeed, it is the reason why some people have them, to act as an early warning system. 'Prevent' acts upon 'barking' in the same way as 'stop' does on 'clock' and 'cut off' does on 'telephone'.
  - 'Silence the pianos', 'muffled drum'.

These two examples are similar. Both instruments create sound and the words 'Silence' and 'muffled' act on 'pianos' and 'drum' in a similar way to the examples already discussed.

- **Stanza two**
  - 'Let the aeroplanes circle'.
    The tension here is not obvious but the usual flight path of an aeroplane is not circular; its function is to move people or freight from one place to another, and therefore its direction is linear. The narrator is suggesting that the aeroplanes counter this natural movement and 'circle' instead.
  - 'crepe bows'/'white necks'.
    You will see this tension only if you are aware that 'crepe bows' are black and were traditionally worn at funerals. The contrast then, is between black and white.
  - 'public'/'my' (stanza three).
    The communal element that is suggested by words such as 'aeroplanes', 'scribbling on the sky', 'public' and 'traffic policeman' contrasts with the private grief expressed in 'my North, my South, my East, and West' and the other references to 'my' in stanza three.

- **Stanza three**
  - 'North'/'South', 'East'/'West'.
    There is, in this contrast, a sense of his lost love having been all things to him. The object of his affection was everywhere and he was the narrator's direction in life.
  - 'working week'/'Sunday rest'.
    This creates a sense of the dead person having been the focus of his life in terms of time. He was there while he worked and when he rested.
  - 'noon'/'midnight'.
    This is similar to the previous point, in that the loved one's presence permeated his life at all times.
  - 'talk'/'song'.
    This is an indication of the way in which his lost love pervaded all areas of social activity in his life.
  - 'thought'/'was wrong'.
    The effect of this conflict is to highlight the narrator's flawed belief that 'love would last forever'.

- **Stanza four**
  - 'stars'/'put out'.
    The visual imagery here serves to create a picture of light (and therefore, in connotative terms, hope) being extinguished. Bearing in mind also the millions of years that many stars have existed, this instruction reinforces dramatically the narrator's feeling that the world's most established natural patterns must stop, now that his love has gone.

- 'Pack up the moon'/'dismantle the sun'.
  Contrast between 'moon' and 'sun' suggests that neither extreme of natural light, nor the night or day that each represents, can continue now. 'Pack up' and 'dismantle' work on 'moon' and 'sun' in a similar way to 'stop' and 'cut off' in stanza one.
- 'Pour away the ocean', 'sweep up the wood'.
  'Pour away' and 'sweep up' are everyday domestic actions that take place when something is no longer required and needs to be removed. 'Pour away' acts on 'ocean' in such a way that we sense a conflict; the ocean is vast, far beyond the ability of humans to 'Pour [it] away' as one would an unwanted glass of water. The verbs and their objects function similarly in 'sweep up the wood'. Notice the opposites referred to in this stanza: the fluidity of the ocean and the solidity of the wood.
- 'nothing'/'any good'.
  This statement of despair rests on the narrator's belief that everything in life is hopeless. There is tension in this because life itself offers some form of hope.

# Track the themes and develop the themes elsewhere

Looking at the language reveals some interesting developments in terms of the themes that we have now established by examining the conflict in the poem.

**Stanza one:**   The diction is organised largely around references to sound: 'clocks', 'telephone', 'barking', 'Silence', 'pianos', 'muffled drum'. The imagery is also to do with the domestic scene.

**Stanza two:**   The language focuses more on sight: 'circle', 'scribbling', 'sky', 'message', 'crepe bows', 'white necks' and 'black cotton gloves'. The imagery here tends to be more public; the message is to be proclaimed from the air, the doves and the traffic policemen (nature and humankind) are to be suitably attired.

**Stanza three:**   Here the language is private, with repetition of 'my'. The narrator's inner life seems to be the focus; 'I thought' and 'I was wrong'.

**Stanza four:**   The language is to do with nature, with references to 'stars', 'moon', 'sun', 'ocean' and 'wood'. The scale of thought is vast and the language emphatic, with 'nothing', 'ever' and 'any'.

The tone is sombre and deliberate throughout. There seem to be few rages of passion; this narrator's pain is comparatively 'quiet' and he wants the world to stop functioning because 'Nothing now can ever come to any good'. There is a note of melancholic resignation and the tone is nihilistic.

Notice the language of death: 'drum', 'coffin', 'mourners', 'crepe bows' and 'black', and the way in which all the verbs refer to cessation (stopping). They are all negative directives in the sense that they all represent something not happening any more: 'Stop', 'cut off', 'prevent', 'Silence' and so on. It is easy to connect the two strands of meaning; the narrator wants everything to stop because his loved one has stopped living. It is a common feature of the grieving process that survivors do not want *the world* to continue with its usual, inevitable patterns when they feel that *their world* has stopped. Notice the sense of isolation in the first stanza. This gives the poem a cold feeling, which reflects the narrator's sense of emptiness.

The imperatives issued throughout the verse could be the narrator's attempts to gain control over a world in which he feels he has lost all power. The issue of control can also be seen, perhaps, in the rhyme scheme. The regular AABB rhyme that pertains throughout gives the verse a sense of regulation and management. Finality and rationality seem not to be too far away from this grieving narrator. It could be an attempt to create order out of chaos – a way of reorganising and manipulating a world that has taken away his reason for living. This narrator's expression of grief seems to be a reasoned argument: stop all these things from happening now because there is no point in any of them any more. There is despair in his voice but it is strangely mixed with a grief-stricken reason.

## How does it end?

It ends on a note of despair that seems to be the product of some sort of logical process. The 'for' in the last line suggests that the narrator is offering an *explanation* for his desire for everything to cease. That final line comes as a heavy blow, a sudden full stop, and there is a powerful sense of hopelessness. We understand his argument; if it is true that 'nothing now can ever come to any good', then his desire to stop the world really is quite reasonable.

## Summarise your response

The opening lines of the poem establish the tone for the rest of it and we are prepared from the start for the long list of negative instructions by this melancholic narrator.

The vastness of the scale on which he expresses his grief is impressive and we are left in no doubt as to the effect that this loss has had on him. Pathos grows stanza by stanza as he shares with us the extent and intensity of his feelings, and the rhythm of the whole poem continues unabated until the abrupt conclusion in the last line. As we are given long lists of all aspects of human and natural life that should cease to function, we start to follow this stream and move with it. We almost become accustomed to the nature of this narrator's thinking and are swept along to the end of the poem, only to be faced with what feels like a brick wall in the last line with its abrupt sense of utter despair.

What we are left with is the sense that a human being has shared with us his most intimate thoughts and feelings. We have heard his deepest sorrow expressed in terms of deliberate and, at times, seemingly rational thought, but the extent of his pain is no less for this; in fact, it seems arguably greater. The fires of passionate grief are not to be found in this verse, but the chill that comes with this narrator's approach is no less effective than Cleopatra's in communicating his sorrow.

Now that we have completed an analysis of both texts, the next step is to return to the question and try to answer it specifically.

## Return to the question

What do the extract and the poem *have in common* and how do they *differ*? In your answer you should consider the *feelings* and *attitudes* as well as the *language* and the *style*.

### Similarities

- Both texts are direct expressions of grief, which results from the loss of a loved one;
- Both are intensely personal;
- Both are emotional, although this feeling is expressed differently;
- Both engage the reader/audience by the strength of their reaction to death;
- Both express a sense of hopelessness without the loved one; and
- Both work towards a climactic end which is nihilistic in tone.

### Differences

- One is drama and the other verse;
- One is an extract and the other a complete text;
- One is set in BC Egypt and the other in contemporary society; and
- One narrator is female and the other probably male (W. H. Auden was homosexual). *object?*

### Feelings and attitudes – *Antony and Cleopatra*

- Cleopatra's grief is such that she feels that what was best in the world has gone – 'The crown o' th' earth doth melt';
- She feels that there is nothing special in life without Antony – 'there is nothing left remarkable/Beneath the visiting moon';
- She feels that now she is, 'No more but e'en a woman'; her immortal quality has vanished with Antony;
- She feels that life holds nothing for her now – 'All's but naught'; and
- Change in mood/feeling: lines 1–7 sadness; lines 9–13 despair; line 14 quietness; lines 15–20 despair.

## Language and style – *Antony and Cleopatra*

- **Dramatic language**: exclamation marks reflect the passage's intensely emotional and dramatic style. There is overt strength of feeling from Cleopatra and both her maids.
- **Fractured language**: the language of the maids is fractured and dramatic, seen in the short, rather gasped lines.
- **Symmetry/reflective language**: there is a noticeable symmetry in Cleopatra's speeches in that, while being dramatic and intense, they are also more reflective and thoughtful. This is suggested by the length of her lines and the nature of her language; for example, in lines 15–17: 'commanded/By such poor passion as the maid that milks/And does the meanest chares'. These longer and more contemplative lines frame the shorter, rather 'breathy' lines of the maids in the middle of the extract.
- **Language on a grand scale**: the language operates on a large scale with references to 'crown o' th' earth' (line 2); 'this world' (line 19); and 'gods' (line 18).
- **Public nature of language**: line 2 'crown o' th' earth', 'garland of war' and 'soldier's pole'.
- **Language of nothingness**: line 2 'melt'; line 3 'withered'; line 4 'fall'n'; line 5 'level'; and line 6 'nothing'. Monosyllabic finality in the last line: 'All's but naught'.
- **Apocalyptic language**: the sense of nothingness increases in intensity as the extract develops. Iras opines that, 'She's dead too, our sovereign'; and at the end of the extract Cleopatra declares with awful finality, 'All's but naught'.
- Because it is **drama**, we see Cleopatra expressing her grief to those on stage with her, and witness the interaction between these characters. The intensity of her grief is confirmed when we see the responses of her maids – 'She's dead too, our sovereign'. This interchange constitutes an intimate sharing of grief with her attendants.


## Feelings and attitudes – 'Funeral'

- **Stanza one**: the desire for the cessation of everyday life comes from the references to stopping sound: 'clocks', 'telephone', 'barking', 'Silence', 'pianos', 'muffled drum'. The domestic scene is the site for this death of sound.
- **Stanza two**: the feeling of grief comes from the focus on sight: 'circle', 'scribbling', 'sky', 'crepe bows', 'white necks' and 'black cotton gloves'. This constitutes a public display of grief.
- **Stanza three**: here the feeling is one of a private response to grief, with repetition of 'my' and details of the narrator's life.
- **Stanza four**: the feelings are transposed on to the natural world, with references to 'stars', 'moon', 'sun', 'ocean' and 'wood'. The narrator has no need for the romantic elements of nature as his lover has gone.
- The scale of thought is vast and the language emphatic, with 'Nothing', 'ever' and 'any'. There is a nihilistic note that runs throughout the verse, but intensifies dramatically in the last line with 'Nothing now can ever come to any good'.

## Language and style – 'Funeral'

- **Sombre diction**: the tone is gloomy, thoughtful and deliberate throughout: 'Stop', 'cut off', 'Silence' and 'muffled'.
- **Language of death**: 'drum', 'coffin', 'mourners', 'crepe bows' and 'black'.
- **Imperatives**: there are numerous imperatives throughout the verse, which could reflect the narrator's feelings of powerlessness and his attempt to gain control over his world. The issue of power/control is also suggested in the rhyme scheme.
- **Reasoned argument**: finality and rationality are strangely mixed with sorrow in what is perhaps an effort to bring order out of chaos. There is despair in his voice but it is suffused with a grief-stricken reason.
- **Coldness**: the language is coldly dramatic. While the instructions to 'Stop', 'cut off' and 'Prevent' are extreme and emotional, they also create a certain chill. They are the first steps in creating a cold, silent, empty world (without barking dogs, music or stars) which, in the narrator's mind, is the only true reflection of life without his loved one.

There is now plenty of material from which to write the essay, a sample version of which follows here.

## Sample essay – *Antony and Cleopatra* and 'Funeral'

Here are two pieces linked, it seems at first glance, by their theme alone. A piece of Shakespearian drama set in Egypt before the birth of Christ meets a contemporary poem by a notorious homosexual, and a mourning 'Empress' surrounded by her maids meets a lonely, urban, male lover. Closer inspection reveals differences between the pieces, but also a number of similarities.

From the first word of the *Antony and Cleopatra* extract we are aware of an outpouring of emotion as Cleopatra exclaims, 'O' and attracts the attention of her attendants and therefore the also audience. This exclamation is repeated four times in the extract to hold our attention and heighten the impact. 'See my women' entreats *us* to mark the situation and appreciate her loss and the resulting pain. This is not only a private grief, it is to affect 'th' earth'. She paints a very public figure – 'the crown o' th' earth', 'the garland of war', 'the soldier' and her repeated use of 'the' suggests that Antony was a universal figure – not '*a* soldier' but '*the* soldier' and thus the effects of his passing influence everything. 'Young boys and girls/Are level now with men. The odds is gone/And there is nothing left remarkable/Beneath the visiting moon'. Nothing escapes untouched by the loss of this man.

This conflict between what was and what should be, and the 'nothing' that is now in its place is reflected in the images of the melted crown, 'withered ... garland' and the 'fall'n' pole. Each of these – crown, garland and pole – is a symbol of status and significance, and with Antony's death they are 'level[led]'. Nothing is 'remarkable', nothing sets things apart now; 'The odds is gone'. Thus we see that, as the saying goes, 'death is the great leveller' and we are left with a sense of empty, flat, deflated hopelessness.

The first seven lines of reflection are then mirrored by the last six lines of the extract, which are another expression of Cleopatra's responses to the impact of Antony's death. This time, however, her focus is a more personal one, as she reveals to her confidantes the effects on her. Her maids' panicked, disjointed and fractured speech is an appeal to Cleopatra in her many roles – as 'Lady', 'madam', 'Royal Egypt' and finally 'Empress'. It is interesting to see them relate to her, first as a woman, then as a boss, then as Egyptian sovereign, and finally as a woman of power and position. Thus her status grows, but is then suddenly cut down by her own retort, 'No more but e'en a woman' whom, she believes, is no longer in control, but rather is 'commanded/By... poor passion' so that she assumes the 'meanest' of social roles 'as the maid that milks'. Women of this rank tend animals and are therefore of an even lower status than the maids in whom she is confiding.

This conflict in position and rank is highlighted when she refers again to her status; 'my scepter' becomes a potential weapon against the gods. This arguably is reminiscent of Hamlet's 'arms against a sea of troubles', but neither protagonist's efforts can be effective; both are trying to fight the intangible with the tangible. Cleopatra's thoughts of hurling her scepter at the gods are futile; she and her weapons are mortal and the gods are not – she must fight like with like. 'This world ... [is *not*] theirs', although with Antony as part of it, it *had*, at least, been 'equal'.

Just as Antony's loss of stature is reflected in the imagery of Cleopatra's first lament, so her own lowliness and impotence is expressed in the second lament, for this was not just *any* man; Antony was hers, her all, and so she can conclude that, 'they had stol'n our jewel. All's but naught', which itself reflects the 'nothing left remarkable' of line 6.

Auden's 'Funeral' ends on a similar note, as he concludes that since the death of his lover, 'Nothing now can ever come to any good'. Both thus present us with what seems to them a logical, reasoned conclusion to their losses. Auden's reasoning up to this point, however, takes a very different tone from that employed by Shakespeare. Beginning as it does with an instruction, this poem continues with a list of imperatives as the narrator coldly directs the world to respond to what is, for him, an earth-shattering loss. He begins with the cessation of everyday life on a domestic level as he attempts to silence his immediate world, to 'Stop all the clocks, cut off the telephone/Prevent the dog from barking [and] ... Silence the pianos'. In short, nothing is allowed to continue doing what it naturally does. There is here a clear correlation with Cleopatra's reference to 'The crown of the earth [which] doth melt', 'withered ... garland' and 'fall'n' pole and in its appeal to the domestic, can also be seen as similar to Cleopatra's 'meanest chares'. Indeed, Auden does not keep his representation of grief within the domestic sphere, but rather metaphorically 'Bring[s] out the coffin [and] let[s] the mourners come' as he appeals to the aeroplanes to change their course, to 'circle moaning overhead' and announce to the world that 'He is Dead'. What is more, the 'public doves' and 'traffic policemen' are instructed to show their respect with traditional symbols of death such as the 'crepe bows' and 'black cotton gloves'.

Just as Cleopatra claims her grief as her own, dragging it from the public into the private, so Auden's narrator does the same in the third stanza, repeating the word 'my' eight times in three lines and many times privileging it and the word 'I' with positions at the beginning of a line or following a caesura, for emphasis. It is in this stanza that the scale of the narrator's feelings becomes abundantly clear as he describes the all-encompassing nature of his lover's role in his life. Opposites are used for this purpose: 'North'/'South', 'East'/'West', 'working week'/'Sunday rest', 'noon'/'midnight' and 'talk'/'song'. The sense of conflict created by this list of opposing forces is further reflected, heightened, and its impact and source encapsulated in the strong, emphatic yet simple final line of the stanza:

I thought that love would last forever; I was wrong.

In much the same way, the final stanza forms a tightly packed and very fitting conclusion to the whole poem. The 'Pack[ing] up', 'dismantl[ing]', 'Pour[ing] away' and 'sweep[ing] up' that the narrator orders, once again allude to the domestic world of the first stanza as well as to its theme of cessation. At the same time, the references to the 'stars', 'moon', 'sun', 'ocean' and 'wood' imply a grandness of scale and public influence referred to in the second and third stanzas, as does the fact that this marks the bringing together of opposites, such as night and day in 'sun' and 'moon', and liquid and solid in 'ocean' and 'wood'.

Thus in the world of both grieving lovers everything is reduced to nothing. Things are turned on their heads and can no longer be relied upon to fulfil their purpose. The whole of life is affected and it no longer holds any meaning. Yet each expresses this devastation in a very different way. Cleopatra is passionate, desperate, employing dramatic language and long lamentations, the impact of which is enhanced through the juxtaposition of her maids' fractured discourse. The narrator of 'Funeral', however, is cold, methodical and closely reasoned, and Auden's use of a strict AABB rhyme scheme and a tight rhythm keeps the whole piece controlled.

Auden and Shakespeare, poetry and drama, male and female, past and present thus come together to provide equally intense and moving expression of private and public grief.

# ◼ ▼ 14 Examination preparation

## Common problems

### I don't understand the question

The whole exercise of practical criticism will be a non-starter if you fail to understand the question. It is essential that you practise the focusing exercise explained in Chapter 5 every time you exercise your practical criticism skills, because by doing this you will identify the key areas of the question that demand your attention. Many students think that they can get away with merely 'writing about' a text in some vague, and possibly even extremely perceptive, way – that so long as they are saying *something* about the text, this is all right. This is not the case. The examination question may require you to focus closely on specific areas, and if you fail to do this, no matter how sensitive and well-expressed your response might be, you will not have answered the question and therefore will not be awarded a high mark.

### Read the question carefully

So, *read the question carefully* for clues. If it says, 'Discuss what you find interesting in the poet's treatment of the subject of death', it is clear that the question is giving you complete freedom to discuss whatever it is that interests *you* about the *way* in which the poet writes about death. You will know this if you do a focusing exercise as below.

> **Discuss** what **you find interesting** in the poet's **treatment** of the subject of death in John Donne's 'Holy Sonnet X – Death be not proud'.

Death be not proud, though some have called thee
Mighty and dreadful, for thou art not so,
For, those, whom thou think'st, thou dost overthrow,
Die not, poor death, nor yet canst thou kill me.
From rest and sleep, which but thy pictures be,
Much pleasure, then from thee, much more must flow,
And soonest our best men with thee do go,
Rest of their bones, and soul's delivery.
Thou art slave to Fate, chance, kings and desperate men,
And dost with poison, war and sickness dwell,
And poppy, or charms can make us sleep as well,

And better than thy stroke; why swell'st thou then?
One short sleep past, we wake eternally,
And death shall be no more; death, thou shalt die.

John Donne

## Focus on the question

**Discuss** means 'talk about'. The *Concise Oxford Dictionary* offers 'examine by argument' as a definition for discussion in written debate. In short, if 'discuss' features as a key instruction in the question, you must 'examine by argument' what you find interesting about a text. In other words, *look closely* at it and *argue your case* by substantiating your claims with close textual reference.

**You find interesting** suggests a highly personal response. The examiner is looking for a discussion of what *you* have responded to in the text. What do *you* think is strange, humorous, impressive, unusual, original, contradictory, dramatic (or anything else that could be described as 'interesting') about the text? If you can describe *the way* in which a certain feature is 'interesting' and use textual evidence to support your claim, then you can answer the question.

**Treatment** reminds us that the focus should be on *the way* in which the writer handles a subject. We need to look at what he or she *does with* it. *How* does he/she *deal with* death? In the case of Donne's sonnet, your responses might include such things as personification of death, direct address to 'him/her', emasculating death, using the language of conflict and victory, and a tone of challenge and defiance. There are many other features that could have been discussed; this is merely an example of some of the things that come under the heading of 'treatment'.

## Learn the critical terms

Another problem emerges when candidates fail to understand questions because of an inability to interpret correctly what the question requires in the sense of critical terms. Make sure that you know what is meant by terms such as 'form', 'structure', 'style', 'diction' and so on. Check your understanding of critical terms by reading Chapter 4 'Tools of analysis – features of text' and consulting the Glossary at the end of this book. If the question asks you to consider the poet's use of form and you do not know exactly what is meant by this, you have a real problem but one that is easily prevented by acquiring before the examination a sound grasp of the basic terms used for critical analysis. Many students have thrown away golden opportunities to excel in examinations simply because they have not learnt the basic vocabulary required to discuss literature. This is quite unnecessary and you should take steps to avoid this happening. Every field of academic study has its own terminology, and you should be able both to understand and to use this competently.

## I don't understand the text

Every examination paper offers you a choice of questions, so you are clearly in a position to choose, to some extent, which ones to answer. However, we all know that this choice can be limited, and it may be that none of the options seems particularly appealing. The obvious answer might seem to be to opt for the text that is most easily understood, and there is a certain amount of common sense in this course of action, but should neither option seem to be entirely fathomable, you should neither despair nor panic.

No text that is set at either Advanced or degree level will be instantly understandable. Any teacher of practical criticism will tell you that he/she reads a text several times before attempting to analyse it with a group of students. Even then, there are aspects that surface only after many practical criticism exercises have been done on it. In an examination, you do not have time for the luxury of reading the text umpteen times, nor of contemplating its larger issues over long periods.

## Close reading

Close reading is your key skill in practical criticism, and the harder the text is to understand the more closely it needs to be read. Skimp on this and your chances of comprehension are greatly reduced. However, basic comprehension is not the whole story, and practical criticism, often called critical appreciation, involves just that – appreciation – and this can be achieved without *total* comprehension. It is accepted that few, if any, candidates will be able fully to understand a previously unseen text in such a short space of time. What *is* expected is that candidates can go on to express an appreciation and a response to that text despite perhaps a lack of complete understanding of *all* aspects of it.

You might be asking yourself, 'How can I possibly respond to something that I don't understand?' Think of an act of communication with another person. For example, a distressed friend might confide in you in an emotional, irrational and passionate way, and you may well not understand everything he or she is saying. In fact if he/she is extremely emotional, then this is very likely. What you probably *would* be able to appreciate, however, is *how he or she is feeling*. If the purpose of your friend's communication with you is to convey how he/she is feeling then your lack of complete comprehension in terms of what he/she is saying is far less important than your grasp of *how he or she feels*. The same can be said of some literature, especially poetry. As was discussed earlier, poetry is about *emotions*, and if you can identify these then you *can* understand some of the text's most important messages.

## Feelings in the tone

In short, all is not lost if you cannot fully understand the content, so long as you can tune into the *feelings*, and the best way of doing this is to identify and respond to the *tone* of the writing. Going back to your emotional friend, one of the most significant clues as to his/her state of mind is his/her tone of voice. If he/she is distraught then his/her tone of voice is likely to reflect this. We must all be able to recall occasions on which our name has been called out by a parent in a tone of voice that quite clearly indicates that we are in trouble. It is not *what* the parent says but *the way* in which he/she says it that communicates most powerfully its meaning.

Tone is a key feature of all writing, and if you have failed to establish the nature of this you have failed to understand the text. You have only to imagine the number of different ways in which you could say, 'Hello. Where have you been?' to see that the *way* in which something is said conveys the meaning. For example, if you miss the ironic or satiric tone of a text, a whole area of meaning is obscured and your appreciation of the writing will be severely impoverished.

Interpreting tone is a skill that is highly developed in most people who do not have physical or neurological difficulties, and one we all use all the time in everyday life. You should not lose sight of this in your study of literature. You need to use this same skill to appreciate and understand texts; the only difference being that the tone of voice is written down and you cannot hear it literally. You must 'listen' for it by close reading, but it is there none the less, and you *can* hear it if you 'listen' carefully.

## Ambiguity

One of the biggest stumbling blocks to understanding complex literary texts is ambiguity and, as has been discussed before, this is an inherent part of any text that has enough depth to be set as an examination text, so you can be sure of encountering it. There is no point in shying away from ambiguity; it has to be met head on, and you have to try to interpret meaning from it. However, it needs to be handled sensitively; if you barge into the murky waters of ambiguity asserting that your interpretation is the correct one, and furthermore, the only one, you are likely to alienate any examiner.

Put a number of English teachers or lecturers in a room with an ambiguous text and you are likely to get several interpretations. The secret is to be confident but not arrogant. Offer your interpretation as a possible explanation; 'it could be that the narrator feels that...' is preferable to 'quite obviously the narrator feels...'. Back it up with solid evidence in the form of close textual reference and, unless your reading of it is wildly out, you will be given credit for trying to draw meaning from what is essentially ambiguous.

It is possible that you will be able to see more than one interpretation and you should offer this alternative meaning as well, explaining carefully *why* you interpret it in this way and, again, providing textual evidence for your argument. Little is written in stone, and as a reader you play an active part in helping to construct meaning. Be active, engage with the text, but always ensure that you can substantiate your opinion.

## Identifying the central conflict

Lack of textual understanding may also result from failing to recognise the nature of the central conflict. In Chapter 5 there was a detailed discussion of the methodology that should be used when approaching all practical criticism exercises on previously unseen texts, and by now you should be familiar with this. The second stage is always to focus on and summarise the central conflict/s, and this has to be done early in the process if your analysis is to be accurate. The central conflict is a text's driving force; once you have identified that, you have established what it is 'about' on a fundamental level. Everything else is built on that.

Look for signs of binary opposition or contrast, and then examine the tension that is created in this conflict. This tension is likely to be part of the text's central meaning.

Looking at Donne's sonnet we see 'Mighty and dreadful'/'slave', 'overthrow'/'Die not', 'swell'st'/'die' and 'sleep'/'wake'. If we think carefully about these opposites it becomes clear that Donne is telling Death that although it thinks it is 'Mighty and dreadful', it is in fact a slave to 'Fate' and other mightier influences, that while it believes that it 'overthrow[s]' some people, they 'die not'. He asks Death 'why swell'st thou then?' when only Death itself will die, and he ends by reminding Death that it is merely 'one short sleep' from which man will 'wake eternally'.

Unless you identify the central conflict in a text you are unlikely to uncover its deeper meanings. This process has been dealt with in detail in previous chapters so there is no need to repeat it here. Suffice to say that this stage in the process of practical criticism is an essential one, and if you find that you are 'locked out' of a text it is likely to be because you have failed to grasp the nature of the conflict that drives it. Detailed guidance on this is given in previous chapters and you should refer to these if you are still in any doubt as to how to do this.

## Language

It is essential in the study of any text that candidates analyse the language used, as it is this element that provides us with some of the most significant clues to meaning. Candidates frequently fail to identify key meanings because they have not examined the language and seen the *patterns* that emerge. For example, identifying the poet's use of language that is to do with power and fighting is an essential step in uncovering the theme of conflict in Donne's 'Holy Sonnet X – Death be not proud'. This theme is central to the meaning of the text, because Donne's sonnet is a challenge to the forces of death; his narrator refuses to acknowledge death's power in the light of resurrection, which, as Christians believe, renders physical death impotent in terms of spiritual immortality. Without a consideration of the pattern of language, this essential discussion would be impossible.

Language can cause problems but, again, you must address this issue confidently. Always look at the context of a word about which you are unsure. You will usually be able to discern its meaning from what is going on around it. Rest assured that if you find it challenging, so will most other candidates.

Long before your examination you should take steps to enlarge your vocabulary by reading good-quality literature. When you encounter a new word, learn its meaning and try to use it. Students of English literature are expected to have a well-developed vocabulary, but this requires work that must be undertaken long before the date of your examination.

If the diction is noticeably complex it is worthy of comment, because it is like that for a reason. Perhaps it is there to make the writer sound learned. Maybe it serves to exclude those who are not familiar with it. Language is used as a barrier as well as to communicate; it can be a means of exerting power. Perhaps it adds an air of formality to the text, or a sense of objectivity. It is not always essential that you understand every word in a text; language can still function successfully in terms of the *effect* it has on a text.

Alternatively the diction may be quite different – informal, colloquial, perhaps containing non-standard variations and dialect. Again, nothing is random, and it is there in order to create an *effect*, which you *must* discuss.

## Structure

It can be helpful when struggling with the comprehension of a text to consider its structure. How has the writer built up his/her argument? In what direction is it going? Where did we start and where do we end up? This is covered in the methodology used to analyse texts, and is dealt with in the six-step approach to practical criticism with which you will, by now, be familiar.

## Expression

If the feedback you receive from teachers and lecturers suggests that your expression is faulty, you should ask them for more detailed advice about ways in which you might improve it. Students frequently fail to do justice to their responses to literature because of the poor quality of their expression. Detailed advice on this is given in Chapters 2 and 6, under 'Expression', and you should refer to these sections if this is a problem for you.

## Timing

Time is one of your greatest enemies, and this inevitably limits the quantity and quality of your responses to a text. However, *all* candidates are in the same position; you are not alone.

Your teachers or lecturers will probably discuss this aspect with you at some point in the course. It is important to know precisely what you have to do, and how long you have to do it. In some examinations the previously unseen paper is three hours long, and in this time candidates have to write three essays. While the obvious strategy would seem to be simply to allow one hour per essay, it is not quite that simple. You need to take into account the time required to read the whole exam paper before choosing your passages for analysis. If one of the passages comes from a 'seen' text, as is sometimes the case when the drama section is a Shakespeare play, you can afford to spend slightly less time on this question than the others that are truly 'unseen'. The prose passages are often quite lengthy, and you must allow time for this.

Successful timing in an examination is a matter of discipline and organisation. Once you know a rough time allocation for each question it is your responsibility to keep to this, come what may. It is of little use to write six pages of response to one text and barely one to another. You might say that this does not matter, because it is the quality of your response that counts and not the quantity, and to some extent this is true. However, there are only so many marks that you can be awarded for any one essay and there is little point in writing endlessly on one text to the detriment of another. Try to spread your time allocation as evenly as possible over all the questions, taking into account any necessary deviations as discussed above.

Should you run out of time however, all is not entirely lost. A sensible course of action is to indicate briefly somewhere on your script that you have run out of time and then put down as concisely as possible in note form what you want to say. You will of course get no credit for your style but the *content* of your notes will be taken into account by the marker.

In the unusual event of time being on your side I would suggest that you review your material carefully. Examinations at Advanced and degree level (or at any level come to that) are *not* designed with spare time in mind. You are *supposed* to be pushed for time; this is part of the discipline that examinations impose upon candidates, and you are assessed to a large extent on the material that you choose to include and exclude from your essay according to the time available. If you have a large chunk of time left, then unless you are of extremely high ability or can write unusually concisely, something is wrong, and you should think again about your essay in terms of both content and style.

## Content

- Have you read and analysed the text closely enough to discover its deeper meanings?
- Is your argument clearly structured?
- Have you developed your ideas fully?
- Are your paragraphs linked to give your material cohesion?
- Is there a clear sense of direction in your essay?
- Are there sufficient pieces of close textual reference/quotations?
- Is there a concise overview at the beginning and a meaningful conclusion at the end?

## Style

- Is your expression clear? Check your sentence structure.
- Is it precise?
- Is it concise?
- Is it formal? Check for slang or colloquialisms.
- Is it legible? If it can't be read you won't get any credit for it however good it is.
- Have you explained fully?
- Are your ideas expressed as elegantly as possible?
- Check your punctuation, grammar and spelling.

# Using quotations

Some candidates struggle with correct use of quotations and it is important to acquire this skill early on in your course. Quotation is an essential part of any textual study and you are expected to be able to use it correctly. Ideally, you should aim for short, appropriate and embedded quotations and you have seen numerous examples of these in the sample essays at the end of each practical criticism exercise.

If it is necessary to quote at length and the quotation is longer than one line of poetry you should leave a line, indent the quotation, leave another line and continue writing, like this:

Donne's narrator hopes to disabuse Death of the idea that it is powerful in its victory over the human body:

> For, those, whom thou think'st, thou dost overthrow,
> Die not, poor death, nor yet can'st thou kill me.

His tone is defiant and he ridicules Death by calling it 'poor', as if it deserved our pity.

Short quotations are preferable, as it shows the candidate's ability to sift the text for concise references rather than present the examiner with a large chunk from which he or she is expected to choose relevant words or phrases to substantiate the argument.

Aim to provide a quotation or a close textual reference *for each point being made.*

## Linking paragraphs

If you have been told that your material is disjointed and lacks cohesion, the most likely cause is that you are not providing enough 'connective tissue' with which to link your paragraphs.

Each paragraph should contain a separate point that you:

- *Make clearly*, preferably near the start of the paragraph;
- *Substantiate by quotation*; and then go on to
- *Discuss and develop.*

When you have dealt fully with that point, begin another paragraph and go on to another point. What can happen is that there appears to be a substantial break between the paragraphs because the points seem to be completely disconnected. Sometimes the points *are* very different and this is, to some extent, inevitable; you cannot go on making the same point over and over again, otherwise you will not cover any ground at all. What you do need to do though is to try to *link* the points together so that your essay 'slides' smoothly from one point to another without any discernible chasms between the paragraphs.

Students frequently ask how this can be achieved, and it is really a simple task. You need to pick up the meaning from one paragraph and trail it into the next, rather similar in effect to the way in which enjambment works in poetry.

Suppose you are dealing with the point about Donne's narrator's use of a direct address to Death in one paragraph, and wanted to go on to discuss the idea of the narrator attempting to emasculate Death in the next. A simple way would be to say something like this at the beginning of the paragraph on emasculation:

> The force of the narrator's direct address to Death is enhanced by his desire to rob Death of its power over mankind. This narrator is not afraid to challenge Death and he does so boldly when he tells Death that '[he is] slave to Fate, chance, kings and desperate men'.

While the two points about direct address and emasculation are distinct from each other, they are brought together to form a cohesive whole that progresses smoothly from one stage of its argument to the next.

## Overview

It is important to make a good impression on the examiner as soon as possible, because it is with this initial impression in his/her mind that he/she will respond to the rest of your essay.

Your opening paragraph should be an overview, and this is discussed in some detail in Chapter 6 under 'Topping', so you should refer to that if you have difficulty with this skill. It is important to be able to write a sharp, concise overview paragraph that enables *you* to concentrate on the key elements of the text while impressing upon the *examiner* that you are focused and clear about its most significant meanings.

It might be helpful to think of it as an upside-down funnel. The overview is the narrow neck that later expands. The concisely expressed ideas established in this first paragraph will later be allowed to enlarge and develop as you discuss and substantiate them.

## Conclusion

Remember that your conclusion is the last thing that the examiner reads before he or she puts his/her mark on your script, so for this reason it needs to be as good as you can make it.

Again, this is dealt with in detail in Chapter 6, under 'Tailing', so you should read this now if this is one of your areas of difficulty. If your conclusions are weak it is well worth your working on this skill as the course progresses. Many a good essay has petered out at the end and 'died', and this can be avoided. Try always to go out 'with a bang, not a whimper'.

## Panic

Panic is another of your worst enemies and you *cannot* allow this to set in. Accept that the text will present you with ambiguities and therefore difficulties, but that does not mean that you cannot formulate a sensitive and worthwhile response. Think of it as an opportunity to prove what you can do.

In *Hamlet*, the prince says that 'there is nothing either good or bad but thinking makes it so' (Act 2, Scene 2). If you *think* of the examination as an intimidating affair, then no matter how good the paper, that is how it will *feel*, and you will respond accordingly, with a lack of confidence. If, however, you go into the examination determined to be constructive and to prove that you can do practical criticism, then it does not matter how challenging the paper; your positive approach will be evident in all your responses. You will *actively engage* in trying to make meaning, and this is what the process is all about.

Panic is a luxury you simply cannot allow yourself because it paralyses analytical and creative thinking, both of which are essential requirements for practical criticism.

# Specific questions asked by students

## Do spelling, punctuation, grammar and handwriting matter?

The simple answer to this question is 'yes'. One of the many aspects of your essay writing that is assessed by the examiner is your expression, and spelling, punctuation, grammar and handwriting are all part of this. As has been said before, students of English literature are expected to express themselves clearly, concisely and accurately. By now you will be familiar with the concept of the 'how' of any text being part of the 'what'. It is the same for *your* writing; *how* you say it is part of *what* you say.

Spelling, punctuation, grammar and handwriting all aid clear, concise and accurate expression. If any of these elements is below standard, your expression will be the poorer for it, and this will be reflected in your final grade. That is not to say that for every spelling or punctuation error a number of marks will be deducted, but when the examiner asks him/herself whether your essay meets the criteria in terms of its expression for a high grade, the answer will be 'no'.

## What happens if everyone else is writing and I'm not?

First, you should make up your mind to *ignore* everyone else in the examination room. Your focus should be on the examination paper, the clock and yourself; nothing else matters.

In the early stages of the examination you should *not* be writing; your task is *close reading*, and this should be done with your full concentration. The only writing you might be doing at this stage is making notes in response to the text. It is essential to remember that the quality of your writing will depend largely on the quality of your reading and thinking. Remember that the first stage of *all* analysis for practical criticism is 'read closely and think'.

Those candidates who rush into their analysis and start writing almost as soon as the examination starts are either geniuses with extraordinary powers of speed-reading, or they are seriously misguided into thinking that they can formulate a meaningful response to any text at such an early stage. The average candidate who is aiming for a sensitive answer to the question *must* spend time reading and thinking *first*. You should expect to read the text carefully *at least twice* before you begin to formulate your responses to it.

## What if I change my mind about the text as I'm analysing it and writing my essay?

This is not as disastrous as it sounds, and in many ways we all do this all the time as we respond to literature. It is impossible to come up with a full, informed and perceptive response to any text instantly. As was discussed earlier, our reactions to texts change with time, even over the comparatively short space of time in an exam.

Once you have established the central conflict, which is the second stage in the process, you have gained a sense of direction. This issue is bound to be developed as the text proceeds; the third and fourth stages of the process prove this – tracking and developing the themes elsewhere. It is important to 'move' *with* the text and to *keep responding to it* throughout your essay.

Should you uncover something that suggests that there might be another interpretation, offer this as a possible reading also. Remember never to assert, but to suggest confidently, stating your reasons for your reading of it in this way.

Perhaps one of the most important things to remember is that little is set in stone; practical criticism is about an informed, personal response and the word 'response' suggests that you react to the text and to its twists and turns. Establishing the central conflict will give you firm ground upon which to base your argument, but you must accept that a degree of flexibility is essential in this sort of exercise.

## Surely it's easier to avoid a comparative question?

The answer is a clear 'no', you should *not* automatically avoid the comparative question if there is one. It is not as daunting as it sometimes appears to be, and you should not discount this as a viable option in any examination. There are advantages and disadvantages to this choice; careful reading of both texts will help you to decide whether or not to opt for this type of question.

This matter is dealt with in Chapter 12 – 'Practical criticism of poetry – comparison' and you should refer to this now for a fuller discussion of the subject.

## How can I prepare for a practical criticism examination?

Some examining boards include a set text (often Shakespeare) in their previously unseen paper and, of course, students sitting this type of exam will be well prepared for this during their course. While sound textual knowledge can be an advantage, it is important to remember that if this text is set as part of a practical criticism/ critical appreciation paper, the approach should remain one of analysing 'the words on the page', and candidates should not be drawn into a discussion of the whole text unless this is specifically required by the question.

If your examination includes critical appreciation of a set text, you can prepare for this easily by doing repeated exercises in analysis on chosen extracts. Select the key speeches first and work towards the less significant.

For boards that do not include a set text, and for the poetry and prose sections of the examination, your best approach is to get plenty of practice of doing the analysis yourself. In the early days of your course you will gain both insight and confidence by doing practical criticism with other students. Sharing responses and ideas is a valuable process, and you need this, but as the course proceeds you must learn to do this on your own as well. Remember that there will be no one with whom to share ideas when you are in the examination room, and you need to develop the skill of being able to apply the six-stage method outlined in this book in complete isolation.

Another useful method of preparation is to read widely (see 'Wider reading' on page 249–52). This gives you practice in responding to texts, and that is what lies at the heart of the process of critical appreciation. Read some of the reference books listed under 'Recommended reading – reference' on page 249; breadth of approach is essential, particularly at degree level. You will find that no two methods of analysis are identical, but that all tend to follow a similar direction in their approach to practical criticism. At degree level you should encounter different schools of critical theory, and your study of these will have a bearing on the approach you choose to adopt towards textual analysis.

Remember that this is a skill, and like any skill it is only perfected through practice. The word 'practice' implies error, and you must be prepared to accept this, just as you would scrunching the gears or kangarooing down the road when you are learning to drive. We are not all born knowing how to do practical criticism, and there is no body of knowledge that can be conveniently packaged and passed on to you. It is a case of trying and, inevitably sometimes, getting it wrong.

Confidence is a key ingredient for success in this skill. It is a journey of exploration into every text, and for this you need to have the courage of an explorer.

# Examination questions

It is essential for your examination preparation that you work through a wide range of questions on texts from *all* the genres. This book is intended to help you to understand the principles of practical criticism and to see it in practice, but *nothing can replace doing it yourself*. You will derive most benefit from this book if you implement what you are learning *as you read it and after you have finished it* with exercises in the skills it teaches.

As you practise these skills by writing responses to texts, you will benefit from referring again to sections such as Chapter 4 'Tools of analysis – features of text' and the reference section, as well as the glossary. You should also read it through again at various points in your course to remind yourself of the key skills to practise.

## Where do I find the questions?

Probably the best source of examination preparation material is the **examining boards**. Past papers can be bought directly from the boards, or your teacher/lecturer/tutor will have a stock of these for you to borrow. The head of department will be able to provide you with addresses and telephone numbers for the examining boards should you wish to approach them directly.

You can set yourself some practice questions with the co-operation of your **teacher/lecturer/tutor**, who will probably be pleased to see that you are taking examination preparation seriously.

You can set **yourself** preparation questions on your own, by focusing on any substantial piece of literature from any genre. Do not be tempted to opt for a text that you find 'easy'. Although it might seem to be the simplest option at the time, you will often find that very 'transparent' texts are actually quite difficult to discuss *because* it is all so obvious. While 'stained glass' is not easy to look *through*, there is at least plenty to look *at*. Explore texts which offer a challenge; you will not improve your critical appreciation skills by 'playing safe'.

## What questions do I set myself?

### General questions

To start with, it is best to set yourself very general questions, which will allow you to *explore* texts freely. In this way you will gradually acquire the finely-tuned skills needed for a more directed and specific approach.

Try writing responses to some of these general questions when exploring a text:

1. What do you find interesting about this poem/extract?
2. What, if anything, do you like about this poem/extract?
3. What do you think is the poet/author/playwright's view of... (focus on the main theme of the text, such as love, loss, the past and so on). How does he/she express this?
4. Analyse the poem/extract in any way you choose.
5. Explore the poet/author's attitude to... focus on the main theme of the text).
6. Write a critical appreciation of the poem/extract.
7. In your opinion, how successfully does the poet's/author's style make vivid his/her subject matter?
8. What are the writer's thoughts and feelings about his/her subject matter? What techniques does he/she use to express them? Are they effective?
9. What do you think is unusual about the way in which this poem/extract has been written?
10. How does the writer try to engage you, the reader? How successful do you think he/she is? What are the effects on your thoughts and feelings as you read this type of writing?

(Questions 9 and 10 might be appropriate to use with modernist texts by writers such as James Joyce, Virginia Woolf or Samuel Beckett, as well as more 'conventional' literature.)

## Specific questions

Try writing responses to these, more specific, questions:

1. Write a critical appreciation of the poem/extract. Include in your discussion a consideration of the writer's use of form, structure and language to express his/her ideas.
2. Comment on the writer's tone. How can we detect it, and in what ways does it influence the text?
3. How convincing do you find the writer's argument? What are the most influential features of his/her narrative style?
4. How successful is the writer's use of humour? What effect does it have on the text and on you, the reader?
5. Discuss the use of imagery in the text. What does this tell you about the writer's feelings towards the subject matter?
6. Examine the contribution made by metre and rhyme to this poem. What effects does the poet achieve by their use?
7. Comment on the effectiveness of the writer's introduction and conclusion. How do they relate to the rest of the text? Are they effective?
8. Discuss the writer's use of symbolism? What contribution do you think it makes to the text?
9. Explore the use of patterning in this text. What effect does this have on it, and how successful do you think it is?
10. Discuss the writer's use of sound to enhance the texture of his/her work? What does this add to the text as a whole?

# Recommended reading – reference

Abrams, M. (1988) *A Glossary of Literary Terms* (5th edn) (London: Holt, Rinehart & Winston).

Belsey, C. (1980) *Critical Practice* (London: Methuen).

Belsey, C. and Moore, J. (eds) (1989) *The Feminist Reader: Essays in Gender and the Politics of Literary Criticism* (London: Macmillan).

Cadden, J. (1986) *Prose Appreciation for A level* (London: Hodder & Stoughton).

Cadden, J. (1986) *Poetry Appreciation for A level* (London: Hodder & Stoughton).

*Casebook Series*, (General ed. A. E. Dyson) (London: Macmillan – now Palgrave).

Eagleton, T. (1976) *Criticism and Ideology* (London: Verso).

Eagleton, T. (1983) *Literary Theory: An Introduction* (Oxford: Basil Blackwell).

Gill, R. (1995) *Mastering English Literature* (London: Macmillan – now Palgrave).

Hawkes, T. (1977) *Structuralism and Semiotics* (London: Methuen).

Jones, R. (1986) *Studying Poetry* (reprinted 1992) (London: Edward Arnold).

Leavis, F. (1948) *The Great Tradition* (London: Chatto & Windus).

Lodge, D. (1972) *Twentieth Century Literary Criticism: A Reader* (London: Longman).

Lodge, D. (1988) *Modern Criticism and Theory: A Reader* (London: Longman).

Peck, J. and Coyle, M. (1984) *Dictionary of Critical Terms* (London: Macmillan – now Palgrave).

Peck, J. and Coyle, M. (1995) *Practical Criticism* (London: Macmillan).

Richards, I. (1924) *Principles of Literary Criticism* (London: Kegan Paul, Trench, Trubner).

Richards, I. (1929) *Practical Criticism* (London: Routledge & Kegan Paul).

Seldon, R. (1985) *A Reader's Guide to Contemporary Literary Theory* (Brighton: Harvester Press).

Showalter, E. (1977) *A Literature of their Own: British Women Novelists from Brontë to Lessing* (Princeton, NJ: Princeton University Press).

Stephen, M. (1986) *Longman Exam Guides – English Literature* (Harlow: Longman).

Walder, D. (ed.) (1981) *Literature in the Modern World: Critical Essays and Documents* (Oxford University Press).

Williams, R. (1977) *Marxism and Literature* (Oxford University Press).

Wright, E. (1984) *Psychoanalytic Criticism: Theory in Practice* (London: Methuen).

# Wider reading

For students to be able to respond sensitively to texts under time pressure, it is essential that this skill is practised. Candidates should ensure that they read widely and closely across a range of writers and periods, and work at responding to texts. It is important that you engage *actively* in this reading process, seeing yourself as autonomous readers and helping to make meaning.

In the examination, what is being tested is your ability to respond quickly and perceptively to pieces of previously unseen literature, and you can only be sure of acquiring this skill if you practise going through the process numerous times, throughout your course. It is of little use leaving this until the last minute; it *must* be done from the start.

The wider reader will build up a bank of reading experience from which to draw on during those crucial few hours of examination. Wider reading will help the candidate to see, in context, the texts before him or her, and to view them against the backdrop of all he or she has already experienced. Note the use of the word 'experienced', as opposed to merely 'read', which suggests a certain passivity – a far cry from the types of skill required in practical criticism. Remember, you cannot learn to drive a car by sitting in a classroom; you must get out on the road.

Recommended reading lists are notorious for evoking mixed responses from experts in the field. Many will express their horror at the omission of certain works, while others will concur with the author's choice. The list that follows is inevitably limited and does not represent the complete range of literature you should try to sample; it merely offers you *some* suggestions for widening the scope of your reading experience and you should use it as a starting point. Your teachers/lecturers/tutors will be able to supplement this list with suggestions of their own, and you should allow them to guide you.

## Poetry

### General

Heaney, S. and Hughes, T. (eds) *The Rattlebag.*
Wain, J. (ed.) (1996) *Anthology of Great English Poetry (Vols 1 and 2)* (London: BCA).

### Seventeenth century

Gardner, H. (ed.) (1973) *The Metaphysical Poets* (Harmondsworth: Penguin).
Milton, J. *Paradise Lost.*

### Eighteenth century

Cowper, W., *The Winter Morning Walk.*
Goldsmith, O., *The Deserted Village.*
Gray, T., *Elegy Written in a Country Churchyard.*
Johnson, S., *London.*
Pope, A., *The Rape of the Lock.*

### Nineteenth century

Blake, W., *Songs of Innocence and Experience.*
Keats, J., *Endymion* (and the Odes).
Rossetti, C., *Goblin Market.*
Wordsworth, W., *The Prelude.*

### Twentieth century

Armitage, S., *Kid.*
Auden, W. H., *Tell Me the Truth About Love.*

Eliot, T. S., *The Wasteland and Other Poems*.
Heaney, S., *Death of a Naturalist*.
Hughes, T., *Crow*.
Larkin, P., *High Windows*.
Nicholls, G., *The Fat Black Woman's Poems*.
Plath, S. and Fainlight, R. *The Bloodaxe Book of Contemporary Women Poets*.
Plath, S., *Ariel*.
Sassoon, S., *The War Poems*.
Thomas, D., *Fern Hill*.
Yeats, W. B., *Collected Poems*.

## Prose

### Seventeenth/eighteenth centuries

Behn, A., *Oroonoko*.
Bunyan, J., *The Pilgrim's Progress*.
Defoe, D., *Robinson Crusoe*.
Donne, J., *Sermons*.
Pepys, S., *Diaries*.
Richardson, S., *Pamela*.

### Eighteenth/nineteenth centuries

Austen, J., *Emma*.
Austen, J., *Mansfield Park*.
Brontë, C., *Jane Eyre*.
Dickens, C., *Great Expectations*.
Eliot, G., *Silas Marner*.
Fielding, H., *Tom Jones*.
Hardy, T., *The Woodlanders*.
Hume, D., *Enquiry Concerning Human Understanding*.
Locke, J., *Essay Concerning Human Understanding*.
Shelley, M., *Frankenstein*.
Swift, J., *Gulliver's Travels*.
Swift, J., *A Modest Proposal*.

### Twentieth century

Angelou, M., *I Know Why the Caged Bird Sings*.
Atwood, M., *The Handmaid's Tale*.
Brookner, A., *Hotel du Lac*.
Hill, S., *A Bit of Singing and Dancing*.
Lawrence, D. H., *The Rainbow*.
Morrison, T., *Beloved*.
Orwell, G., *The Road to Wigan Pier*.
Walker, A., *The Colour Purple*.

Wharton, E., *The Age of Innocence*.
Woolf, V., *To The Lighthouse*.

## Drama
### Sixteenth/seventeenth centuries

Behn, A., *The Rover*.
Dryden, J., *All For Love*.
Shakespeare, W., selection of plays:
   Tragedy:  *King Lear, Hamlet, Othello, Macbeth*.
   History:  *Henry IV, Part I, Henry IV, Part II, Julius Caesar*.
   Comedy:  *A Midsummer Night's Dream, Much Ado About Nothing, Twelfth Night*.

### Eighteenth century

Lindsay, D., ('Introduction'), *The Beggar's Opera and Other Eighteenth Century Plays*.
Gay, J., *The Beggar's Opera*.
Goldsmith, O., *She Stoops to Conquer*.
Sheridan, R., *School for Scandal* and *The Rivals*.
Fielding, H., *The Tragedy of Tragedies, or The Life and Death of Tom Thumb*.
Steele, Sir R., *The Conscious Lovers*.
Lillo, G., *The London Merchant*.

### Nineteenth century

Checkov, A., *The Seagull, Uncle Vanya, The Cherry Orchard*.
Ibsen, H., *Ghosts, Peer Gynt, Hedda Gabler*.
Wilde, O., *The Importance of Being Earnest*.

### Twentieth century

Beckett, S., *Waiting For Godot*.
Miller, A., *Death of a Salesman*.
Priestley, J., *An Inspector Calls*.
Stoppard, T., *Rozencrantz and Guildenstern Are Dead*.

# ■ ☑ 15 Reference chapter

## How to use this chapter

This section is intended as a quick and easy reference guide. The information is expanded on in detail in Chapter 4, 'Tools of analysis – features of text'; this is merely a quick guide for you to use while you are doing a practical criticism exercise.

## Future form/emphatic form of the verb 'to be'

| Future form | Emphatic form |
|---|---|
| I shall | I will |
| You will | You shall |
| He/she/it will | He/she/it shall |
| We shall | We will |
| You (plural) will | You (plural) shall |
| They will | They shall |

## Symbolism

Candidates miss important meanings in literature when they fail to respond to symbolism. The reason for this is a lack of knowledge or understanding of areas of life upon which we draw to create and interpret symbols.

### Christian symbolism

The category that suffers most from neglect is that of Christian symbolism, largely because the teaching of religious education from the later decades of the twentieth century has become all-embracing in terms of world religions, and students now focus less on Christianity.

It is not easy to provide a quick guide to Christian symbolism. It is, of course, exemplified in the Bible, and if you want to acquire a sound foundation in Christian symbolism, this is what you should be reading. However, the following might be useful, as a start:

| Symbol | Meaning/connotations |
|---|---|
| angel | messenger from God, purity |
| apple | original sin, temptation/Eve |
| bread | life, sacrifice, forgiveness, the body of Christ |
| clay | fallibility, human nature |
| cross | crucifixion, sacrifice, death, resurrection (if the cross is empty) |
| crown | sovereignty |
| dove | peace, forgiveness, new beginnings |
| fig leaf | shame |
| garden | Garden of Eden |
| lamb | innocence, sacrifice, Christ |
| one | unity, three persons of the Trinity in one |
| red | sin, blood |
| serpent | the Devil, temptation |
| seven | creation of the world (seven days) |
| ten | commandments |
| thorns | pain, suffering |
| three | Holy Trinity (Father, Son and Holy Ghost), three crosses on Golgotha |
| tree | Tree of the Knowledge of Good and Evil |
| twelve | disciples of Christ |
| water | cleansing, new life |
| wine/blood | death, sacrifice, forgiveness, suffering, blood of Christ |
| white | purity, godliness, forgiveness |

Writers use a variety of symbols as carriers of meaning. These include the following:

## Agricultural symbolism

| Symbol | Meaning/connotations |
|---|---|
| spring | sowing seed/new life and hope |
| summer | crops growing/fullness |
| autumn | crops harvested and ploughing/ripeness and reaping |
| winter | resting land/death and sleep |

## Seasonal symbolism

| Symbol | Meaning/connotations |
|---|---|
| spring | new life, hope, youth, growth, beginnings |
| summer | sun, warmth, joy, ease, colour, fullness |
| autumn | ripeness/maturity before decline, sadness, mellowness, nearing the end |
| winter | death, despair, loneliness, emptiness, colourless, cold, old age, the end |

## Colour symbolism

| Symbol | Meaning/connotations |
|---|---|
| black | death, darkness, unknown, sadness, fear |

| | |
|---|---|
| blue | coolness, sadness, peace |
| gold | money, power, rarity, sovereignty |
| green | nature, youth, innocence |
| grey | uncertainty, mystery |
| orange | fire, warmth, brightness, joy |
| pink | femininity, flesh, softness |
| purple | royalty, wealth |
| red | danger, fire, heat, immorality, passion |
| white | purity, spirituality, peace, surrender, cowardice, ice, heat |
| yellow | sun, joy, warmth, cowardice |

## General symbolism

| Symbol | Meaning/connotations |
|---|---|
| books | education, knowledge |
| chain | bondage, restriction, suffering, interdependence |
| clock/calendar | time |
| crown | monarchy, power |
| day/light | hope, sanity, clarity |
| farm | nature, productivity |
| gate/door | entry, exclusion |
| hearth/fire | warmth, domesticity |
| junction | time of choice, options |
| lily | purity |
| mountain | obstacle, challenge, hardship |
| mist/fog | uncertainty, mystery |
| night/dark | despair, madness, unknown |
| ring | eternity, cyclical, exclusivity, belonging |
| road | journey, passage of time |
| rose | beauty, optimism, love, secrecy |
| sleep | death |
| snow | cold, purity, harshness |
| sunrise | new beginning |
| sunset | ending |
| thorn | pain |
| throne | authority, sovereignty |
| tree | life, family, origins, nature |

# Sound

## Texture of words

### Vowels

**Long vowels**

- **a** as in 'cape';
- **e** as in 'reed';

- **i** as in 'pine';
- **o** as in 'hope'; and
- **u** as in 'cute'.

**Effect**: slow, soft, fluid, light, thoughtful, languid and feminine *depending on the context*.

### Short vowels

- **a** as in 'cap';
- **e** as in 'red';
- **i** as in 'pin';
- **o** as in 'hop'; and
- **u** as in 'cut'.

**Effect**: fast, firm, solid, heavy, emphatic, harsh and masculine *depending on the context*.

## Consonants

**Hard consonants**: b, c, d, g, k, p, q, s, t, x, z.

**Effect**: harsh, severe feel.

**Soft consonants**: c, f, g, h, j, l, m, n, ph, s, sh, z.

**Effect**: sense of softness or tenderness.

The letters 'g', 's' and 'z' can shift between the two consonant groups. The harshness or softness of these two sounds depends to a large extent upon their *context*.

## Metre

The terms for the number of feet in a line are as follows:

Monometre = one foot/unit of metre per line.
Dimetre    = two feet/units of metre per line.
Trimetre   = three feet/units of metre per line.
Tetrametre = four feet/units of metre per line.
Pentametre = five feet/units of metre per line.
Hexametre  = six feet/units of metre per line.
Heptametre = seven feet/units of metre per line.
Octametre  = eight feet/units of metre per line.

## Types of Feet

| Name of foot | Symbol | Example | Effect |
| --- | --- | --- | --- |
| Iambic foot | ~ / | 'begin' | like human speech |
| Trochaic Foot | / ~ | 'hollow' | solemn mood |
| Dactylic Foot | / ~ ~ | 'elephant' | sombre |
| Anapestic Foot | ~ ~ / | 'serenade' | excitement, energy |

There are also: the Spondaic foot (/ /); the Pyrrhic foot (~ ~ ); and the Amphibrach foot (~ / ~ ).

## Rhyme

| Location | Effect |
| --- | --- |
| end rhyme | depends on the type of rhyme |
| internal rhyme | enhances pace and emphasises rhymed words |

| Type | Stress | Example | Effect |
| --- | --- | --- | --- |
| masculine | last syllable stressed | before/adore | emphatic |
| feminine | last syllable unstressed | hollow/follow | vanishing/uneasy |
| half | incomplete | escaped/scooped | unsatisfactory |
| eye | visual | love/prove | discordance/disruption |

# Modes of writing

While it is often possible to identify certain modes or types of writing in any piece of literature, it should be remembered that these categories are, to some extent, quite *arbitrary* in that prose is usually a *combination* of several modes (of which there are infinite numbers) and *rarely* purely one or another.

## Narrative

Narrative prose is the most common form, found in novels and short stories. It quite simply refers to prose that tells a story or develops a plot.

Its two areas of **focus** are:

- key situations and events; and
- characters.

It fulfils two main **roles**:

- to *inform* the reader *about* events and characters; and
- to sustain the reader's *interest in* events and characters.

For a fuller and more detailed discussion of different types of narrative you should refer to the section on narrators earlier in this chapter. Here is an example:

Having been condemned, by nature and fortune, to an active and restless life, in two months after my return, I again left my native country, and took shipping in the Downs, on the 20th day of June, 1702, in the *Adventure* – Captain John Nicholas, a Cornishman, commander – bound for Surat.

(From Jonathan Swift, *Gulliver's Travels*)

Notice how the prose is full of *information* relating to events and to the character of the narrator. We are told 'what happens', and in this way the plot is developed.

## Descriptive

This mode of writing involves creating atmosphere, and often a sense of place, by the use of evocative description. Characters are carefully drawn and there is feeling in the writing. By the nature of the description it is possible to identify the attitude of the writer towards that particular place, event or character. Descriptive prose often employs figurative language and imagery that can give it a 'poetic' quality. The reader's feelings are invariably involved in this mode of writing.

Detail is a key feature here and it should serve to bring the subject of it to life. An example follows:

> Generally, the faces (those of children excepted) were depressed and subdued, and wanted colour. Aged people were there in every variety. Mumbling, bleareyed, spectacled, stupid, deaf, lame; vacantly winking in the gleams of sun that now and then crept in through the open doors, from the paved yard; shading their listening ears, or blinking eyes, with their withered hands; poring over their books, leering at nothing, going to sleep, crouching and drooping in corners.

> (From Charles Dickens, *A Walk in the Workhouse*)

## Discursive

This word describes prose that 'rambles' along the path of an issue. It refers to writing in which the writer shares with us his/her thoughts and deliberations on a particular subject; for example, 'the benefits of growing older' or the belief that 'youth is wasted on the young'. The tone is usually light and the remarks spontaneous.

In a narrative, discursive prose often provides the author with an opportunity to explore a character's thoughts and feelings by having him or her 'be discursive'. It is a more subtle and interesting way to do this than to have the narrator explaining directly to the reader the workings of a character's mind. Here is an example:

> Do you see, Arren, how an act is not, as young men think, like a rock that one picks up and throws and it hits or misses, and that's the end of it. When that rock is lifted the earth is lighter, the hand that bears it heavier. When it is thrown the circuits of the stars respond, and where it strikes or falls the universe is changed. On every act the balance of the whole depends. The winds and seas, the powers of water and earth and light, all that these do, and all that the beasts and green things do, is well done, and rightly done. All these act within the Equilibrium. From the hurricane and the great whale's sounding to the fall of a dry leaf and the gnat's flight, all they do is done within the balance of the whole. But we, insofar as we have power over the world and over one another, we must *learn*

to do what the leaf and the whale and the wind do of their own nature. We must learn to keep the balance. Having intelligence, we must not act in ignorance. Having choice, we must not act without responsibility.

(From Ursula Le Guin, *The Farthest Shore*, 1973)

## Contemplative

Contemplative prose is similar to discursive writing but tends to be on a more profound level. The writer will express deeply held beliefs and feelings about a more weighty issue than that dealt with in the discursive prose. The tone is likely to be more serious and often it will arise when a character is trying to reconcile a dilemma by weighing up both sides of an issue. For example:

> Give me a night in the midst of such weather, and then think of the farm atop the hill, to which two good miles of deep, wandering lane go climbing, and mix the rain with a great wind from the mountain: and then think of entering the place which I have described, set now for the old act of winter...A man will leave his place, snug in shelter, in the deepest glow of the fire, and go out for a moment and open but a little of the door in the porch and see all the world black and wild and wet, and then come back to the light and heat and thank God for his home, wondering whether any are still abroad on such a night of tempest.

(From John Cadden, *Prose Appreciation for A Level*)

## Philosophical

If a passage deals with a simple encounter that one person has with another, it is *discursive*. If this develops into the deeper thoughts and responses of the writer about this person and himself it is *contemplative*. When it goes on to consider the relationship between man and his fellow human beings, it becomes *philosophical*. This type of writing tends to be more formal and more carefully structured than the other two varieties, and typical topics include politics, religion and philosophy. There will often be evidence of a debate or analysis, and an effort to support a specific thesis or belief. The style will be more complex and the language more elevated than other types of writing, suitable for the more serious subject matter.

A distinction needs to be made between the writer's *mode of writing* and his or her own philosophy; it is a philosophical *way of writing* and not the philosophy itself that is referred to when we talk about philosophical writing. See, for example:

> Everyman's nature is a sufficient advertisement to him of the character of his fellow. My right and my wrong is their right and their wrong. Whilst I do what is fit for me, and abstain from what is unfit, my neighbour and I shall often agree in our means, and work together for a time to one end. But whenever I find my dominion over myself not sufficient for me, and undertake the direction of him also, I overstep the truth, and come to false relations to him. I may have so much more skill and strength than he, that he cannot express adequately his

sense of wrong, but it is a lie, and hurts like a lie both him and me. Love and nature cannot maintain the assumption: it must be executed by a practical lie, namely, by force. This undertaking for another, is the blunder which stands in colossal ugliness in the governments of the world.

(From John Cadden, *Prose Appreciation for A Level*)

## Didactic

Didactic prose seeks to instruct the reader, to influence his/her thinking and/or behaviour. Its purpose is to persuade its audience, to varying degrees of intensity, to think in a certain way. The issues with which it deals are usually moral or political, and this type of writing is perhaps most evident in sermons and political speeches. Journalism and propaganda also bear the signs of didacticism; degrees of subtlety will inevitably vary according to the medium and purpose.

The writer of didactic prose makes no claims to be impartial; this writing is usually passionate in nature and the writer burns with a desire to right perceived wrongs. The style is intense and powerful – designed to move the reader. Look at this example:

> The bourgeoisie, wherever it has got the upper hand, has put an end to all feudal, patriarchal, idyllic relations. It has pitilessly torn asunder the motley feudal ties that bound man to his 'natural superiors', and has left no other nexus between man and man than naked self-interest, than callous 'cash payment'. It has drowned the most heavenly ecstasies of religious fervour, of chivalrous enthusiasm, of philistine sentimentalism, in the icy water of egotistical calculation. It has resolved personal worth into exchange value, and in place of the numberless indefeasible chartered freedoms, has set up that single, unconscionable freedom – Free Trade. In one word, for exploitation, veiled by religious and political illusions, it has substituted naked, shameless, direct, brutal exploitation.

(From K. Marx and F. Engels, *The Communist Manifesto*)

A distinction should be made between 'didactic' and 'directive' prose. While the former is the appropriate term with which to describe the passionate prose of the sermon, 'directive' writing is unemotional and objective, its aim being to instruct; it tells the reader what to do.

## Parody

Parody is a work that is written in imitation of another work, usually with the intention of mockery or ridicule. Particular features of the original are exaggerated, making them appear absurd. The term is applied to a *specific* text and not to a style in general, whereas 'burlesque' is used to describe such a method when it targets a *whole style or approach*, which might be found in several texts. Consider the following example:

> When the little girl opened the door of her grandmother's house she saw that there was somebody in bed with a nightcap and nightgown on. She had

approached no nearer than twenty-five feet from the bed when she saw that it was not her grandmother but the wolf, for even in a nightcap a wolf does not look any more like your grandmother than the Metro-Goldwyn lion looks like Calvin Coolidge. So the little girl took an automatic out of her basket and shot the wolf dead.

*Moral:*   *It is not so easy to fool little girls nowadays as it used to be.*

(From James Thurber, *Fables of Our Time*)

## Burlesque

Here is an example:

The case seemed wholly desperate and deplorable; and this magnificent palace would have infallibly been burnt down to the ground, if, by a presence of mind, unusual to me, I had not suddenly thought of an expedient. I had the evening before drank plentifully of a most delicious wine, called *glimigrin* (the Blefus-cudians call it *flunec*, but ours is esteemed the better sort) which is very diur-etick. By the luckiest chance in the world, I had not discharged myself of any part of it. The heat I had contracted by coming very near the flames, and by my labouring to quench them, made the wine begin to operate by urine; which I voided in such a quantity, and applied so well to the proper places, that in three minutes the fire was wholly extinguished; and the rest of that noble pile, which had cost so many ages in erecting, preserved from destruction.

(From Jonathan Swift, *Gulliver's Travels*)

## Satire

It could be argued that satire is more of an *aim* than a mode of writing. The original and literary meaning of the word 'satire' refers to the method by which a writer exposes human folly in all its forms. This type of writing brings the reader's attention to immorality by exaggerating it and thereby making it laughable.

Satire is didactic in nature because it seeks to warn the reader against such behaviour by showing him/her the stupidity of it. If we mock someone because of his/her folly, it is likely that we shall try to avoid emulating that behaviour ourselves.

Look out for the following elements of satire:

- sarcasm;
- exaggeration;
- excessive emphasis on certain characteristics;
- ridicule; and
- irony.

Look at this example:

The king's son was going to be married so there were general rejoicings. After the banquet there was to be a ball. The bride and the bridegroom were to dance the Rose dance together and the king had promised to play the flute. He played very badly but no one had ever dared to tell him so because he was the king. Indeed he only knew two airs and was never quite certain which one he was playing; but it made no matter for, whatever he did, everyone cried out, 'Charming! Charming!'

The last item on the programme was a grand display of fireworks, to be let off exactly at midnight. The little princess had never seen a firework in her life, so the king had given orders that the royal pyrotechnist should be in attendance on the day of her marriage.

'What are fireworks like?' she had asked the prince one morning as she was walking on the terrace.

'They are like the Aurora Borealis', said the king, who always answered questions that were addressed to other people, 'only much more natural. I prefer them to stars myself as you always know when they are going to appear and they are as delightful as my own flute-playing. You must certainly see them.'

(From Oscar Wilde, *The Remarkable Rocket*)

# ◼ ⓜ Glossary

## How to use this glossary

It should be stated clearly that this glossary is *not* a comprehensive guide to *all* literary terms. That is not its purpose, nor is it possible to include such an aid in a book of this nature. In the section entitled 'Recommended Reading' (pp. 249 ff) there are titles of more detailed and far-reaching guides that you might find helpful.

What this glossary does do is offer you a simple definition of a number of literary terms you are likely to encounter as you study the skills of practical criticism.

It is important that you resist the temptation to use it as a checklist for practical criticism exercises. This would *not* enhance your personal response in any way and would merely create a formulaic feel to your answer. It exists as a dictionary for you to refer to when you need to clarify the meaning of a technical term of which you are not entirely sure. It may also serve to help you to understand terms with which perhaps you are not already familiar.

Many, but not all, of the terms in the glossary are discussed in detail in Chapter 4, 'Tools of analysis – features of text' and you should cross-reference this section whenever possible in order to consider the *contribution* that each literary technique makes to a text. Remember that it is never enough merely to spot the device; *you must explain the effect it has on the text*.

| | |
|---|---|
| **allegory** | A narrative where the surface events and characters represent abstract ideas; for example, in George Orwell's *Animal Farm*. |
| **alliteration** | The repetition of the same consonant sound, especially at the beginning of words; for example, 'faltering forward'. |
| **allusion** | A reference to a person, place or incident outside the world of the text, or to another literary work. It makes the text denser and draws parallels between it and other areas of life and art. |
| **ambiguity** | Language with uncertain meaning or the possibility of multiple meanings. |
| **amphibrach** | A metrical foot: ~ / ~ . |
| **anachronism** | An event that is historically inaccurate; for example, the clock that strikes in Shakespeare's *Julius Caesar*; clocks had not been invented in Roman times. |
| **anapaest** | A metrical foot: ~ ~ / . |
| **archaism** | The use of old or out-dated language; for example, 'beyond yon straggling fence that skirts the way'. |
| **assonance** | The repetition of vowel sounds. |
| **ballad** | A narrative poem with an often lengthy story told simply. |
| **bathos** | Anti-climax, either intended or unintentional. |
| **binary opposition** | Two terms that represent opposites; for example, light/dark, good/evil. |
| **blank verse** | Poetry written in unrhymed iambic pentameters. Rhythms are usually persistent. Used in narrative, or for expressing thoughts and feelings. |
| **burlesque** | A work of literature that mimics and ridicules a whole style of writing (not one specific text). |
| **caesura** | A pause in a line of poetry, often signified by punctuation. |
| **canon** | A list of authors/works of literature that are recognised as being great. |

| | |
|---|---|
| catharsis | The emotional release that occurs at the end of tragedy. |
| chorus | Originally a group of actors in Greek drama who comment on the action in the play before them, often reciting or chanting their lines. Nowadays, any character who acts as a commentator. |
| cliché | A phrase or saying so over used that it has lost its freshness. |
| colloquial | Ordinary, everyday language, not formal or literary. |
| conceit | An elaborate and extended metaphor that compares two very different things, and at first seems unlikely or startling. Initially intriguing but ultimately convincing. Pleasure follows our appreciation of the image. Common in metaphysical poetry; for example, 'The Flea' by John Donne, in which he compares himself and his lover to a flea which, having sucked the blood of both, acts as a unifying force in their relationship. |
| connotation | Connotative meaning or additional meanings, other than denotative, that surface through suggestions, associations or the emotional undertones attached to words; for example, 'black' when describing a day suggests sadness, gloom or despair. |
| consonance | The repetition of similar consonant sounds preceding and following different vowel sounds; for example, 'pool' and 'pale'. |
| couplets | Two consecutive lines of verse that rhyme. Elizabethan playwrights often ended a scene with a rhyming couplet. It rounds off the action and sometimes points to future events. |
| dactyl | A metrical foot: / ~ ~ . |
| denouement | The ending in drama (which has three stages: exposition, complication and resolution). Order is re-established and characters re-adjust to change. |
| diction | A writer's choice and organisation of words. Same meaning as 'vocabulary' in everyday language. |
| didactic | A work that deals with a moral, philosophical or religious theme. The same as teaching a lesson in everyday language. |
| dimeter | A verse line of two feet. |
| dramatic irony | When a character says something that has a totally different meaning for the audience or for the other characters on stage; for example, in *Macbeth*, when Duncan says, 'This castle hath a fine and pleasant seat', the audience knows from what has gone before that this is where the king is going to be murdered. |
| elegy | A poem of lamentation, about loss or mourning, either for a dead person or a lost ideal. |
| empathy | Ability to identify with another's thoughts and feelings. |
| end rhyme | Rhyme that occurs at the end of a line of poetry. |
| end stop | A pause or a stop at the end of a line of verse, marked by punctuation. |
| enjambment | The sense of one line runs over into another. |
| epic | A long, narrative poem with heroic subject matter, written in an elevated style. |
| epigram | A short, pointed, often witty saying found in all forms of literature. |
| epistle | A literary work in the form of a letter or series of letters. |
| epitaph | Short piece of writing in memory of a person who has died. |
| euphemism | A mild expression used in place of something more unpleasant or harsh. |
| euphony | Pleasant or melodious language. |
| eye rhyme | Rhyme based on the appearance rather than the sound of words; for example, 'through' and 'rough'. |
| fable | A short tale that teaches a moral lesson. |

| | |
|---|---|
| fabliau | A brief comic or satirical tale with an element of bawdiness; for example, Chaucer's 'The Miller's Tale'. |
| farce | A comic play containing elements of fun and confusion. Complicated plot, shallow meaning. |
| feminine rhyme | Weak rhyme – two rhyming syllables, one stressed followed by an unstressed, for example, 'measure'/'pleasure'. |
| figurative language | Non-literal use of language. |
| foot | A group of syllables that form a unit of verse. |
| form | The way an author presents his/her ideas. There are three general forms: poetry, prose and drama, and within each are finer distinctions; for example, sonnet, ode, ballad. |
| free verse | Verse without a regular metrical pattern. |
| genre | A kind or class of writing; for example, poetry, prose or drama. The term also applies to categories such as comedy, tragedy, epic, lyric and satire. |
| gothic | Dealing with the supernatural, passion and violence. |
| half rhyme | Rhyme that is imperfect or incomplete; for example, in Wilfred Owen's 'Strange Meeting': 'escaped'/'scooped'. |
| heptameter | A verse line of seven feet. |
| hero | The main character. Also called the protagonist. The hero in literature does not always mean someone noble or brave as in everyday language; he can be either good or amoral. |
| heroine | The female equivalent of hero. |
| hexameter | A verse line of six feet. |
| hyperbole | Deliberate exaggeration. |
| iamb | A metrical foot: ~ / (the most common in English poetry). |
| iambic pentameter | A line of verse with five iambs (ten syllables). |
| imagery | The use of: (i) similes and metaphors; and (ii) actual objects, feelings and actions in a text (concrete as opposed to abstract representation of these). |
| internal rhyme | Words that rhyme within a line rather than at the end. |
| invective | Use of insult or ridicule to denounce. |
| irony | Stating one meaning and intending another. Irony occurs when the apparent meaning differs from that beneath the surface. |
| lyric | Originally a song accompanied by a lyre, now a song-like poem or a short poem in stanzas or some recognised form, expressing the emotions and reflections of one speaker, usually the poet. |
| masculine rhyme | Strong rhyme – a single stressed syllable; for example, 'fall'/'all'. |
| metaphor | Comparison of two elements by suggesting that one is the other. |
| metre | The regular and patterned use of stressed and unstressed syllables in poetry. |
| mock heroic | Treatment of insignificant subject with the elevated style of the epic mode in order to ridicule the subject and provoke laughter. |
| monometer | A verse line of only one foot. |
| motif | An image or event that occurs frequently; for example, 'nothing' in *King Lear*. Much smaller than a theme. |
| objectivity | A detached, unemotional and impersonal style. The author handles the subject impartially. It is doubtful whether any writer can be truly objective, but there are degrees of objectivity. |
| octameter | A verse line of eight feet. |
| ode | A long and elaborate lyric poem that addresses a person, an object or an idea; for example, *Ode on Melancholy*. |

| | |
|---|---|
| **omniscient narrator** | The narrator who can see all that happens in the plot and to the characters. |
| **onomatopoeia** | The use of words, the sounds of which enact or echo their meaning; for example, 'splash' or 'cuckoo'. |
| **oxymoron** | The combination of two apparently opposite or contradictory terms; for example, 'sweet sorrow'. |
| **paradox** | A statement which at first seems self-contradictory but which on closer consideration is seen to contain truth. Unexpected and intriguing, it forces the reader to analyse the connection made between the two apparently contradictory elements; for example, 'Fair is foul and foul is fair' from *Macbeth*. |
| **pararhyme** | Another term for half rhyme. |
| **parody** | A work that imitates another with the intention of ridiculing it. See *also burlesque*. |
| **pastoral** | Literature that contains elements of peaceful country life. Typically includes references to shepherds and shepherdesses, who live an idyllic rural life, falling in love and singing. |
| **pathetic fallacy** | John Ruskin's term for the way in which natural objects are given human qualities; for example, 'The waves beside them danced' (from Wordsworth's 'Daffodils'). Ruskin saw this as fallacious. |
| **pathos** | The quality that evokes pity or sorrow in the reader. |
| **pentameter** | A verse line of five feet. |
| **personification** | Giving human qualities to inanimate objects or ideas. |
| **protagonist** | The central character of a book or play, not necessarily one that is a hero or heroine. |
| **pun** | A play on words that have similar sounds but different meanings. |
| **pyrrhic** | A metrical foot: ~ ~ . |
| **refrain** | Repetition of a phrase, line or series of lines throughout a poem. Acts as the chorus in a song. |
| **rhetoric** | The art of using language to persuade and influence an audience. Part of English grammar school education in Shakespeare's day, and studied by Greeks and Romans. These days refers to empty and meaningless statements. |
| **rhetorical question** | One that does not expect an answer because it is implied in the question. |
| **rhyme** | Unity of sound between words or their endings. |
| **satire** | Mode of writing intended to ridicule human vice and folly. Can be light and humorous or savage and biting. |
| **scansion** | Analysis of poetry's metrical patterns. |
| **septet** | A seven-line stanza. |
| **sibilance** | Hissing quality to the sound. Can be sinister or soothing, depending on the context. |
| **simile** | Comparison between two elements when one is said to be like another. |
| **soliloquy** | An extended speech in which a character expresses his/her thoughts and feelings aloud, usually alone on stage. |
| **sonnet** | Fourteen-line poem with a complex structure and rhyme scheme. |
| **spondee/spondaic foot** | A metrical foot: / /. |
| **stanza** | A group of lines separated from the rest. Correct term for a 'verse' of poetry. |
| **stream of consciousness** | An attempt to replicate the experience of thoughts and feelings as they flow through a person's mind. |
| **structure** | Refers to the way the text is constructed; its shape. How the interconnecting parts fit together. |

| | |
|---|---|
| **style** | The way an author writes. Individual characteristics of his/her writing. |
| **subjective** | An involved, personal approach. The author deals with the subject emotionally, expressing his/her own individual response. Opposite of objective. |
| **sub-plot** | The secondary plot in a novel or play that interacts with the main plot, either to mirror it or suggest another outlook on its themes. |
| **symbol** | A tangible representation of an abstract idea. Associations between the concept and the object become widely accepted in a community; a type of cultural shorthand. |
| **sympathetic background** | Setting and natural conditions that reflect what is happening in the human world; for example, the storm on the heath in *King Lear*, which coincides with the tempest in the hero's mind. |
| **sympathy** | Sharing the feelings of another person. In drama, most often evoked by characters in a soliloquy. |
| **tetrameter** | A verse line of four feet. |
| **theme** | The central idea or concept with which the author deals in a text. |
| **tone** | The attitude of the author to his/her subject and the reader. Identifiable by establishing what tone of voice you would use to read it aloud. |
| **tragedy** | A text dealing with tragic events and an unhappy ending. Features include the downfall and death of the main character. A feeling of catharsis exists at the end. |
| **trimeter** | A verse line of three feet. |
| **trochee/trochaic foot** | A metrical pattern: / ~ . |
| **unintrusive narrator** | A narrator who does not intrude upon our reading of a text by passing judgements and commenting on the characters or the action. An omniscient narrator can be all-seeing but unintrusive. Most realistic novels adopt this form of narration. |
| **unreliable narrator** | A narrator whose understanding of character is limited and whose perception of the action is highly subjective. We cannot entirely trust his/her interpretation of events. |
| **verse** | The correct term for 'poetry'. |
| **villain** | The antagonist who counters the hero, although the hero can also be a villain, as in *Macbeth*. The villain's wicked actions frequently disturb the social order. |
| **weak rhyme** | Another term for feminine rhyme. |

# ■ ⩔  References

W. Auden, 'Funeral', from *Tell Me the Truth About Love* (London: Faber & Faber, 1999) p. 33.

S. Beckett, *Waiting for Godot* (Norwich: Faber & Faber, 1977) pp. 13–15.

H. Belloc, 'Tarantella', from S. Heaney and T. Hughes (eds) *The Rattlebag* (London: Faber & Faber, 1982) p. 416.

W. Blake, 'A Poison Tree', from *The Oxford Anthology of Great English Poetry Vol. II* (London, New York, Sydney, Toronto: BCA, 1996) p. 10.

W. Blake, 'London' (*Songs of Experience*), from *The Rattlebag* S. Heaney and T. Hughes (eds) (London: Faber & Faber, 1982) p. 251.

W. Blake, 'The Divine Image' from W. Yeats (ed.) *The Poems of William Blake* (Thetford: The Thetford Press, 1979; reprinted 1983) p. 54.

D. Brazier, 'Vegetarian Verse', from D. Kitchen (ed.) *Axed Between the Ears*, (Oxford: Heinemann Educational, 1987; reprinted 1990) p. 68.

C. Brontë, *Jane Eyre* (Harmondsworth: Penguin English Library, 1976) p. 51.

E. Brontë, *Wuthering Heights* (Harmondsworth: Penguin Classics, 1988).

B. Chatwin, *On the Black Hill* (London: Picador, 1982) pp. 38–41.

C. Dickens, *A Christmas Carol*, from *Christmas Books* (London: Thomas Nelson, n.d.).

C. Dickens, *A Walk in the Workhouse*, from A. Clayre (ed.) *Nature and Industrialisation* (Oxford University Press, 1977; reprinted 1984; copyright The Open University, 1977) p. 160.

J. Donne, 'Holy Sonnet – Death be not Proud', from *The Complete Poetry of John Donne, Introduction, notes and varian*, John T. Shawcross (New York: New York University Press; London: London University Press Ltd, 1968) p. 342.

J. Donne, 'Holy Sonnet X – Death be not Proud', from A. Clements, (ed.) *John Donne's Poetry* 2nd edn (New York and London: Norton, 1991) (A Norton Critical Edition) p. 114.

C. Doyle, *The Adventure of the Empty House*, from *The Penguin Complete Sherlock Holmes* (Harmondsworth: Penguin, 1981) pp. 483–96.

T. S. Eliot, 'The Love Song of J. Alfred Prufrock', from *The Oxford Anthology of Great English Poetry, Vol. II* (London, New York, Sydney, Toronto: BCA, 1996) p. 615.

M. Esslin, *The Theatre of the Absurd* (Harmondsworth: Pelican, 1972).

U. Fanthorpe, *Family Entertainment* from Associated Examining Board (AEB) examination paper.

H. and F. Fowler, *The Concise Oxford Dictionary* (London: BCA, 1991).

O. Goldsmith, 'The Deserted Village,' from *Poetry Please* (London: J. M. Dent, 1996; reprinted 1997) p. 41.

T. Hardy, 'At Castle Boterel', from *The Oxford Anthology of Great English Poetry, Vol. II* (London, New York, Sydney, Toronto: BCA, 1996) p. 520.

T. Hardy, 'The Voice', from *The Nation's Favourite Love Poems* (London: BBC, 1997) p. 141.

S. Heaney, 'The Wife's Tale', from *Seamus Heaney New Selected Poems 1966–1987* (London: Faber & Faber, 1990) p. 13.

R. J. Joyce, *Ulysses* (Oxford University Press, 1993) p. 409.

J. Keats, 'To Autumn', from S. Heaney and T. Hughes (eds) *The Rattlebag* (London: Faber & Faber, 1982) p. 434.

J. Keats, 'Eve of St Agnes', from *The Oxford Anthology of Great English Poetry, Vol. II* (London, New York, Sydney, Toronto: BCA, 1996) p. 255.

J. Keats, 'Ode on a Grecian Urn', from *The Oxford Anthology of Great English Poetry, Vol. II* (London, New York, Sydney, Toronto: BCA, 1996) p. 268.

P. Larkin, 'The Explosion', from S. Heaney and T. Hughes (eds) *The Rattlebag* (London: Faber & Faber, 1982) p. 144.

D. H. Lawrence, 'Last Lesson of the Afternoon', from *The Complete Poems of D. H. Lawrence, Vol. 1*, V. de Sola Pinto and W. Roberts (eds) (London: Heinemann, 1964) p. 74.

U. Le Guin, *The Farthest Shore* (London: Gollancz, 1973) pp. 74–5.

W. de la Mare, 'Silver', from *The Complete Poems of Walter de la Mare* (London: Faber & Faber, 1969) p. 181.

C. Marlowe, 'The Passionate Shepherd to His Love', from *Complete Plays and Poems* (London: Dent, 1976) p. 485, lines 1–2.

A. Marvell, 'To His Coy Mistress', from *The Oxford Anthology of Great English Poetry, Vol. I* (London, New York, Sydney, Toronto: BCA, 1996) p. 381.

K. Marx and F. Engels, *The Communist Manifesto* (London: Verso, 1998).

R. McGough, '40 – Love', from *After the Mersey Sound New Volume* (London: Penguin, 1983) p. 94.

S. Milligan, 'The Dog Lovers', from D. Kitchen (ed.) *Axed Between the Ears* (Oxford: Heinemann Educational, 1990) p. 64.

J. Milton, 'Paradise Lost', Book IV, (Harmondsworth: Penguin, 2000) p. 99, lines 977–90.

W. Owen, 'Arms and the Boy', from *The Collected Poems of Wilfred Owen* (London: Chatto & Windus, 1963; reprinted 1971) p. 43.

W. Owen, 'Anthem for Doomed Youth', from *The Collected Poems of Wilfred Owen* (London: Chatto & Windus, 1963; reprinted 1971) p. 44.

W. Owen, 'Dulce et Decorum est', from *The Collected Poems of Wilfred Owen* (London: Chatto & Windus, 1963, reprinted 1971) p. 55.

W. Owen, 'The Sentry', from *The Collected Poems of Wilfred Owen* (London: Chatto & Windus, 1963; reprinted 1971) p. 61.

W. Owen, 'Strange Meeting', from *The Rattlebag*, S. Heaney and T. Hughes (eds) (London: Faber & Faber, 1982) p. 407.

B. Patten, 'Dead Thick', from *Storm Damage* (London: Unwin Paperbacks, 1988) p. 23.

A. Pope, 'The Rape of the Lock', from *The Oxford Anthology of Great English Poetry, Vol. I* (London, New York, Sydney, Toronto: BCA, 1996) p. 488.

I. A. Richards, *Practical Criticism* (London: Routledge & Kegan Paul, 1929).

P. Roche, 'Plug In, Turn On, Look Out', from D. Kitchen (ed.) *Axed Between the Ears* (Oxford: Heinemann Educational, 1987; reprinted 1990) p. 84.

V. Scannell, 'A Case of Murder', from D. Kitchen (ed.) *Axed Between the Ears* (Oxford: Heinemann Educational, 1990) p. 62.

W. Shakespeare, *Antony and Cleopatra* (New York: Signet, 1964).

W. Shakespeare, *Hamlet* (Cambridge University Press, 1969).

W. Shakespeare, *King Lear* (Harlow: Longman, 1974) Act 1, Sc. 2.

W. Shakespeare, *Macbeth* from *Cambridge School Shakespeare* (Cambridge University Press, 1994).

M. Stapleton, *The Cambridge Guide to English Literature* (London: Book Club Associates, 1983).

R. L. Stevenson, 'Song at Dawn', from J. A. Smith (ed.) *Robert Louis Stevenson Collected Poems* (London: Rupert Hart-Davis, 1950) p. 89.

J. Swift, *'Gulliver's Travels' Introduction, Bibliography and Chronology* (London: Random Century, 1991).

D. Thomas, *Under Milk Wood* (New York: New Directions Publishing Corporation, 1954) p. 1.

D. Thomas, 'Fern Hill', from *Poetry Please* (London: J. M. Dent, 1996; reprinted 1997) p. 97.

J. Thurber, *The Thurber Carnival* (Harmondsworth, Penguin, 1965) p. 283.

O. Wilde, *The Remarkable Rocket*, from D. Kilvington (ed.) *A Level Exam Success Guide – English* (Deddington: Philip Allan, 1998) p. 64.

M. Wollstonecraft, *A Vindication of the Rights of Woman: an authoritative text*, C. H. Poston (ed.) 2nd edn (A Norton Critical Edn) (Series title) (New York; London: Norton, 1988).

V. Woolf, *Mrs Dalloway* (Harmondsworth: Penguin, 1992) p. 88.

V. Woolf, *To The Lighthouse* (London, Glasgow, Toronto, Sydney, Auckland: Grafton, Collins, 1997; reprinted 1988) p. 55.

W. Wordsworth, 'Daffodils', from *A Salem House Pocket Poet – Wordsworth*, (Exeter: Webb and Bower, 1985) p. 23.

T. Wyatt, 'They Flee From Me That Sometime Did Me Seek', from *The Nation's Favourite Love Poems* (London: BBC, 1997) p. 116.

# ◼▼ Bibliography

Burton, S. (1973) *The Criticism of Prose* (London: Longman).

Cadden, J. (1986) *Poetry Appreciation for A-level* (London: Hodder & Stoughton).

Cadden, J. (1986) *Prose Appreciation for A-level* (London: Hodder & Stoughton).

Eagleton, T. (1993) *Literary Theory* (Oxford: Basil Blackwell).

Esslin, M. (1972) *The Theatre of the Absurd* (Harmondsworth: Penguin).

Gill, R. (1995) *Mastering English Literature* (London: Macmillan – now Palgrave).

Gill, R. (1998) *Mastering Shakespeare* (London: Macmillan – now Palgrave).

Hinchcliffe, A. P. (ed.) (1979) *Drama Criticism – Developments Since Ibsen*, Casebook Series (London: Macmillan).

Jones, R. (1986) *Studying Poetry* (reprinted 1992) (London: Edward Arnold).

Kettle, A., G. Martin and D. Walder (1978) *Introduction to Literature* (reprinted 1981) (Milton Keynes: Open University Press).

Kilvington, D. (1998) *Exam Success Guide – English* (Deddington: Philip Allan).

Miller, R. and I. Currie (1972) *The Language of Prose* (London: Heinemann).

Peck, J. and M. Coyle (1984) *Literary Terms and Criticism* (London: Macmillan – now Palgrave).

Peck, J. and M. Coyle (1995) *Practical Criticism* (London: Macmillan – now Palgrave).

Richards, I. A. (1929) *Practical Criticism* (London: Routledge & Kegan Paul).

Stephen, M. (1986) *English Literature, Longman Exam Guides* (Harlow: Longman).

Walder, D. (1993) *Literature in the Modern World* (Oxford University Press).

# ■ ⅄ Index